ALSO BY GORDON GRICE

THE RED HOURGLASS: LIVES OF THE PREDATORS

DEADLY KINGDOM

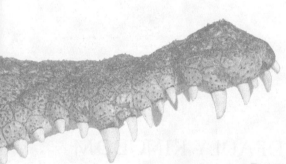

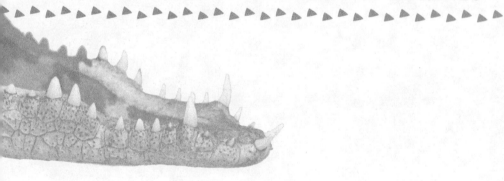

THE BOOK OF **DANGEROUS ANIMALS**

DEADLY
KINGDOM

GORDON GRICE

The Dial Press  New York

Published in the United States by The Dial Press, an imprint of
The Random House Publishing Group, a division of Random
House, Inc., New York.

DIAL PRESS is a registered trademark of Random House, Inc.,
and the colophon is a trademark of Random House, Inc.

Portions of this book originally appeared in *Arkansas Literary Forum,*
Discover, Granta, and *Oklahoma Today* in different form.

Photo permission credits can be found beginning on page 309.

LIBRARY OF CONGRESS CATALOGING-IN-PUBLICATION DATA
Grice, Gordon (Gordon D.)
Deadly Kingdom: the book of dangerous animals / Gordon Grice.
p. cm.
Includes index.
ISBN 978-0-385-33562-1
eBook ISBN 978-0-440-33890-1
1. Dangerous animals. I. Title.
QL100.G75 2010
591.6′5—dc22   2009033933

Printed in the United States of America on acid-free paper

www.dialpress.com

9 8 7 6 5 4 3 2 1

FIRST EDITION

Picture editor: Vincent Virga

Book design by Simon M. Sullivan

For Tracy, Parker, Beckett, Griffin, and Abilene

Philosophy is really there to redeem what lies in an animal's gaze.

—THEODOR ADORNO

CONTENTS

OTHER MAMMALS · 229

"But why can't we go look at it?" I asked my mother.

"Because it's dangerous," she said.

"We could watch from the car."

"We'll go back into town and let Granddad handle it."

"We never get to do anything fun," I said, but the argument was lost already, the red cedar fence posts clicking by faster and faster outside the car window. I picked at the threads in the green upholstery of the backseat. Mom was putting miles of safety between us and the cougar treed in front of our farmhouse. My grandfather had waved us down as we drove home from errands and told us to proceed no farther. I was six; it didn't occur to me to worry about my grandfather. I only knew I was missing out on something.

The next time I saw him, Granddad was the same as always, tossing his silver head as he told his jokes, smiling in his broad but mysterious way, like the man on the Quaker Oats box. He had little to say about the fate of the cougar. Only with the distance of years do I understand what must have passed among the adults of my family, how they must have felt to see a predator like that in the elm tree my sister and I played beneath each day.

We lived in the Oklahoma Panhandle, where the soil was black as coffee and could be coaxed to grow anything if only you could pipe enough water to it. It was a land of extremes, of tornadoes and droughts and dust storms, and the sense of history I absorbed from my family was centered on the apocalypse of the Dust Bowl. It was a land where things that ought to seem strange happened as a matter of course. One clear summer afternoon, we felt a rumble low in our bones, and then the house seemed to quiver like a drop of water thinking of falling. It was over in a second.

MY GRANDFATHER ON HIS HORSE, OLE CHARGER.

"Earthquake!" my sister Meg and I shouted as one. Mom was dubious; whatever it was had made a sound, and the sound had seemed to come from the corral. Granddad sipped his tea calmly. Meg and I tore out to the corral, shouting back to Mom that we promised to be careful.

Near the cattle tank we came upon a smoking scatter of stones, clearly the breakings of a single rock. The original mass must have been bigger than a basketball.

"Volcano rocks!" I said.

"But where's the volcano?" Meg said. We looked all around us. The horizon was flat in every direction. There were no peaks, nothing that might have passed for a volcano, even with imagination. We came speeding back into the house to report our findings.

"It must be a meteor," Granddad explained. It was a new idea for us.

"Don't touch it," Mom said. "It's probably still hot."

The pieces looked different after they cooled—smooth green

wedges, like slabs cut from mint ice cream. They were heavier than they looked, heavier in fact than any rock I'd ever hefted. Meg and I used them when we played *Star Trek;* they were moon stones, valuable ore, some transmutative substance. Meg came home from school with a set of terminology—meteor, meteoroid, meteorite—that she drilled into me, and when we next saw our cousins, we all went out to watch for meteorites and make fun of people who called them falling stars. And we went on with our lives as if nothing much had happened.

But the Panhandle oddities that interested me most were biological: a two-headed Hereford calf at the local museum, plagues of grasshoppers and rabbits, mastodons dug out of the fields, the tracks of allosaurs found in stone. Carnivals came through, displaying five-legged sheep and three-legged hens and, once, a pickled two-headed human baby. One summer when I was ten, prodigious congregations of black crickets rose from the soil. They seethed beneath the outdoor lights. Once they came pouring over the edge of our front porch, where a friend and I had just squashed a grasshopper. It seemed, for a panicky moment, like retribution.

Only as I write this do I realize how forbidding the Panhandle must seem to outsiders. To us, it was home. My father's family had lived there since 1904, which was virtually as long as cattle and railroads had been there in place of bison and mustang herds. The lives of my ancestors were riddled with ghost towns and vanished homesteads, but here they had made the earth yield. All of my grandparents were farmers, and that occupation was understood to call for a kind of integrity others couldn't muster.

But we were a family falling away from the land. My mother would have been happier in town. My father liked the country, but not the life of a farmer. By the time I was a teen, he owned a fleet of tow trucks, and my mother held an office job. They'd become townies. I still spent a lot of time in the country with kinsmen and friends, but I'd lost something. I never got it back.

THE REAL COUGAR passed from my life permanently. I never even glimpsed him. But the memory of him was written in fire. It seemed a special cruelty for my elders to deny me his company, for I was already

obsessed with wild animals and wanted to see him more than I can perhaps make clear. Already I had heard the voice of the bobcat and followed the delicate and sinuous track of the rattlesnake; soon I would
begin to keep insects and spiders in jars; within a few years I would fill
notebooks with my observations and drawings of wildlife. I have spent
much of my adult life in the same pursuits.

A COUGAR BEGINS BY OPENING THE BELLY....

It was decades before I encountered another cougar in the wild. As
before, I never laid eyes on it. I had to use other senses to detect it. I
came into the territory of this particular cougar by accident when
friends invited me to spend a few days at a ranch in Wyoming.

My friends and I went out for a ride. Our horses' shoes clapped
against the steep granite as we worked our way around the mountain's
shoulder. Then we were into a stretch of open field. My horse, a big, unruly bay, trudged through a clattering pile of bones. I reined him in and
asked Virgil, the wrangler, about the carcass. We dismounted.

Virgil handed me the skull. It was about as long as my hand,
equipped with broad molars for chewing vegetation. The front of the
mouth lacked teeth.

"Pronghorn antelope," Virgil said, untying his ponytail to bind it tighter. "They don't have front teeth. They use their lips to pull in grass and leaves." He used his own lips to hold the rubber band while he worked on his hair.

The horns themselves were gone. We looked the bones over to see if we could figure out what had killed the pronghorn. We found plenty of marks, but what to make of them?

"These look like something chewed on them," I said, holding up a femur and an uncertain fragment.

"Could be," Virgil said. "We've got coyotes and cougars. Of course, anything could chew on it once it was dead. God knows how long it's been here."

Some soft gristle and a flap of hide remained on the skull. It had too much heft to be empty. I didn't think it was old. I tied it to my saddle to take back to the bunkhouse. A pair of sluggish insects built like gray bullets emerged from an eye socket and crawled down opposite sides of the nose: carrion beetles.

At the ranch house I scrounged a five-gallon bucket and filled it with water. When I immersed the skull, dozens of beetles came struggling out from the eye sockets and the infinite papery complications of the nasal cavity. A three-year-old boy with a disconcerting tendency not to blink watched me. This small kinsman of my hosts turned to whisper something to his uncle. I had seen them earlier hiking a little way into the hills. They had stood over the leg bones of a deer and talked a long while. The uncle reported the conversation to me: the boy asking how the bones "fell out" of the animal, the uncle trying to explain death as "going back to the earth." Now they huddled again, apparently discussing the pronghorn skull and its colonizers.

I went to work cleaning the skull and forgot about the little boy. When I looked up I found him standing on the porch above me, staring. I had just plunged the skull into a fresh bucketful of water, and a new set of carrion beetles came out in a panic, as if they had slept through the first dousing. They struggled over each other to stay above the surface. The boy stared at the troubled water, the skull gazing back from the bottom of the bucket.

"The bugs help him go back to the earth," the boy said, fingering a toy six-shooter.

As I walked to the kitchen the next morning, led by the smell of bacon, I had to pass a pigpen. I stopped to lean on its rails and look the pigs over. There were five, all patched with brown and white except for one plump pink hog. I wondered what pigs think of that savory smell.

Virgil came up and leaned on the rail next to me. I declined the bent Marlboro he offered. A fresh piece of lumber stood out among the weather-beaten planks and posts; I kicked it idly.

"I put that on last week," Virgil said. "Cougar tore the old board off."

He told the story, pausing three times to light the recalcitrant cigarette. He'd woken one night to the screams of the pink hog. The cougar had it by the hind leg and was trying to drag it through the break in the fence. Virgil fired a shotgun in the air to scare the cat off. I could see a deep black seam of healing wound on the hog's leg. I asked whether the cat had been back since.

"Not up here close to the house," Virgil said. He'd gone fishing at a stock pond the day before yesterday. When his horse started acting spooky, he packed his gear and headed for the ranch house. He returned to the pond later that afternoon. The cougar's tracks led down to the fallen log at the water's edge where he'd sat fishing.

Near dusk Virgil asked me to help him drive a few head of cattle into their evening pasture. The cattle knew the drill; all we had to do was keep them moving. We did it on foot.

We were walking a dirt road. The cattle, with their hides of rust and cream, hustled ahead of us. On our left was a fenced pasture; on our right was a bank of heavy brush. The road changed abruptly from hard-packed dirt to a patch where frequent runoff from a hill had left soft, smooth undulations of dirt. On this softer ground the cattle kicked up a little dust. It was on this stretch I spotted the pugmarks of the cougar. They dappled the road for several yards, obscured in two places where the cattle had crossed them. A good rain had fallen about two hours earlier. The tracks must have been made since then.

Soon we had the cattle in their pasture. Virgil needed a minute to wrestle the broken gate shut. Suddenly we both looked toward the brush, then at each other, then back at the brush. I scanned the ditch tangled with grass and stunted trees.

Virgil whispered a long string of profanities. He told me later he had heard something at that moment, a subtle click that might have been the breaking of a twig. I wasn't aware of hearing anything. I just suddenly got a cold feeling in my scalp, and I knew I was being watched. We started toward the ranch house, Virgil cursing steadily. We walked slowly. I puffed myself up to look large. Virgil was smaller than I and would make a more inviting target, I reflected. I noticed he kept me between himself and the brush. "Wish I had my damn shotgun," he said.

We stopped simultaneously. No signal passed between us, but we must have been thinking the same thing. A thick clump of brush jutted into the road ahead of us, and neither of us wanted to go near it. I stomped on a branch that lay in the road, breaking off a manageable truncheon. Virgil picked up a chunk of sandstone. We walked past the clump, and suddenly we were talking about the weather in loud, angry voices, agreeing that it was nice but a little damp in tones that suggested we meant to kill each other.

We could see the ranch house up the road. Soon we could see our friends lounging on the veranda. We walked slowly, taking turns proclaiming the damn niceness of the weather over our shoulders.

A conversation about politics drifted down from the veranda; someone quipped and several laughed. Why couldn't they shout down the road to us? Or decide to meet us halfway? Finally we were in the yard and away from the brush. Our friends told us we were the victims of imagination.

The next day I followed our tracks along the road to the evening pasture. A fresh set of pugmarks led toward the house. They ran between Virgil's prints and mine, and occasionally turned a circle before rejoining our path. One pugmark fell neatly within the spade-shaped impression of my left boot, four blunt toes and a trapezoidal foot pad deepening the dent of my print.

I took the pronghorn skull home when I left the ranch. A fizzing denture cleaner hardly changed its dirty exterior. I had to throw it out after a couple of days, when it began to smell like bad chicken broth.

That incident provoked me to the investigations that led, eventually, to this book. It was not the first time I had felt the sensation of being watched by a predator, nor the first time I had found myself in some danger in the country. What was different here was the clash in my head between instinct and learning. I had spent much of my indoor life reading books and scientific articles about animal behavior. Those sources claimed that, no matter what my granddad might think, the cougar is not a predator of humans. I had met them in other settings: in zoos, in a sideshow attraction where people were invited to pose with a chained and languid specimen for a picture, even in a junkyard where a big haggard tom was set loose to guard the place at dusk. All my reading and experience made me think cougars weren't dangerous. And in fact I might have been safe enough. One biologist later told me I might have been the object of mere feline curiosity. Still: I'd felt a cold mortality in my belly under the scrutiny of the cat.

It was lucky for me that I'd been ignoring the news for a few years, in another of my periodic fits of disillusionment with my own species. If I had been up to date, I would have known what happened to an eighteen-year-old jogger near Idaho Springs, Colorado. In January 1991, this young man was found disemboweled and literally defaced. One of the searchers who found the body assumed he was looking at a murder scene—until he spotted a cougar five yards from the body.

When I looked into the matter further, I found that the relation between humans and cougars traced an odd U-shaped pattern. From the earliest European settlements in the Americas, the animal was considered dangerous. In the late nineteenth and early twentieth centuries, writers as diverse as Ambrose Bierce and Laura Ingalls Wilder mentioned cougar attacks as ordinary events. But by the time James Clarke came to write his classic study *Man Is the Prey* in the 1960s, authentic cases were hard to come by. He judged cougar attacks rare, and he could produce only one case of a cougar eating a human. Around the same time, Roger Caras turned up several attacks, but called them "rare" and "abnormal." This wasn't, as some suspected, a mere case of a myth debunked. It represented a real change in behavior.

Recently, writer Kathy Etling found no records of fatal attacks between 1949 and 1971, and only a few in the decades on either side. Then, starting in the late 1980s, predatory attacks on humans became an undeniable reality. There were a dozen fatal attacks between 1988 and 2001. Naturalists had been in the habit of blaming the rare fatalities on the aberrant behavior of rabid or starving animals. But these new cases made it clear cougars were treating humans as prey. The attacks happened in widely separated places—California, Colorado, British Columbia. It was not a common occurrence, of course, but it used to be almost unheard of. What to make of this odd trend?

Thanks to the work of scientists like Lee Fitzhugh of the University of California, Davis, we can make some sense of it. Fitzhugh's investigations confirm that cougars really have changed their behavior over the decades. The reasons for this change are complex, and they begin with human culture.

There was in North America, and still is, a culture of extermination. Our ancestors here didn't simply hunt down specific animals that had killed human beings or taken livestock; they killed all animals of dangerous or undesirable species. They organized "drives" to round up and kill coyotes, for example. It's still common practice in some rural areas to shoot any coyote, cougar, or bear on sight.

The result of these practices, besides reducing the numbers of such animals, was to teach the survivors that human beings are dangerous. The large predatory mammals learned to fear humans. And because big mammals learn a lot about life from their parents, this fear was passed down. Zoologists call this transmission of knowledge, which parallels our own, "culture." We have strong evidence of culture in great apes, crows, killer whales, and others. Among the species potentially aggressive toward us, each population varies in its familiarity with, and response to, humans. In North American wolves, the cultural distrust of humans seems to be holding firm. A wolf will often go miles out of its way to avoid the smell of a human being. Among cougars, the case is different, because they are less social and spend part of their youth, when their tastes and habits are developing, solo. When a surge in cougar population in the 1990s pushed the cats into closer contact with humans, older cougars typically kept their established territories, away from humanity. Presumably they also kept their established definitions of what constituted a decent meal, and this did not include humans, because when they were young soloists, they rarely encountered humans and never experimented with the notion of eating them. As adults, they were set in their ways and unlikely to consider new dietary options.

But younger cats, forced to seek territories in human country, tended to be more adventurous in culinary matters. They saw no objection to eating people. At the same time, a shift in the culture of American humans was under way. The practice of exterminating predators gave way to a more environmentally conscious habit of appreciating wildlife. People even chose rural or suburban homes for their proximity to wildlife. Unarmed people met cougars unfamiliar with human violence. A few people, and a great many cougars, died.

To consider animal behavior without history is to misunderstand it.

HERODOTUS, THE FIRST true historian, was also the first human being we know of to write empirically about the habits of dangerous animals. In his *Inquiries,* written more than 2,400 years ago, he tells us how venomous snakes limit their own numbers. The female bites the male in the neck while they mate, delivering a mortal wound. The young, in turn, eat their way out of the womb, killing their mother. The wise gods supplied vipers with these habits to keep them from overrunning the earth.

These ideas are wrong, of course, but sound observations lurk behind them. The mating of the vipers in the Mediterranean does involve a lot of thrashing about that looks hostile, and the young do eventually issue live from the belly of their mother, already equipped to deliver venomous bites. It's only the interpretation Herodotus got wrong. We now know that the apparent death struggle is a harmless ritual combat between rival males or, in other cases, a courtship dance between the mating pair; that it's not a bite, but a harmless ritual licking of the neck, and delivered by the male rather than the female; and that the live birth of the young doesn't harm the mother. The interpretation Herodotus (or his informants) gave these observations must have come from a prejudice, a preexisting belief that vipers are all about violence and harm.

This, in a nutshell, is what has happened in reports about animals ever since, from travelogues to newspaper stories to scientific papers. We start from observation, but even as we're seeing something, we're seeing it through eyes trained to take a certain perspective. Belief is a part of seeing. It's hard to filter out the interpretation and leave mere facts. Even the words we use can betray us into error. For example, I look back on my correction of Herodotus and see that I've used words such as "courtship" and "ritual." "Courtship" is a quaint Victorian euphemism. "Ritual" is hard to define; we hardly understand the meaning of our own rituals. Even careful scientists are stuck with a language that can skew their observations.

The violence some animals inflict on humans would seem hard to skew. Either somebody got hurt, or he didn't. But in fact, this aspect of zoology has been more liable to distortion than most. The trouble, besides our usual biased views of all the parties involved, is that violence rouses strong emotions. We are almost forced to take sides with the injured humans or the slandered animals. Many accounts of violence simplify on one side or the other. For example, I often read accounts that point out what the human victim did "wrong" before she was attacked by a bear or a shark. Many writers depict virtually all animal attacks as "provoked" by the victim. On the other side, some writers are at pains to paint dangerous animals as monsters of cruelty. All of these views are simplistic.

Subtler distortions are a problem, too. When I was a child with an avid interest in animals, the prevailing view was that natural selection had sculpted each species to respond to a given stimulus in a predictable way. If you studied a few wombats, you understood them all. But, as the case of the cougar shows, animal culture complicates behavior. Individual animals also differ because of their circumstances, their stressors, and even their genetics. A mother bear tolerant of human presence may become aggressive when she has cubs; she may become even more aggressive when she scents a male bear in the area, since he's a danger to her cubs. We now know that many animals, from elephants to dogs, live in dominance hierarchies, and that we can unwittingly become involved in these hierarchies with disastrous results. For example, the training of elephants as work animals or circus performers involves impressing on them, through physical punishment, that the human trainer outranks them socially. But when an elephant sees his chance to move up in the hierarchy, he can give his trainer an alternate impression.

All of these new insights guided me as I interviewed scientists and read journal articles, talked to hunters and ranchers, reviewed the old literature, and even went to see and touch for myself whenever I could. My aim here has been to survey the dangers our fellow animals pose to us. I wanted to be complete; as far as I know, nobody has even tried that since Roger Caras wrote *Dangerous to Man* (1964; revised 1975). Many species have proved as changeable as the cougar, and I will draw on cases both historic and recent to show what we now understand about these species. Caras distinguished between "provoked" and "unprovoked" attacks. He didn't count the "provoked" attacks, because they could be blamed on the human victim rather than on the essential nature of the animal. My view is a little different. I'm not out to blame anyone, only to report and understand. So I've included some cases that surely wouldn't have happened without human cooperation. It may be that in our twenty-first-century world, no attack is truly unprovoked. Some biologists suspect that animals as diverse as sun bears, chimpanzees, and great white sharks may be more likely to attack people in response to stresses caused by the shrinking of their habitats. It's become uncomfortably clear that our own actions are always relevant to animal attacks.

In fact the whole context of an attack is important. Many of the attacks Caras classed as "unprovoked" seem, with the perspective of today's science, the opposite. For example, a captive pilot whale named Bimbo was released from Marineland in 1967 because it had attacked its fellow captives and roughed up trainers. Caras reported that this behavior was considered "psychotic." Since then, we have come to appreciate that captivity is not a healthy situation for most animals. It's particularly harmful to whales, who see the world partly through echolocation. To put them in a small enclosure is essentially to blind them. Bimbo's aggression was a response to his treatment at the hands of humans, not some inherent flaw in him. His story provides an ugly example of human presumption.

You'll see even uglier things in the pages ahead. This is, after all, a book about what happens when things go terribly wrong. I'll relate many tales of violence deployed against both humans and other animals. For me, the worst revelation of my researches was just what a brutal world this is for children. The smaller the person, the more likely she will fall within the range of sizes acceptable to a predator. Living in the United States, I never had to face this truth before. I have the wealth to buy a good weapon if I ever decide I need one; my house is solid enough to keep out the most dangerous animals; police will rush to help me guard my children when I call. In much of the world, things are different.

My youngest son is seven, the same age I was when a cougar showed up in my yard. He's never seen the farm I grew up on. Not long ago my parents visited that farm and sent me photos of fence posts, cattle, the Siberian elm where the cougar perched. The buildings are gone, burned to the ground, their very foundations reclaimed by grass. No one recalls the year of the fire, or even the decade. Another unlikely event hardly worth mentioning.

I suppose it's strange to frame natural tragedies with my personal life. But this book is ultimately about the behavior of human beings as well as our fellow earthlings. It's a brutal world for all of us, really, and some aspects of it are not comfortable for the sentimental or the squeamish. Somehow that's never dimmed my love for all animals. I celebrate their beauty, even the darker side of it.

THE CARNIVORIDS

THE SNOUT OF A
DOG CONCEALS
CARNASSIAL TEETH
THAT CAN CRACK BONE.

1. WOLVES, DOGS, AND THEIR KIN

ORDER CARNIVORA: FAMILY CANIDAE

MR. PECK, THE YELLOW DOG who shared my childhood, could not let prey pass. Almost any small animal that crossed his path was game: field mice, for which he would dig with ferocious energy, pausing to listen for them in their tunnels; porcupines, despite the beard of painful barbs they left him with; skunks, despite the sewer-and-cabbage smell; cats, even the ones we loved. One day, when our kitten was too slow, Mr. Peck left him dead beneath the Chinese elm he'd been racing for, his black coat littered with bits of leaf and twig. I recalled the rubbery scream I'd ignored hours earlier. I felt guilty for not seeing its importance at the time. Long days of misery followed before I could forgive Mr. Peck, days during which my mother told me again and again that he was following his nature, that he'd never learned not to hurt cats and couldn't be blamed for this.

Rabbits tempted him above all. Their zigzag escape routes didn't fool the yellow dog. He often brought one home and lay on the lawn, bracing it between his forepaws as he chewed. The largest jackrabbit I ever saw was his kill, a monster that might still, after two days of his gnawing, have been a red head of lettuce. My mother grimaced at this kill every time she passed him on the lawn.

"Pecky, I wish you'd take that elsewhere," she said to him, but he merely turned his head to the side so the jagged carnassial teeth along his jaw could shear off a chunk of meat and bone.

Our dog's carnivory was so much a part of my landscape that I hardly remarked it. I learned not to walk too close when he was on a kill, lest he growl to warn me off; otherwise, the bones and blood were routine. What made me notice them afresh was a new item on his menu. Strung through the buffalo grass of our backyard was a skeleton, dragged into disarticulation, the meat mostly gnawed off. The size of the thing startled me—bones strung out for a dozen feet, white in the sun except where they were filmed with red. At the end of the string Mr. Peck lay struggling with a femur. He put its bulbous end between his jaws and bit, but the thing went sliding out the side of his mouth with a clatter.

I found no skull, and had to ask my mother to identify the animal.

"A steer," she said.

"Is Pecky supposed to kill the steers?" I said.

"He didn't kill it. It was already dead when he found it."

"What killed it?"

"Coyotes, probably."

The next stage in my education about dog carnivory came with the visit of our neighbor's dog, a broad-chested border collie. I enjoyed its presence at first, because it was always game for a chase. Border collies generally are: they must herd, and will try to guide and turn running geese or sheep or children—even, I have read, a string of ants. This border collie cavorted with my dogs and me, always pushing its side against me to keep me with the pack.

But then it began to kill our hens. We had six of them, five white leghorns and a slender auburn one. They died one at a time, and I would go out after school and track them by the feathers they lost as the border collie chased them.

"Shoot him if you have to," our neighbor said. He was a kindly old man with great patience for children. "I got cattle, so I can learn him off of them, but I can't learn him off of chickens." It was a delicate point of etiquette, the shooting of someone else's dog. Letting your dog roam free was a major attraction of country life; your dog's freedom represented your own. But costing someone else his livelihood had consequences. I relayed the permission to my parents. They said we'd be moving soon, that we would have to get rid of the chickens anyway, so there was no need to hurt the dog.

One day I found my favorite hen, Fat Feet, near death. Her feet had always looked like the tubers of irises, extravagantly fleshy even for a white leghorn. I found her in the carport beside Dad's shop. The border collie did not eat the chickens; he only chased them down to kill them. Fat Feet had hated being handled before, but now when I touched her she raised her head and looked at me and slowly put her head back down. She made low sounds, like the raw material for her normal clucks. I had a vague impression of blood among her white feathers. I told Mom—expecting, I guess, that she could do something to save Fat Feet. She told me to leave the bird alone and let her die.

I couldn't. I went back again and again and stroked her feathers, and she raised her head more feebly each time, and the weird monotone she made grew softer as the afternoon went on. I said things to comfort her, though all promises at this point had to be empty.

Back in the yard I told the border collie to go away. He licked my hand. He was big enough to be an adult, but, as my neighbor had told me, he was still a puppy, and killing was his way of playing.

I went back to the carport and found Fat Feet dead. The next day I told my second-grade teacher about the episode. She asked why I hadn't grabbed the hen up and put her in the freezer.

Peck and the border collie were good dogs, but imperfectly trained, each killing certain animals we humans would have preferred they didn't touch. My mother taught me, in effect, that dogs hunt by instinct; my neighbor's comment about training taught me that instinct can be shaped to suit our own needs. I didn't really understand the border collie's herding behavior, but that, too, is important: it's an example of an instinct heightened and refined so that it lingers through generations, though it dissipates when we stop making dogs mate within their own breeds. In fact it is a modification of hunting behavior, the pursuit warped so that capture is less important than the chase itself.

IN MUCH OF the world—the parts where people have extirpated the large native predators—the dog is the most dangerous large animal except for the human being. In the United States, for example, an estimated 4.7 million dog bites occur each year. These bites cause some 800,000 people per year to seek medical help, nearly half of them at emergency rooms. The U.S. government's Centers for Disease Control and Prevention, which is the source of these statistics, puts the annual death rate from dog attacks at about a dozen. Other Western countries have similar rates. In the UK, postal workers alone are attacked by dogs at a rate of nearly five thousand a year.

People view most of these incidents as something of a different order from, say, an attack by a crocodile or bear. It is this very difference in perception that allows dogs to be a danger. Because we perceive them as belonging among us, we are more vulnerable to them and more frequently hurt by them. Of course, this is only true in gross numbers. The average dog is unlikely to hurt a person, and most bites are minor events.

The most serious attacks tend to involve children (who comprise half the victims of medically significant bites) and old people. These victims are, of course, less able to defend themselves once an attack is launched, but that's only part of the reason why they are disproportionately victimized. The main reason lies in the social structure of wolf packs.

The dog, despite the remarkable diversity of its body types, is simply a kind of wolf. Wolf packs are structured partly according to a dominance hierarchy, with stronger, more intimidating animals taking roles of privilege and leadership. These roles within a pack are always subject to revision. A low-ranking wolf can improve his standing by outfighting or cowing a higher-ranking one. In the right situation, a wolf will instinctively attack a pack mate of higher standing who looks weak, even if only momentarily. For example, if a wolf is injured in a hunt, he becomes a target of his social inferiors.

A domesticated dog seems to see itself as a low-ranking member of human society. Most dogs settle happily into their subordinate roles, once those roles are made clear to them. But this is not always the case. Sometimes dogs well past puppyhood try to rise socially by hurting children. I have known badly trained puppies to constantly rough up the youngest children in a house. The puppy is trying to improve his rank by establishing his dominance over the child. I've even known badly trained puppies to attack the adults in a household when they bend to pick something up. Bending over seems to the dog a sign of weakness or submission.

A setter I knew had lived amicably with my friends for years. One day he approached the four-year-old girl, who was just tall enough to look him in the eye. He opened his mouth and seized her face. Her father kicked the dog and pursued it into the woods. The girl was left with a scar on her lip. The family was broken up, the human members remaining, the setter exiled to live with other people. Traumatic as it was for all concerned, this scenario is commonplace. Fifty percent of dog bites to children are on the face. It is the eyes that provoke them; a direct gaze is a claim of social superiority, and the dog may challenge that claim from the weakest member of a human pack.

Old people are vulnerable when they appear infirm. An unsteady walk, for example, is a classic mark of weakness in wolf society; it will often draw a challenge. Possibly a quavering voice strikes a dog's ear as a similar mark.

Some dogs are, of course, bred for attack. Just as the border collie I knew would try to herd children, running alongside us to control our paths, other dogs have a heightened desire for inflicting injury. This is simply a different part of the hunting protocol brought to the fore. We humans have kept attack dogs since prehistoric times. The benefit to the wolves was the opportunity of eating human refuse; the benefit to the humans was the wolves' sensory adaptation to the dark. Wolves could hear or smell danger and give warning. They did this, of course, for their own benefit. But gradually the cultures of wolf and human integrated more fully, and the wolf began to serve not just as warning, but sometimes as actual guard, attacking other creatures that invaded a camp. Eventually dogs were bred specifically for this purpose, and they could be made to attack another creature solely for human benefit. For example, a dog does not gain by attacking a bear. Wolves generally do so only if their numbers are strong enough to give them a strong chance of victory. But dogs have been trained to attack bears in defense of humans, or even for human amusement.

Similarly, dogs can be bred to attack invading humans; and, by a very slight extension, they can be induced to selectively attack humans who are not invading. In medieval Europe, great mastiffs were used in combat. They could disembowel men or horses; they could run beneath the horses with vessels of fire strapped to their backs.

Dogs were invaluable tools of colonialism. Columbus used them as attack animals to help eradicate the Taino people of Hispaniola. In the United States, this colonial use of dogs continued. Histories are full of cases in which white settlers trained dogs to attack Native Americans or white Southerners trained dogs to attack African Americans. When race

ATTACK DOGS HELPED ERADICATE THE TAINO PEOPLE.

riots broke out in the 1960s, many white Americans acquired German shepherds. They'd seen police turning shepherds on black rioters.

Open warfare, conquest, riot control, racist oppression, and territorial defense do not exhaust the violent uses to which we humans have put dogs. There's also torture. At Abu Ghraib prison in Iraq, American interrogators threatened prisoners with attack dogs, the objectives including the amusement value of making prisoners soil themselves. Dogs were used as weapons of torture against political prisoners by a Uruguayan regime of the 1970s and by Robespierre's revolutionary government.

It's difficult to nail down the dangers of specific breeds. News reports often, and without sufficient evidence, blame the breeds considered dangerous at the time. Today, for example, pit bull terriers and rottweilers take the blame for attacks from all sorts of dogs. In the past, Doberman pinschers and German shepherds were similarly blamed. These breeds can be more aggressive than others, but the degree of this difference may have been exaggerated.

Larger breeds are generally more dangerous than smaller ones, even when we haven't designed them for attack. Saint Bernards, which may weigh more than 200 pounds, have killed people. Dog breeders and owners have made various claims about the temperaments of different breeds. It is said with some evidence, for example, that chows begin life as suitable companions for children but sometimes turn mean in their old age—old age for a chow being about eight years. The very process of creating a pure strain involves inbreeding, which tends to create unforeseen behavioral anomalies such as inappropriate aggression.

WOLVES EAT A wide range of meat, from field mice to elk and moose. They succeed against larger, more powerful animals by teamwork. Typically, they separate a vulnerable member of a herd from the rest, then chase it in relays. Exhaustion helps bring the prey down; so does the traumatic injury of any bite the wolves can manage on the run. By making exhaustion part of the killing strategy, wolves avoid at least some of the kicks and gorings they might otherwise receive. They may finish the prey with a strangling bite to the throat. This strategy depends for its success on the fact that hoofed mammals typically don't cooperate to save each other from predators. Each deer, for example, saves itself. There are some exceptions among the hoofed animals; bison defend their young against wolves by forming a circle, their horned heads outward. But a wolf pack's success often depends on its superior teamwork.

The same factors are at play when wolves prey on humans. During the Black Death of the fourteenth century, wolves came out of the hills to feast on the bodies of the dead and the ill. The comrades who would normally protect these people were themselves disabled by the disease. Other disease outbreaks have provided similar opportunities for scavenging and mass predation on the weak or wounded, as have wars. This may be one way in which a population of wolves is educated to eat people. Famine offers the same opportunity. In northern China, famine killed 9 to 13 million people between 1876 and 1879. Wolves and dogs were minor contributors to this toll. Presumably they also scavenged among the abundant corpses. As is the case with many animals, wolves are not especially impressed by the distinction between preying on the weak and scavenging the dead. The custom among many human cultures of defending corpses against scavengers—by burying them, for example—probably has its roots in the need to keep predators from learning to take us as food.

But we don't have to look to the great disasters of history to see these principles in play. Wherever human communities have trouble guarding their weakest members, wolves learn all over again that we're viable prey. For example, wolves took twelve children in southeast Holland in 1810 and 1811 and injured others. Similar depredations occurred continually in Estonia during the eighteenth and nineteenth centuries, where 136 people were killed by wolves; in Vimianzo, Spain, in 1957, 1958, and 1959, where wolves attacked six children, killing two; in the Bihar region of India, where wolves took sixty children from 1993 to 1995; and in Uttar Pradesh, India, where, in a seven-month span of 1996, wolves attacked 76 children, killing at least 22. The common factor in these diverse times and places was an economic reality: unsupervised children had to do farmwork, generally tending livestock. This economic factor helps to account for the variable danger of wolves across their range. In the last fifty years, wolves have killed hundreds of people in Asia, especially in India, where children remain a large part of the rural workforce.

WOLVES SUCCEED AGAINST LARGER, MORE POWERFUL ANIMALS BY TEAMWORK.

In North America, where small children rarely have to work without supervision, the death toll for the same period was only one.

Seventeen are known to have died from wolf attacks in Europe during that period, all in rural areas where people must work or travel alone. Hans Kruuk reported a series of attacks in remote villages of Belarus in 1995 and 1996. In one case, a sixty-year-old man traveling alone between two villages went missing. Wolf tracks were found around a bloody patch of disturbed snow. Near the village of Hvoschno, a fifty-five-year-old woodcutter did not return from the forest one day. Parts of him were found surrounded by wolf tracks. In Usviatyda, a teacher kept a nine-year-old girl after school. It was dark by the time she set out for home alone. Her father became concerned and went looking for her. On a stretch of snow darkened by blood and marked by the prints of wolves, he discovered her severed head. He later killed the teacher.

The same agricultural situation prevailed in the most famous series of wolf attacks on record. From 1764 to 1767, something popularly called the Beast of Gevaudan took at least sixty-four people in the Cévennes Mountains of south central France. Though this case is well documented, it is also cluttered with myth and exaggeration. There is the tale of a child decapitated in an instant, her head rolling along the ground; there is the tale of a boy's shoes left standing in the road when the Beast took him. The fame of the wolf drew the notice of the king and an assortment of journalists. The depredations ended after two large but unremarkable wolves were hunted down and killed.

PEOPLE BROUGHT DOGS to Australia about four thousand years ago. The dogs developed into a breeding population in the wild. Feral dogs lose the characteristics of individual breeds, blending into a sort of standard wild dog form—about the size of a German shepherd, yellowish, with upright ears and long snouts. Australia's feral dogs are called dingoes.

Like other canids, dingoes possess a social structure based on dominance. Their play is often a sort of ritual enactment of social rank. It can easily turn into a bid for promotion. Since they are capable of playing with humans, finding us sufficiently similar to be ranked, attacks sometimes evolve from playing. This happens fairly frequently because people purposely play with, photograph, and feed dingoes in parks, in the suburbs, and in the wilds. Besides social-climbing violence, dingoes occasionally treat children as prey. Like people, they need not act according to clearly separated motives.

In 1980 occurred the most famous of all dingo attacks on humans. At a campground near the tourist attraction Ayers Rock, a dingo slipped into a tent and seized Azaria Chamberlain, who was less than ten weeks old. Lindy Chamberlain, the baby's mother, witnessed the attack, but arrived too late to stop it. Mrs. Chamberlain was subsequently charged with murder, then convicted on incompetent scientific evidence. She served four years in prison, was released, and eventually won a settlement for wrongful imprisonment. Books and films made the case more famous. Decades later, people still parody Meryl Streep's line from *A Cry in the Dark*: "The dingo took my baby."

The most astonishing aspect of this tragedy is the incredulity with which Mrs. Chamberlain's story was met. Much of it arose from the rarity of dingo attacks. Dingoes were already biting people in Australian parks, but somehow people tended to define this the same way we define bites by domestic dogs—as accidents that go with pets. A minor bite from, say, a nonvenomous snake almost always provokes more concern than a blood-drawing bite by a pet dog or cat. Just as the dingo sometimes accepts people into its own social ranking system, people have long since accepted dogs and cats into our family systems, and we react to their attacks as we would to the naughty pranks of children. This reaction helps explain why most people were not particularly alarmed by the nips and bites of dingoes around campgrounds.

At the same time, a very different feeling was in play, one that cast the dingo, like the North American wolf, as a symbol of untainted nature, of predatory grandeur. People—both Australians and foreign tourists—saw the dingo as a national symbol, and the part of the nation it symbolized was its rugged natural heritage. One could argue the logic of this view, since the dogs are not native and not genetically distinct from basset hounds; but it was a feeling rather than an argument. People want to touch nature, whatever that may mean. Just as tourists in the United States feed bears from car windows, tourists in Australia feed dingoes, despite rules and warnings. A peculiar fallacy accompanies this urge to touch the wild: people feel, somehow, that nature will not hurt them because they are themselves approaching it with a kindred feeling.

So it was that the death of Azaria Chamberlain ran counter to prevailing beliefs—for some people, deeply held beliefs that might as well be called spiritual. It was the general view, even among some biologists, that large predators do not view human beings as prey. The idea that our efforts to touch the wild would result in the killing of a baby was shocking, sacrilegious. There's a contradiction in valuing a predator for its death-dealing powers and simultaneously believing those same predators harmless, but I frequently find these opposed beliefs cohabiting a single human head.

In the death of the baby, it seemed a moral imperative to find a human culprit. Otherwise, nature itself was something different than we'd like to believe.

In 2001, dingoes attacked two brothers, aged nine and seven, on Fraser Island, part of a national park. The younger brother was injured, the elder killed.

• • •

OCCASIONALLY MY CHILDHOOD nights were shattered by shouting and gunfire and the panicked racket of the chickens. I would rise from my bed, pleased at the excitement, to see my father standing on the porch in his underwear holding a thirty-thirty. His shots brought Mr. Peck and our two younger dogs growling to his aid. Somewhere out there the coyote that had meant to take a chicken went hurtling into the night. Usually the coyote wasn't hurt; he was too fast for the dogs, and my father couldn't see him in the dark and could only fire in the air to scare him.

I also knew coyotes from their midnight songs and the flensed bones they left behind. In my childhood, we saw coyotes as distinct from dogs. So did the scientists. Nowadays we know they belong to the same species. They are both wolves imperfectly adapted to the presence of people. The coyote is a small subspecies of wolf, generally weighing less than 50 pounds. It adapts to diverse environments. In rural areas where people routinely shoot at them, coyotes almost never attack people except when rabid. In that setting, people come into conflict with coyotes mostly when protecting livestock.

In recent decades, however, coyotes have proved capable of living in suburbs and even within cities like Los Angeles and Chicago. Most dangerous encounters occur in the suburbs, where coyotes preying on cats and small dogs meet people ill armed to deal with them. Dozens of attacks have been documented in the United States. As with dingoes and domestic dogs, most of these encounters resulted in nothing more than minor bites. Some attacks on small children were clearly attempts at predation. In Glendale, California, in 1981, a coyote fatally broke the neck of a three-year-old girl.

The urban coyote is dangerous because it's become habituated: it meets the scent and sight of people often without dire consequences. Experts note that killing these bold coyotes probably wouldn't help. It would merely open their territories for different coyotes to move in. What *would* help, ironically, is shooting at them and missing often. Canids pass their knowledge to their young. If we kill a few but leave most of them alive to teach their offspring we're dangerous, then hu-

RABIES KILLS MORE
THAN FIFTY THOUSAND
PEOPLE A YEAR.

mans, pets, and coyotes could all occupy the same territory more amicably. It's too bad the unfettered use of guns in suburbs would create far worse problems.

Habituation also leads to danger when dogs breed with wolves or coyotes. Because these three animals are not really distinct species, they can mate and produce viable offspring. Their matings are unpredictable: sometimes they simply prey on each other instead. Sometimes wolves mate with dogs, then kill and eat them. In fact, the red wolf of Texas and Mexico, once regarded as a separate species, is now recognized as a hybrid of wolf and coyote. In any event, hybrids are common, and sometimes breeders produce them on purpose. There's a brisk pet trade in hybrid animals. A wolf-dog can be a volatile combination of wild and domestic traits, as comfortable around people as a dog, but as prone to dominance brawling as a wolf. They have killed several people.

. . .

IN 1833, A SINGLE wolf went on a rampage in Wyoming, biting dozens of people and killing thirteen. It was a clear case of rabies. The history of the Old West is sprinkled with such accounts—a mad wolf traveling scores of miles in a day, killing cattle and dogs and people, leaving many of the survivors to suffer the disease themselves.

Because of our close relationship, dogs share more diseases with us than most animals do. They play a part in the transmission of diseases as diverse as plague and anthrax, and they spread such parasites as fleas, mites, and worms. But rabies is the greatest danger canids pose. They are the major reservoir of the disease worldwide.

The disease, whether in human or other animal, progresses thus: The virus spreads from the bite wound into the surrounding muscle tissue, where it reproduces, gathering its strength. This latent period may last days, months, or even years. Then the virus migrates to the nerves near the wound. The wound, though long since healed, may itch, burn, and tingle. The virus travels along the nerves toward the spinal cord and brain. It may take it a few days or a few months to reach these central locations. When it does, the outward symptoms hit, prompted by the sudden swelling of the brain and spinal cord. In dogs, the behavior becomes depressed; their human companions can hear the change in the tenor of their barking. In humans, there is a battery of symptoms that might go with almost any illness—fever, headache, nausea, malaise, stiffness, sore throat. There are also more troubling symptoms: an excess of saliva, pupils wide like those of an addict in withdrawal, an intolerance to heat, cold, noise, light. This phase lasts a few days at most.

Next is the famous part of the disease, the mad phase. It does not occur in all cases. The mad phase is unknown in some animal species, and with some strains of the virus; beyond that there is blind luck to tell whether you will get it. In people, it comes in the form of insomnia, confusion, delirium, hallucinations, convulsions, psychotic fear, and, yes, foaming at the mouth. In canids, the mad phase sometimes includes chewing, an urge to eat anything in reach, even inedible things. The wild attacks come now. To the extraordinary stamina of the wolf or dog is added an utter disregard for its own safety. Every moving thing it sees will suffer.

Foxes are too small to see even young children as prey, but they become dangerous during the mad phase of rabies. They come into yards to attack people. In 2007, a gray fox attacked a woman in New Kensington, Pennsylvania, as she went to a neighbor's house. She repelled the attack, but it was renewed moments later when she returned home. This time she used a mop to defeat the attacker, which fled to a nearby house. There it entered unbidden and did battle with the two resident canids. A human inhabitant of the house took shelter in a bedroom. The dogs killed the fox. Another spectacular attack took place in 2008, when a fox seized an Arizona jogger. Knowing she'd want the fox tested for rabies, she ran a mile with it clamped on to her arm, then tossed it into the trunk of her car and drove to the hospital. When the trunk was opened, the fox bit an animal control officer.

The mad victim, canid or human, cannot drink, not even his own saliva—the attempt at swallowing makes his throat spasm. The sight of water can make him panic and gasp. He feels he is choking, and he is: the neurological mechanisms that time our breathing and drinking and eating, that keep us safe without our notice, are breaking down. The victim may die now, during this period of wildness. If he lives long enough, he lapses suddenly into lassitude. Paralysis takes him entirely, and he dies when it closes down his breath.

Without treatment, the mortality rate is 100 percent. A vaccine is effective if administered promptly, but even with treatment, only a handful of people have survived once symptoms appeared. Worldwide, some fifty thousand people a year die of rabies. In some nations it remains among the most feared diseases. China, for example, ranks it among the top three human-killing infectious diseases. In the United States, where dogs are routinely vaccinated, it claims only one or two people a year. Americans are more likely to get the disease from skunks, bats, raccoons, and foxes.

But it is the madness of dogs that has bitten most deeply into our psyches. What rabies taught us in the recesses of history is our fundamental equality with the canid: it makes dog and man, or wolf and man, equal, both reducible to savagery. A dog can revert to the wild, and so can a man, a woman, a child. Perhaps this is the basis for the myth of the werewolf.

THE HERBIVOROUS
GIANT PANDA IS
DANGEROUS ONLY
WHEN PROVOKED.

2. THE BEARS

ORDER CARNIVORA: FAMILY URSIDAE

FROM BIOLOGISTS AND RANCHERS in the Southwest, I learned a crude kind of forensic science. You read the carcass of a steer and deduce the killer. A cougar, for example, generally begins by opening the belly, as neatly as if it owned a scalpel. It removes the stomach and sets it aside—for the vegetable matter in an herbivore's stomach is distasteful to a cat. It begins its meal with the heart and lungs. When it must leave some of the carcass for later, it kicks dirt and dead weeds onto it, though this disguise doesn't always fool badgers or crows. Coyotes often leave tracks circling a cougar kill at a distance. The smell of meat tempts them, but the smell of a cougar is a strong deterrent—for the cougar will sometimes track down the canine despoilers and kill them. When the cougar has time and appetite, it leaves nothing but spatters of blood and the fur, flensed from the carcass with its abrasive tongue.

Other kill sites show the marks of a different style. The carcasses are peeled like bananas. Their skulls may be broken, as if with a sledgeham-mer, the neck deeply plowed with parallel furrows. The grass all around is tangled and trampled and smeared with the feces of the killer. If crows and coyotes have not yet spoiled the ground, it reveals tracks that might have been left by a stunted man with blunt, bent feet. These kills are the work of a black bear.

The North American black bear is an elusive presence, hard to find except when, at odd intervals, it shows itself, snuffling around a garbage pail or walking onto a porch. One day an uncle of mine in Oklahoma came upon a canyon his horse refused to enter, and when he asked the old men of the county, they told him that meant the horse smelled bear. One night the owner of a bed and breakfast in my uncle's town heard a ruckus in the front yard of her establishment. She looked out into the darkness, expecting to find drunken men. Instead she saw one burly man standing silent at the metal gate a few yards away. The man sud- denly dropped to all fours and walked away. One morning a friend of mine in Wisconsin went for her usual jog along a heavily used road, and when she finished her miles and turned in to her own driveway, she saw a dark stranger in the sunshine.

In all these cases, a human being got nothing but a fright. The black bear rarely has more to offer. It is unusual among the predators of human beings because predation is not its preference. It may take as lit-tle as 10 or 15 percent of its nutrition from meat, and some of that comes from carrion. Mostly it eats fruit, nuts, roots, honey, and insects. When it meets a human, its usual response is retreat or lack of interest. But sometimes—when the blueberries are sparse, for example, or when the bear is pregnant—its hunger for meat is greater.

In 1997, a woman was making a move from Texas to Alaska with her two children. They took a sightseeing tour along the way. At a park on the Liard River, British Columbia, they went hiking among hot springs. Other tourists were nearby; it must have looked safe enough. As they walked, a black bear charged out of the woods and attacked. Others tried to help, pelting the bear with rocks and sticks, but it was not to be distracted. Two men, one an experienced hunter, the other a college stu-dent conducting research, came to the rescue and were mauled. Another tourist ran for his gun and killed the bear. The woman lay dead, as did the hunter. The woman's thirteen-year-old son and the college student were hospitalized. Her seven-year-old daughter escaped injury.

A similar story unfolded in 2006 in the Cherokee National Forest in Tennessee's Smoky Mountains. A woman had brought her two young children to a swimming area they knew well. A black bear attacked the younger child, a two-year-old boy, biting through his skull. The woman fought the bear, but it overpowered her. As in the Liard River attack, other tourists came to the rescue, throwing rocks and striking the bear with sticks. It retreated into the woods. The other child, a six-year-old girl, had run away when the bear attacked. No one saw her for an hour. A man searching for her found the bear standing over her dead body. Someone else shot at the bear, scaring it away. The woman survived with spinal injuries and numerous puncture wounds requiring skin grafts. Her son survived after brain surgery.

Black bears have taken children from yards and even, in one case, from a baby carriage. They have killed more than sixty people in the past century. But purposeful predation is a minor source of conflict between these bears and people. We're far more attractive to them as a source of stockpiled food. It's fairly common for bears to raid garbage cans and even break into cabins. In 2001, a ninety-three-year-old Cleveland, New Mexico, woman died when a black bear, having broken into her house in search of food, repeatedly bit her. In wildlife parks, many people, perhaps not appreciating the danger, like to feed, pet, or photograph bears. In *A Walk in the Woods,* Bill Bryson tells of a toddler whose mother smeared his hand with honey so she could shoot video of him playing with a black bear. It ate his hand.

Asia has a closely related species called variously the moon, Himalayan, Tibetan, or simply Asiatic black bear. It is about the same size as the American version, the biggest topping 300 pounds. Moon bears have attacked many people. In 1999, one of them killed a man gathering plants in the woods of Hokkaido, Japan. Later that day, it mauled two women in the same area. They arrived at the hospital in serious condition. As is the case with most of the large carnivores, captive specimens have taken their toll. In 1999, a moon bear on display at a zoo in Lahore, Pakistan, pulled an eighteen-month-old boy into its cage and dismembered him. In 2004, in Weedsport, New York, a woman reached into a cage housing two moon bears and lost half her arm.

THE FIVE-INCH CLAWS
OF THE BROWN BEAR
CAN DISMANTLE THE
HUMAN BODY.

In China, the bile of the bear is believed to have medicinal properties, and hundreds of bear farming operations supply the demand for it. The bile is removed by several methods, including catheters. It is perhaps not surprising that bears in this situation become irritable. In 2005, a man was cleaning a bear pen when six of the animals killed and ate him. Police tossed raw meat into the cage to distract the bears while they recovered what was left of him.

The most formidable member of the family, and in fact the most formidable predator on land, is the brown bear, a type that includes such subspecies as the grizzly and the Kodiak. It evolved in Asia and spread across the northern parts of Europe and North America as well. It is armed with remarkable muscles. The force generated by a big grizzly moving its two thousand pounds up a steep hill, without laboring, is phenomenal. A less obvious but perhaps even more impressive feat of strength occurs when a bear sliding down a snowy mountain stops its tremendous momentum in midslide to walk away without seeming effort. When turned against the mighty American moose, these muscles are capable of delivering a literally skull-shattering blow. Against a human being, which is built on a considerably lighter scale than a moose, the destructive capacity is even more impressive.

Add to this power the usual carnivore weaponry of claws and teeth, but on a large scale. A grizzly can often fit a human head into its mouth for a crunching bite. If the person is lucky, the skull slides out like a pinched marble. That's what happened to Al Johnson, who survived being scalped by a grizzly. He found himself wondering why he wasn't dead; it was only later he realized the bear's teeth had merely scraped the naked bone of his skull. Another victim, Jacob Fowler, also thought he heard his skull breaking in the jaws of a grizzly. He was right. His comrades discovered a hole in his temple. He died soon after. Others, however, have survived fractured skulls.

The claws of a big brown measure five inches and can wreak tremendous injuries on human victims. One survivor ended up with fifty staples in various parts of her body and a set of stitches across her face. It is not unusual for a victim to be eviscerated or for the eyeballs to be sliced from their sockets. Few animals can ruin a human body so thoroughly.

As is the case with wolves, brown bear populations vary in their propensity to attack people. Siberian browns are more likely to attack than European ones, for example. And as with all the other carnivores, the behavior of both humans and bears comes into play. Conflicts over livestock frequently lead to attacks. In Romania, where brown bears take sheep and other livestock, people defending their animals are the most likely to come to grief with bears. One report mentions eighteen people killed by brown bears in Romania from 1990 to 1997.

Hunting is another dangerous situation. Hunters who merely wound a bear may pay with their lives. People who kill deer or other enticing prey sometimes find bears willing to fight them for the meat. In Alaska, the majority of bear attacks result from hunters stumbling upon bears in the brush. Being surprised often triggers a bear's defensive attack.

In fact, brown bears take what seems to us an oversensitive view of their own safety. A sow may attack people who walk, inadvertently or otherwise, between her and her cubs. The social interactions of bears are

A BEAR CUB TAKES REFUGE IN A TREE.

relevant to their dispositions. In one attack, for example, a sow seems to have been unusually defensive because she was aware of a male nearby who posed a threat to her cubs. When a human appeared on the scene, she mauled him; she might otherwise have been more inclined to simply avoid him. Even loud noises seem capable of provoking some bears to attack.

Like wolves, chimpanzees, and many other animals, brown bears operate partly on the principle of social dominance determined by intimidation and brute force. They may see humans as rivals. They perceive the direct gaze of a human as a challenge, which they meet by battering the human into submission. This is why playing dead sometimes works with brown bears: the bear has no need to further dominate a dead or utterly submissive opponent. Even screaming while being mauled may encourage the bear to continue an attack. Black bears do not seem to perceive humans as rivals for dominance, so playing dead doesn't work with them.

Like black bears, browns get most of their nutrition from vegetation and even insects. Predation is a minor concern for them most of the time. Nonetheless, they sometimes stalk and kill people as they would any other prey. In *Bear Attacks: Their Causes and Avoidance,* Stephen Herrero mentions the case of a hunter who was found with his belly mostly eaten away. Tracks showed that the bear he was hunting had trailed and ambushed him. In 2005, a couple camped on Alaska's Hulahula River were killed and eaten by a 300-pound grizzly. Evidence showed they had taken considerable precautions to make sure their campsites didn't smell of food. When another couple, accompanied by a guide, discovered the ravaged campsite, the bear chased their raft downriver for forty-five minutes. Rangers killed the bear.

Brown bears learn to associate humans with garbage and other food. They may ambush campers in their tents as well as raid their supplies. In fact, any attack, regardless of the original motive, may turn into predation. For example, a professional photographer working in Yellowstone National Park seems to have provoked a grizzly into a defensive attack by running after it for a closer shot. Searchers found the lower half of his body more or less intact; even the clothes were in place. The bear had eaten much of the rest, caching a few leftovers in various locations across the face of a hill.

THE ONLY URSINE as big as the brown is the polar bear, which can weigh nearly a ton and stand more than 12 feet on its hind legs. All bears are omnivorous, but polar bears eat a higher percentage of meat than the others, subsisting mostly on seals. They occasionally take large prey like walruses, beluga whales, reindeer, and musk oxen.

The polar bear has traditionally been regarded as extremely dangerous, prone to stalk and kill human beings. Because many of them live beyond our range, they show no awareness of us as dangerous creatures and thus no fear. For the same reason, however, they rarely have occasion to prey on people. Where the two species overlap, polar bears invade campgrounds, houses, and even restaurants in search of food. They have killed at least three people in Norway. In 2003, one of them tore into the tents of an American hunting expedition in Nunavut, Canada, mauling a guide. The bear inflicted many lacerations on the man, broke two of his ribs, and flensed his scalp from his skull before one of the hunters killed it. Doctors needed some three hundred staples to reattach his scalp.

Around the world, polar bears in zoos have proved dangerous. They are popular exhibits; one at the Como Zoo in St. Paul, where I often take my family, spends hours doing underwater somersaults. His enclosure is always surrounded by children. In 2000, a zoo specimen in Kazakhstan amputated the leg of an eleven-year-old girl who was feeding it dried apricots. She survived the injury. In 2009, a suicidal woman visiting a German zoo climbed over a barrier and plunged into a moat where polar bears swam. She was rescued by zoo employees, but not before one bear ravaged her arm and leg.

A purely herbivorous bear is the giant panda, which inhabits the mountain forests of China and Tibet. It's best known as the mascot of a certain conservation group and as a sexually reluctant object of human scrutiny in zoos. Pandas rarely encounter people in the wild, and they retreat when they do. Panda-on-human violence occurs only when people attempt to trap the animals or get too close to them in zoos. For example, a fourteen-year-old Chinese boy on a field trip to a breeding facility was bitten when he tried to pet a panda. He suffered wounds to his head and arm. A keeper at the same facility suffered bites to her legs in 1999 when she fell into the pandas' pen. In 2006, an American woman volunteering at a panda research and conservation facility in Sichuan Province, China, lost the tip of her thumb to a cub she was feeding. The same year provided another example of the drunk-meets-animal sort of violence: a man well saturated with beer leaped into a pen at the Beijing Zoo in hopes of touching a panda named Gu Gu. Gu Gu bit him on the leg; the man retaliated with a kick; a catch-as-catch-can match followed, with each party scoring some bites on the other before a keeper turned a hose on the brawlers. The panda suffered no injuries, but the man was hospitalized. Since then, Gu Gu has injured a student who wanted to cuddle him and a father who tried to retrieve a dropped toy from Gu Gu's cage.

THE OTHER BEAR species don't prey on us, either, but two of them are so aggressive in their own defense that they often hurt people. The sun bear (aka Malay or honey bear) is a creature of the tropics, found in the Malay Peninsula and the adjacent Indonesian islands as well as parts of India. It is the smallest kind of bear, reaching only about 140 pounds. Its short fur is generally black; a russet marking on its chest gives it its name. Its usual diet is insects, especially termites and bees; of the latter it will take everything, including adults, grubs, and honeycomb. It also eats prodigiously of earthworms and the delicate parts of coconut palms. It takes any small vertebrate—bird, rodent, lizard—it comes across. It divides its time between the trees, where, like an ape, it sleeps in platforms made of branches, and the ground, where it digs and tears into rotting logs in search of prey.

For such prey-pursuing activities it is equipped with long claws that double as weapons. Malaysians report that the sun bear attacks without provocation. It claws its victim energetically, then vanishes. Even tigers avoid it. Statements about lack of provocation are always problematic, however; an animal whose senses and instincts differ from ours simply has a different threshold for provocation.

A typical attack occurred in January 2000 in the jungles of Borneo. A researcher who was there to study orangutans heard a sound like swarming bees. It seemed to emanate from a log. She soon realized the sound was more like heavy breathing. She tried to run, but a sun bear landed on her backpack and knocked her down. It clawed her legs. She kicked and yelled; the bear retreated. She was left with scars.

Some scientists claim sun bear attacks in Borneo have increased recently because of deforestation. Fewer resources means the bears are under greater stress and react more aggressively. This hypothesis fits the facts, but has not been proved. The general idea that man-made environmental changes such as deforestation, climate change, and urban encroachment increase animal attacks has been proposed for a great variety of species, from great white sharks to chimpanzees to cougars, in some cases with impressive evidence. The human toll of such attacks is, of course, minor compared to the loss of life these changes promise to virtually all species.

THE URSINE MOST likely to attack a human is neither the meat-hungry polar bear nor the mighty grizzly, but another modest-sized species with hair-trigger defenses. Wherever people and sloth bears both live, fighting breaks out. A five-year period in Central India produced 735 sloth bear attacks on humans. Forty-eight of these were fatal.

The sloth bear, like the sun bear, has long claws (about three inches) for digging into termite mounds and scratching up windfalls of nuts and fruit. But it's a somewhat bigger animal, reaching five or six feet when it stands to attack a human. It can weigh 300 pounds. In his book *Man-eaters and Jungle Killers,* Kenneth Anderson described the tactics of one sloth bear that killed a dozen people and injured many others:

> [H]e invariably attacked the face of the victim, which he commenced to tear apart with his tremendously long and powerful claws, in addition to biting. . . . Quite half the injured had lost one or both eyes; some had lost their noses, while others had had their cheeks bitten through. Those who had been killed had died with their faces almost torn from their heads.

Anderson agreed to hunt the bear. He soon found himself alone at dusk searching for another victim whose struggle with the bear had been heard from a distance. By the time Anderson reached him, the man was so mangled that only the blood-bubbles of his breath proved him yet alive. Soon the bubbles stopped.

Eventually, tips from local people led Anderson to the verge of a field, where he sat up late one night at the base of a boram tree. The fruit was just coming on, still green but beginning to take the mahogany spots that would deepen into a dull red. Anderson sat with his back to the biggest tree he could find, watching the glimmering leaves grow dark as the sun set. There were few windfalls at this season to draw the bear. It came anyway, snuffling and scratching for roots. A moonless hour passed as Anderson listened and strained to see exactly where it was. At last the silhouette of the sloth bear appeared against the stars. Anderson clicked on his flashlight. The bear rose on its hind legs to gaze into the glare and meet the fatal bullet.

THE PUREST MAMMALIAN CARNIVORE.

3. THE CATS

ORDER CARNIVORA: FAMILY FELIDAE

I WAS NEVER BORED in the cat-owning days of my childhood. I could let a rubber ball fall from my hand and before it had gone a foot, my cat Mink (named for the luxuriance of his black-and-white coat) was on it, and then off the far side of it, crashing to the floor in his eagerness. His claws plucked divots from the orange surface. The ball held still in his grasp for a moment, then sprang out as if alive and sped across the floor. Of course he himself had loosed it, his interest in the chase unfulfilled by the easy catch. He was after it, on it, batting it from side to side. If I tired of the ball, a length of clothesline would do. Mink could be induced to whirl in circles as long as my stamina held, in hot pursuit of a dangling strand. When I tired altogether, he stared at me with his flat face, his cat eyes looking at me in a way that suggested to my human understanding an accusation. If I persisted in my indolence, he might take an interest in the twitching of his own tail.

It was all predation, or practice for it. The same moves served him when he attacked a June bug or a grasshopper: the quick capture, the release, the batting about, the shredding with claws or teeth of a creature still alive, a creature he would then release and chase again. Once he took a cicada big as a shotgun shell in his grip, muffling its headachy song, and then released it to let it crawl away. On the ground a cicada is clumsy and slow; it needs to climb before it can fly, so it was helpless before the cat. Mink took it up again, his ears turning inward each time the buzzing song was muffled or fell silent. Half a dozen times he caught and released it, and the insect's transparent wings became crumpled lace. Soon Mink removed the wings and bit delicately into the thing. It buzzed feebly even in his mouth, just once, causing him to pull it out and swat it gently. After he had done with his meal I collected the wings he'd left behind. They shredded the morning light into little rainbows in my grip.

It is surprising what a range of things a cat will play its death games with. I have seen this catch-and-catch-again routine often with cats I've known, played with everything from a juvenile squirrel to a length of chain dangling from a tow truck. Once, after half an hour harassing what looked like a molding clump of spaghetti, a stray cat brought me her prize. It hung limp from both sides of her mouth, like a mustache. It was a baby rattlesnake.

Once, as I stroked his back, he ducking and pushing to bring his head firmly against my hand, I admired the white blaze on Mink's breast. He yawned. His teeth were like needles, so thin that in the sun their color was vague as watery milk. It only took a second for him to bite me, and he did it by turning his head to the side as he yawned. Along the side of his jaw were his carnassial teeth, a narrow little mountain range meant for shearing meat. He bit me gently, and the tip of my finger was slow to open; when it did it appeared as if someone was drawing a red circle around it. I pushed the cat away and accused him of treachery. He only looked at me with his bright butterscotch eyes.

·   ·   ·

CATS ARE THE purest mammalian carnivores, eating almost no plant matter. Their predatory behavior is remarkably consistent across sizes: though it's not quite true to say a lion is merely a big cat, they do act much the same when it comes to eating other animals. They chase more often than they kill, and they kill more often than they eat. They are armed with hooked claws and piercing canine teeth ideal for puncturing the throats or even the skulls of their prey. The largest can, and do, regard even adult humans as food.

The lion is one of the planet's premier predators of human beings. Although anthropophagy (the eating of humans) is a minority behavior in lions, it has, over the centuries, been the finish of untold thousands of lives. Westerners have traditionally explained predatory attacks on people as aberrations. The term "rogue lion," with its implication of biological abnormality, has been in use for more than a century, and some writers have compared human-eating lions to serial killers. This interpretation doesn't derive from science or even from observation. It comes from a bias about our role in the scheme of things. That bias goes back ultimately to religious texts and teachings. The version I grew up with had Adam being given dominion over birds and beasts, fish and creeping things. Teachings like this put human beings at the top of a

LIONS SCAVENGE THE CARCASS OF AN ELEPHANT.

scale of value, so any information that moves us lower must be explained as abnormal. This view is surprisingly durable. It's still common in discussions of anthropophagy to hear of us being taken out of "our normal place at the top of the food chain." In such claims, the religious explanation has dropped away, but the unfounded belief in our special destiny persists.

In the real world, the significance of things is situational, not determined by some preordained ranking. A human may be food or consumer, as conditions dictate. The whole concept of ranking, for that matter, is an artifact of the human way of thinking; biologists have long since replaced the simple "food chain" with the "food web"—a network of chains, a set of interrelations rather than a pecking order. Lions have for millions of years been predators of primates, including our close cousins the chimpanzees and, it appears, our ancestor *Australopithecus*. They have been predators of human beings as long as we have inhabited this planet. The fact that humans far more often kill lions doesn't contradict the fact that lions still, under perfectly "normal" circumstances, prey on humans.

But this doesn't mean every lion is looking for human prey. The ability, and general willingness, of lions to prey on large primates like us is only the first important condition. Everything else depends on the circumstances, such as the individual lion's learned habits and preferences and the behavior of the human being in question.

Take, for example, the most famous case of lions preying on people. A Victorian pair known as the man-eaters of Tsavo gained fame in the West because they interfered with British commerce—specifically, the building of a railroad in Kenya. The first important condition to note is that these lions were a pair of young males. Lions learn diet from their elders, but as a young adult, a male leaves his pride of origin and, typically, becomes more adventurous in his choices. These two may have learned that humans are food from older lions, a distinct possibility since human-eating was common in that area. Or they may have discovered it on their own, their youthful openness to possibility meeting the opportunity of people clustered in numbers for the construction. (The railroad has been compared to a long smorgasbord.)

J. H. Patterson, an engineer working on the construction, recounted the depredations of this pair vividly, if not always with a firm grasp of biology. The first victim Patterson describes was an Indian officer named Ungan Singh. A lion seized him by the head one night and dragged him from his tent. Patterson tracked the lion by the trail of blood it left. Soon he found the site where it and a companion had set-tled down to eat Ungan Singh. Singh's head lay on the ground, punc-tured by the lion's canine teeth, its eyes wide open. The rest of his body had been reduced to smears and "morsels."

After the first attack, the workers tried to protect their camps with thorn fences and big fires. The lions, having found food in the camps, persisted in spite of these measures. One of them leaped over the thorn fence and wiggled its head under a tent. The men inside slept with their heads toward the middle of the tent—another safety measure. The lion bit one man on the foot and dragged him out. The man grabbed any-thing he could, including a heavy box and then a tent rope, but the lion easily overpowered him. Once it had him clear of the tent, it seized him by the throat and shook him as a dog shakes a rat. This is common predatory tactic, used not only by the mammalian carnivores but even by crocodiles and monitor lizards. It breaks the spine, killing the prey quickly. The man stopped screaming. The lion carried him in its mouth as it ran along the fence looking for a way out. It plunged through a small gap, leaving shreds of flesh and clothing on the thorns. Patterson catalogued the man's remains: "the skull, the jaws, a few of the larger bones and a portion of the palm with one or two fingers attached." Pat-terson had the wedding ring removed from one of these fingers and sent to the man's widow.

The lions varied their points of attack, rarely taking prey from the same camp twice in a row and refusing to revisit previous kills when Pat-terson and others sat in wait for them with guns. They showed consid-erable intelligence, anticipating the moves of the hunters and taking advantage of the routines of the humans. The lion's intelligent observa-tion of human routine is well known from other cases. For example, C.J.P. Ionides reported lions lying in wait where people habitually went to gather food or cook or urinate.

Though they adapt their hunting strategies to the circumstances, lions show a carnivore's typical inflexibility once they have chosen their prey. They have been known to step between, or even on, sleeping men to get to the one they've chosen. The Tsavo man-eaters ignored not only fences and tents, but campfires, flung torches, and even missed gunshots. After months of trying, Patterson was finally able to shoot first one and then the other lion. But others in the same area continued to take human prey.

A recent analysis suggests that lions in Tsavo were more likely than others to prey on humans because the ground there was covered with low bushes, which allowed the lions to lie in ambush. That's their favorite way to hunt people. The brush hadn't always been there. Grazing elephants used to leave little cover for lions. The elephants died off, decimated by ivory hunters and by the viral disease rinderpest. People accidentally catalyzed the epidemic spread of rinderpest by establishing vast herds of livestock in Africa, amplifying the usual pattern of disease transmission.

By killing the elephants (both directly and indirectly), people contributed to the lion attacks. No one recognized this human influence until almost a century after the events. There were other human factors as well. Slave traders had for several decades been tying recalcitrant captives to trees to let predators take them, a punishment meant to intimidate the rest of the slaves into submission. This practice may have helped teach the lions in the area that people are feasible food. In the 1930s and '40s, generations of lions thus acculturated to human food killed hundreds of people in Tanganyika.

Lions often prey on vulnerable members of herbivore herds—the young, the ill, the injured. The same is true of human prey. A lion's perception of vulnerability in a human can prompt an attack, whether it's hungry or not, just as the presence of a dangling rope prompted an attack from my pet cat. Sleeping, having sex, and crouching to draw water are all invitations to carnivory. Ionides tells a story of a lion that "finding a man lying drunk outside a hut, merely nipped a chunk out of his behind, rather as you might take a passing bite from an apple and leave the rest."

People alone are far more likely to be attacked than those in groups. For the last few decades, lion attacks have occurred frequently in South Africa's Kruger National Park. It is here that people most often immigrate illegally from the far less prosperous country of Mozambique. To avoid detection, they typically travel alone or in small groups. Making their chances worse, these people must travel at night (when lions prefer to hunt and human senses are least useful) and typically without adequate weapons. In 1997, a pride of lions attacked five refugees, snatching one from the ground and three from a tree they tried to shelter in. Only the fifth person, highest in the tree, survived. Robert R. Frump described the sights that often meet workers in the park: "Bits of bloody clothes found in the middle of nowhere. A lone suitcase, filled, abandoned in the bush. A single shoe. A full water bottle. Footprints that trekked on, then just ended."

FOR SOME REASON I have never been much impressed by the old circus trick in which the tamer puts his head into a lion's mouth. Cartoons and overexposure have, I suppose, dulled the image for me. But it really is a dangerous stunt, as a circus audience discovered in Belgium in 1991 when a lion took its trainer's head into its mouth and suffocated her. Others came to help her and shot the lion to death. The tamer was already dead. But circus lions have quicker ways to kill audience members as well as workers. During a performance in São Paulo in 2000, a lion dragged a six-year-old boy into the cage it shared with four others. The five lions ate the boy while his father and the rest of the crowd watched. Police fired machine guns into the air to scare the lions off the body. Ricochets wounded two people.

Captive lions have attacked scores of people in the last decade alone, killing more than a dozen, hospitalizing most of the rest, and amputating a few arms. Zoos, safari parks, and animal shelters have all been the scenes of violence. Occasionally lions escape and hurt someone, but mostly they maul their keepers during routine feedings, or else protest being petted through the bars. It is not terribly unusual for big cats in cages to reach out and seize children, who are the proper size to set off the predators' chase instincts. This is the same instinct that made a rolling ball so interesting to my cat Mink.

People can be surprisingly naïve about the dangers of lions. At a safari park, a mother and son were injured while tossing live chickens out the window to feed the cats. In 1995, a woman climbed into the lion exhibit at the National Zoo in Washington, D.C. Her body could not immediately be identified because the lions left her neither face nor fingerprints. I don't know what prompted this woman to her adventure, but mental illness and alcohol have contributed to other, similar incidents. In 2006, a visitor to the Kiev zoo proclaimed, "God will save me, if he exists," and entered the lion enclosure, where a lioness instantly sliced his carotid artery.

It's also surprisingly common for Americans to keep lions as pets, roadside attractions, or advertising gimmicks for their businesses—car lots, restaurants, even a Christmas tree farm in one case. In 2002, a man who owned a roadside zoo entered a cage to pose with his lion, which was said to weigh 500 pounds. The lion leaped on him and dragged him around the cage, in the process puncturing his throat, slicing tendons in his chest and neck, striking bone with its teeth, and popping his right eye out of its socket. The entrepreneur survived, though he was listed as critical for the first eleven days of his lengthy hospital stay.

"Do you know anyone killed by a tiger?" I said. I had to be blunt because we had little language in common.

The man looked hard at me. His short, calloused fingers stopped in the middle of turning a page. I was afraid I'd offended him, but in fact I had only startled him. It had never occurred to him that I might *not* know anyone who'd been killed by a tiger. Then he named a few people and their villages.

In my job of teaching English to Vietnamese refugees in America, this sort of conversation turned out to be a great tool. Everybody could understand the idea of a tiger from a mere picture, and conversation blossomed from that starting point. Over the years, I heard a number of stories about neighbors eaten by tigers. It was especially in their journeys to escape the country that people learned to fear the tiger. In the jungle, without shelter or weapons, that danger was palpable. Hmong refugees attempting to escape to Thailand often avoided roads and the human dangers associated with them; their alternative was wildlife trails, where the tigers could take a person unheard.

Tigers take fewer people than lions do, but this fact says more about the dwindling number of tigers than about their propensities. They are mostly solitary hunters, though cubs may stay with their mothers for several seasons, learning her hunting tactics. They are the biggest cats,

A SOLITARY HUNTER.

sometimes reaching 11 feet and 600 pounds. Like lions, they prey on humans only in certain circumstances. Pockets of especially dangerous tigers occur throughout their range in Southeast Asia and Russia.

"We found the woman's clothes, and a few pieces of bone." This is one of many startling statements the famous hunter Jim Corbett made about the Champawat tigress, which is listed in the *Guinness Book of World Records* as the most prolific animal killer of human beings ever documented. It took 200 victims in Nepal, followed by 236 more in the Kumaon region of India. One victim was observed by eyewitnesses, screaming for help as the tiger calmly carried her away in its mouth, her hair and feet dragging on the ground.

The Champawat tigress took her last victim in 1907. Corbett tracked it into the jungle. He found the victim's beaded necklace next to a pool of blood. Farther along the trail, the young woman's hair was strung like gossamer on blackthorn bushes. Then Corbett came to a bloody patch of ground littered with bone splinters. The woman's lower leg lay neatly severed. Corbett was so disturbed by this sight that he nearly fell victim to the tiger poised 15 feet above him on an embankment. He brought his rifle up; the tiger slipped away. He ran up the embankment in pursuit. He couldn't see the fleeing tiger, but he was close enough behind her to see the grass springing back up where she had passed. She stopped frequently to gnaw at the corpse she carried, but Corbett's approach always made her growl and move on. After hours of chase, Corbett had to turn back; night was falling, and he didn't care to be near the tiger in the dark.

Corbett recruited nearly three hundred men to make noise the next day. His strategy was to drive the tiger out of its hiding place on a rocky, forested mountainside. He'd be waiting for it, assuming it ran in the direction he expected. As the men fired guns and beat on tin cans, the tiger made her appearance, headed for the safety of an overgrown gorge. Corbett put two bullets into her torso. A third blast only caught her in the paw, but she lay down and died anyway; the earlier shots had finally taken effect. The carcass was carried through the neighboring villages so the people could feel sure the man-eater was dead. After Corbett had skinned it, the carcass was cut up and the morsels made into protective charms for the local children.

It's unlikely the Champawat man-eater would hold on to her record if all the facts of the world were known to us. She lived at a time when improved communication was beginning to make such tallying possible and to expose such events to the wider world. Many other tigers have taken human prey serially. At Chowgarh, Corbett encountered a tigress that, sometimes with the help of her nearly grown cub, killed at least sixty-four people and wounded many others over a five-year span. Yet another of Corbett's tigers killed "about 150." The Indian government listed 1,046 people killed by various tigers in 1902. One recent survey of the literature found 12,599 people reported killed by tigers in the entire twentieth century. This number is more than five times the reported deaths for all other wild mammalian carnivores combined. However, the authors of the survey acknowledge that some of the original reports may not have been accurate.

Though the tiger populations of the world soon began a precipitous decline under human pressure, the remnants have continued to take people. In the Sundarbans region shared by Bangladesh and India, several deaths occur annually. It's hard to be precise because some survivors, having ventured into the area to hunt for meat or honey without permits, do not report the deaths of companions. This region has a long history of tiger trouble. In 1971, a single tiger killed 32 people on the Bangladeshi side. From 1956 to 1970, various tigers killed 392 people in this region.

Another region where tigers continue to take people is northern

India. Seven people were killed in this heavily populated area in the first month of 2009.

IT'S AN IRONY of our modern world that a person is almost as likely to be killed by a tiger outside its natural range as in it. In one report on U.S. occupational fatalities, the usual agricultural deaths caused by cattle and horses were joined by three tiger-related deaths in circuses and zoos. (Elephants killed a few workers as well.) Trainers and keepers consider tigers far more dangerous than lions. The reasons lie in the lion's social structure. Because lions often live in prides, they have an instinctual capacity for giving way to a social superior. They learn their place in a pecking order, and the trainer's job is to impress them with the idea that he outranks them. The traditional trainer uses violence to make this point. Any aggression from the lion has to be met with even greater force. A tiger, however, doesn't live in groups in the wild. It respects no authority except its own mother, and she holds this power only until the cub approaches adulthood. A trainer can still intimidate a tiger into following directions, but the tiger never settles into a subordinate role. Any mistake the trainer makes can be his last: it can make him look like prey. In a recent fifteen-year period, news media reported more than a hundred attacks on people by captive tigers, about twice the number reported for lions. Twenty-eight people died in those tiger attacks. Seven survivors lost an arm or a hand.

The most famous victim of a captive tiger was Roy Horn of the Siegfried and Roy act. In 2003, during a stage show in Las Vegas, Nevada, a white tiger mauled him. Horn was an experienced tamer who had worked with this particular animal for six years. Both his partner and his employer at the Mirage explained the attack, rather improbably, as the tiger's attempt to protect Horn when he fell. The fact is that many carnivores take what opportunity offers. Years of association may make a human being—even an experienced trainer—think of an animal as his loyal friend. Tigers don't seem to see things that way. Horn suffered a serious bite to his shoulder and massive blood loss. His heart stopped twice. In the hospital, his suffering was complicated by a stroke. Doctors removed a quarter of his skull to relieve the pressure on his brain. He eventually learned to walk again with assistance.

Another notorious attack occurred on Christmas Day 2007. Three young men celebrated with a trip to the San Francisco Zoo, where they allegedly taunted various animals. The last animal they taunted was a Siberian tiger named Tatiana. The young men probably didn't know that Tatiana had mauled a keeper the year before. Seventeen-year-old Carlos Sousa, Jr., stood atop the railing around Tatiana's cage to shout and wave at her. As they left, the three heard a sound behind them. Tatiana had apparently leaped a 15-foot moat and a 12-foot safety wall to get at them. She attacked twenty-three-year-old Kulbir Dhaliwal. His brother, Paul, nineteen, and Sousa shouted to distract her. She seized Sousa and killed him. The Dhaliwal brothers managed to put some distance between themselves and Tatiana, but she caught up with them near the zoo's Terrace Café. She mauled them in quick succession, biting and clawing their heads and torsos. When police arrived, they found Kulbir Dhaliwal lying on the ground. His brother was sitting on the ground screaming, blood streaming from his head. Tatiana sat in front of him, looking him in the face. Four police officers whistled and called, hoping to draw Tatiana away from the brothers. She swatted playfully at Paul Dhaliwal before she turned her attention to the officers. All four fired. One of them, Chris Oshita, saw his bullet part the tiger's fur as it entered. Oshita was disconcerted to note that the bullet didn't slow her down. But she fell dead before she could reach the officers. Two bullets had struck her in the head. Five were found lodged in her chest.

One need not harass a tiger to draw danger. At Safari Joe's Rock Creek Exotic Animal Park in Adair, Oklahoma, a keeper was filling the water trough for a cage housing several tigers. One tiger seized her by the arm and pulled her into the cage, where its fellows jumped on her. Another employee pounded the tigers with a shovel to get them to release his coworker. He was able to retrieve her corpse in two pieces.

In the wild, lions and tigers have no common range and do not meet, much less mate. Hybrids occur only in captivity. These hybrids are called tiglons, ligers, and other names, depending on which species served as sire and which as dam, and even on the grandparentage. These crosses are a mere stunt of human ingenuity rather than a viable line. Crosses have severely injured children at zoos and circuses. In 2008, a liger killed its keeper at Safari's Animal Sanctuary in Broken Arrow, Oklahoma.

• • •

THE LEOPARD IS much smaller than the lion or tiger—about 200 pounds at most—but it rivals them as a danger to people. Few leopards hunt humans, but some do so very effectively. They generally hunt humans the same way they manage other prey, ambushing them in the dark. They may, for example, take sleeping people from their homes. Many observers have commented on their startling ability to flatten and conceal themselves in almost any cover. This talent, along with a patterned coat that makes them difficult to see in shadow, allows them to move very close to victims before striking. In fact, field biologists sometimes have trouble seeing leopards even when they know exactly where to look. The leopard's strike is remarkably fast, usually ending with a bite that either strangles the victim or pierces his brain.

Jim Corbett recounts an incident that illustrates the leopard's remarkable stealth. Two men were sitting in a dark room in the Indian state of Rudraprayag, smoking and chatting. The door was closed. One man passed the pipe back to his friend, who did not take it. Its embers scattered on the blanket they sat on. It was only when the first man moved to clean up the mess that he noticed a silhouette passing out the now open door. It was the shadow of a leopard carrying his friend in its

A LEOPARD HAS TAKEN ITS KILL INTO A TREE, BEYOND THE REACH OF ITS RIVALS.

mouth. The witness had heard nothing while the cat killed his friend a yard away from him.

The leopard responsible killed at least 125 people in a little more than a decade. It took people tending livestock, drawing water, or cutting wood. It devoured many people making pilgrimages to the shrines of the region. As it grew more experienced, it ripped off wooden doors, burst through windows, and clawed through the walls of thatched huts to reach human prey. Corbett killed it in 1926. In 1910, he had killed another dangerous cat called the Panar leopard, which reportedly killed four hundred people. Africa, too, has known cases of serial predation by leopards. Ionides reports that one killed eighteen children near Ruponda, Tanganyika. Along the Ruponda River, another leopard killed twenty-six women and children without eating any of them. Many carnivores are known to kill far more than they can eat, caching the surplus against a future need. This instinct is untrammeled by the mathematical skills that might otherwise tell an animal when he's overdone it. That behavior may explain the behavior of the Ruponda River leopard. But, like a housecat toying with insects or mice, the leopard may simply have been practicing its hunting skills. We do not know what animals think or feel, but it takes no great leap to suspect that cats enjoy using their skills without practical purpose. Certainly mere enjoyment accounts for much of human behavior.

Leopards still take people throughout much of their African and Indian ranges. In fact, the leopard may be the most prolific mammalian predator of human beings. In the single month of June 2004, for example, leopards took ten people within the city limits of Bombay.

Captive leopards have killed their keepers—and visitors—from Oklahoma City to India. The favorite tactic of leopards in this situation is to seize the victim's head with one broad paw and drag him close enough for a bite.

The jaguar, a Latin American cousin to the lion, tiger, and leopard, can reach 300 pounds, and claims have been made for the occasional tiger-sized specimen. History provides many cases of jaguars eating people. On his historic journey with the *Beagle,* Charles Darwin heard of woodcutters killed by jaguars. He knew of a man who was attacked on board a ship. The jaguar apparently swam aboard at night and seized the first man to show himself on deck. The man lost the use of his arm.

Theodore Roosevelt reported what befell a surveying expedition in the Amazon. A big male jaguar repeatedly raided their stock of jerked beef. The men finally stowed the meat so that the jaguar couldn't get at it. In its next nocturnal visit, it seized a man instead. He screamed once before the cat killed him with a bite through the skull. This is a classic case of habituation: the jaguar learned to associate people with food before actively preying on a human.

Things changed as the human population of South America became relatively well armed. These days, jaguars are, as big cats go, minor predators of humans. Their main interaction with people comes from preying on livestock. People trying to defend their herds, or to track down the jaguars responsible for thinning them, have often been killed.

I HEARD AN interesting story about a cougar a few years ago, and though I was never able to trace it back to its source, I did explore the area and verify the presence of cougars that had taken livestock. As the story goes, a man driving through a rural town in Oklahoma was surprised to see a cougar sitting in a backyard. He wondered whether the people who lived in the house knew about it. He stopped his car and got out cautiously. The cougar did not seem to notice him. It was busy looking at something else. It nodded continually, its gaze apparently on something the man couldn't see. In front of the cougar was a tall fence that separated this yard from the next. Following the cat's gaze on its upward swing, the man saw what it saw. A little girl appeared over the fence every few seconds. He could hear voices now. Children were playing on a trampoline. The man shouted a warning. The cougar turned to look him in the eye. The next moment seemed to last a very long time. Suddenly the cougar swung away. The man remembered its first few steps, but after that it seemed to have soaked into the earth.

The cougar—also known as the puma, mountain lion, or panther—ranges broadly in the deserts, mountains, coastal plains, swamps, and rain forests of the Americas. Because the cougar is stealthy and generally solitary, it can live near human cities without being detected. It prefers to hunt at dawn and dusk, but adapts to working by day or night. It is a generalist predator. It often preys on deer, elk, and other large herbivores, but is also comfortable eating mice and squirrels and even grasshoppers. Occasionally a cougar takes a small alligator.

The animal's physical abilities are impressive. It can see in the dark. It can swim and climb trees. It can fall 40 or 50 feet, landing unharmed on its feet. It can execute 25-foot leaps from a dead stop, and with a running start can leap almost 40 feet. It has been known to clear ten-foot fences and to leap from the ground onto the back of a person on a horse. A cougar weighing 140 pounds can lift and carry three times its own weight in its mouth. At a research facility owned by the University of California, Davis, a cougar once killed a 130-pound deer and carried it over an eight-foot chain-link fence.

I've already discussed the complicated interactions of humans and cougars in the introduction to this book. I'll add here that, unlike many predators, wild cougars hurt people almost exclusively in the course of predation. In May 1992, in Kyuquot on Vancouver Island, a cougar took an eight-year-old boy who was sitting on a log at the edge of a school yard. In August 1996, near Princeton, British Columbia, a woman was riding horses with her children when a cougar attacked her six-year-old son. The boy survived. His mother died in his defense.

Adults, too, have been the targets of predatory attacks by cougars, though taller people generally intimidate them. The young jogger killed in Idaho Springs, Colorado, weighed less than 130 pounds. In April, 1994, in El Dorado County, California, another slender runner was attacked on a wilderness trail. As investigators pieced things together later, the cougar knocked her 30 feet down an embankment to a creek, where she regained her feet and fought back, as evinced by the defensive wounds on her hands and arms. She broke free and ran away, covering another 25 feet before the cougar again seized her. It killed her with a bite that shattered her skull.

No OTHER CATS prey on people, but many can do us harm in the wrong circumstances. The cheetah is a good example of an animal utterly harmless in the wild but potentially lethal when meddled with. This slender spotted cat of Africa droops like a suspension bridge between pelvis and shoulder. Its spine is far more flexible than that of most quadrupeds, allowing the animal to stretch at a full run for greater speed. Its speed, as most people have heard, often betters 60 miles per hour in short bursts, and it's the fastest land animal.

At rest, the cheetah appears unthreatening. Black lines lead down from the inner corners of its eyes, as if it had been crying through its mascara. Its face is small in relation to the length of its body, and this reflects the fact that it is built less for fighting than for speed, since the teeth and jaws of a cat are weapons. Even in defense, the cheetah prefers flight to fight. People have had to resort to ingenious stratagems to get themselves attacked. One such person was Stan Brock, famed in the 1960s and '70s as a personality on the TV show *Wild Kingdom*. He was moving cheetahs from one area to another as part of a conservation effort. He worked from horseback, capturing the cheetahs with a lariat. One cheetah submitted to the lariat with a few snarls and an ineffectual swat. But the director felt this successful first lassoing had not been captured adequately on film, so a second capture of the same animal was arranged. Having learned the procedure from the first take, the cheetah ruined the second by anticipating Brock's blocking. It leaped onto his horse, stared him squarely in the face, and took a bite. Its long upper cuspid punctured the bone just below his left eye. In a flurry of motion, it left the horse's back and the general area. Brock was evacuated by helicopter to a distant hospital, where a plastic surgeon saved his eye and his telegenic looks.

Such incidents with wildlife are common in TV and the movies, because they involve people trying to force animals to act according to expectations. Another case pitted Joan Embry, a Los Angeles zoo worker well known in the United States for her appearances on talk shows, against a cheetah. Embry suffered two slash wounds on her face.

One need not attain celebrity status to suffer the wrath of the cheetah. An eight-year-old boy was the victim in a 1994 attack in Jackson, Mississippi. The cheetah climbed out of its zoo cage, tackled the boy, and inflicted scratches and minor bites before help arrived. In 2007, a Belgian woman apparently hid in the Olmense Zoo until closing time, then found the keys to the cheetah cage and let herself in. No one knows her motive. She was a fan of wildlife and in fact sponsored one of the cheetahs. She was found dead in the morning.

Most of the forty-one species of cats are harmless in the wild, but captivity changes things. Captive snow leopards, ocelots, bobcats, caracals, Eurasian lynxes, and Asian jungle cats have all attacked people. In 2000, in Rensselaer, New York, a man was walking a pet serval when it attacked a four-year-old boy. It bit him in the neck and face. The man tried to control the cat and was bitten on the hand before he succeeded. The man required stitches, the boy plastic surgery. Servals normally live in the long grasses and stream beds of northern and central Africa. They stand about two feet high at the shoulder and weigh up to 40 pounds. Their keen ears guide them in the hunt; often they find lizards and rodents by listening for them as they tunnel underground. The serval also takes small hoofed animals, birds, frogs, and insects. A four-year-old child, weighing perhaps 40 pounds, would be a large but appealing meal for a serval. Only millennia of cohabitation can reduce the instinct of predatory mammals to attack children similar in size to their usual prey. (Even among domestic dogs, as we have seen, this instinct has not altogether vanished.) Children are usually protected by the tendency of smaller wild cats to avoid human presence. Captivity removes that protection.

A FEW OTHER circumstances can bring wild cats into conflict with people. For example, there's the case of a Canadian lynx leaping from a tree onto the back of a trapper carrying a dozen snowshoe hare carcasses. The snowshoe hare is the favored prey of this species. After a brawl that supposedly lasted ten minutes, the trapper strangled the cat. Possibly the lynx had failed to perceive what was carrying the food it wanted. Or perhaps it judged the bounty worth fighting for.

Illness can make a cat aggressive. Rabies is particularly dangerous because it can imbue a cat with almost inconceivable ferocity and persistence. The *Orlando Sentinel* reported an illustrative case in 2002. The victim was a man hiking alone in a park. The hiking trail wound through stands of oaks and past an historic cemetery before it edged up to a pond. It was a summer afternoon in Florida, hot enough to justify a canteen full of ice water. As the hiker broke into the grasslands near the pond, he heard a growl behind him. It was, he thought, exactly like the bobcat growls on old TV shows.

He turned in time to see the bobcat bounding out of the scrub. It went for his throat. He caught it with both hands and held it away from him. The cat thrashed and bit, slicing up the man's arms. The man shook it, as if to bring it back to its senses. It was, in theory, a nocturnal predator that favored smaller prey—rabbits, rodents, and birds, supplemented by the occasional grasshopper or snake and a rare fawn or sheep. Bobcats typically measure two or three feet long and weigh only 15 or 20 pounds, about twice the weight of an average house cat.

The man threw the bobcat. It scrambled off into the woods. He thought he was safe now, but it came back as quickly as it had vanished, heading straight for him again. He picked up a tree branch and swung. The cat went down, unconscious. The man felt guilty: the cat was mad and didn't deserve this cruelty. He also felt he didn't want it to get back up. He bludgeoned it with the branch, aiming for a merciful kill.

He had a first-aid kit and a cell phone. He stopped his bleeding and dialed. It was a two-mile hike through roadless wilderness to get help, and the thought of rabies had rooted in his mind. He expected attacks from every clump of brush, from bears or bobcats or coyotes. At the trailhead, rescuers were waiting for him, but his adventure wasn't over. A park ranger persuaded him to point out the spot where he'd killed the bobcat. They drove there in a truck, and when they arrived, they found nothing. But there was no time to wonder if they'd gotten the wrong spot, because the bobcat came slamming against the door of the truck, clawing futilely to get at the men inside. The ranger came out ready to shoot, but the cat scampered off into the brush again.

After taking the hiker back to safety, the ranger returned with two colleagues. They rattled through the brush to find the bobcat. This is the most dangerous situation for a human; like lions, bobcats like to launch their attacks from the safety of cover, and the undergrowth provided plenty of that. The unlucky member of the trio saw the cat springing out of cover too late. It bit down on her elbow, its canine teeth making four crisp punctures. She shook it off, but it leaped onto her back. She was wearing a bulletproof vest, which protected her from most of the cat's attack. There was a frantic struggle. The cat would not let go. One of the other rangers pushed the barrel of his weapon into the cat's fur and fired. It still didn't let go. Another point-blank round finally made it relinquish its hold. The rangers finished it.

Lab results showed the cat rabid. The hiker and the bitten ranger each took a course of injections.

PROPORTIONALLY, THE HYENA HAS THE MOST POWERFUL JAWS OF ANY MAMMAL.

4. THE HYENAS

ORDER CARNIVORA: FAMILY HYAENIDAE

> The sound of Africa is not the thundering rumble of a distant
> lion, nor is it the hollow trumpet of a bull elephant. If Africa has a
> voice, it is the hyena. . . . From the first, faraway *wooooo-uppp* of
> the pack gathering to the sniggering chitter of the kill, the hyena
> is telling you something you don't want to be reminded of: *you're
> just meat after all and your day will come.*
>
> PETER HATHAWAY CAPSTICK, *Death in the Long Grass*

"HORRIFIED." That was the word Jane Goodall used in *Innocent Killers*
to describe her reaction when she witnessed spotted hyenas eating their
prey alive. While studying the behavior of predators near the Ngoron-
goro Crater in Tanzania, she saw hyenas dismantling a wildebeest,
which continued to bawl for three minutes while the hyenas brawled

with each other, "running off with pieces of gut, giggling." Hyenas have even been known to bite off and eat pieces of a prey animal while it's still running.

A big spotted hyena reaches five feet in length and stands almost three feet high at the shoulder. It weighs as much as 175 pounds. Proportionally, it possesses perhaps the most powerful jaws of any mammal. It also has the largest carnassial teeth—those specialized teeth in the side of the jaw that distinguish carnivores and allow them to shear apart large prey. Its bite can crack bones. In fact, it typically eats the bones of its prey, along with almost everything else. It spares only the horns of an herbivore and its rumen, the forestomach compartment that holds insufficiently chewed vegetation.

The spotted hyena takes an almost unbelievable variety of prey, including such formidable animals as Cape buffalo, sablebuck, and even lions (though this feat requires a four-to-one advantage for the hyenas). Young hippopotamuses, rhinoceroses, and giraffes are also potential food, despite the protection of their dangerous parents. Furthermore: various antelopes (including the largest kind, the eland), hares, zebras, jackals, foxes, snakes, porcupines, dogs, cats, livestock, termites, the feces of other animals (Hugo van Lawick reported that they especially sought that of Cape hunting dogs), placentas from various animals, leather, ostrich eggs, warthogs. And other spotted hyenas, on occasion. The archaeologist Louis Leakey and a companion were once attacked by a party of seventeen spotted hyenas. They shot two of the animals— which were summarily eaten by the rest. The hyena finds prey by sight, by sound, by smell, and even by deduction: it has been observed to follow the flights of vultures to injured or dead animals.

It begins its aggressive ways within hours of birth, when it brawls with its littermates. Sometimes these brawls end in death—an extreme form of sibling rivalry. Once old enough to hunt outside their own den, hyenas may work alone, in small groups temporarily splintered from the clan, or, when hunting large, fast animals such as zebra, in groups of a dozen or more. In defense of territory, the entire clan—up to eighty animals—may cooperate. Like wolves, hyenas increase the range of possible prey by pack hunting.

They generally need no such tactics against human beings. As is the case with most carnivores, preying on humans is a minority pursuit for the spotted hyena, but those that do take up this activity excel at it.

In 1995, a twenty-five-year-old California woman was attacked while on an educational camping expedition to Kenya with nineteen other foreigners. The hyena tore through the tent where she and three others slept. The *Jewish Bulletin of Northern California* quotes her as follows: "The first thing I remember is just this animal landing on my arm. Everyone was screaming. It was biting my arm over and over again. I thought it was a baboon or monkey because its hands were so human, gripping my arm as it bit at my elbow. It was holding on to me, and I couldn't get it off." She then heard the hyena biting her face. It is the sound, specifically, that she remembers, followed by the feel: "My whole face just came open." The hyena dragged her out of the tent. Its ambition was foiled by a local man who stabbed it through the eye. The hyena did not at first find this discouraging. The man stabbed several times, until the hyena finally surrendered and fled. The attack happened in a remote area. The young woman survived twelve hours of transport and three hours of surgery. She eventually recovered with scars on her face and arm.

In 2000, an eleven-year-old boy from Baltimore was on safari in Botswana with his mother. Hyenas took him while he slept in his tent.

THE SPOTTED HYENA FINDS PREY BY SIGHT, BY SOUND,
BY SMELL, AND EVEN BY DEDUCTION.

Despite a quick response, guides were able to recover only part of his body.

Hyenas are not intimidated by numbers. An Ethiopian family was attacked as they slept in a refugee camp. The hyenas killed two of the children by crushing their skulls. Their mother died of evisceration. One of the hyenas seized an eleven-year-old boy by the face and dragged him, severing his nose, destroying one eye and dislocating the other, crushing the orbital bones, and removing most of the left side of his face. The father succeeded in driving off the hyenas before they could take this boy. The father died later that night, possibly of a heart attack brought on by trauma. The eleven-year-old survived and was at last report headed for adoption by an American family. He has undergone extensive reconstructive surgery.

As these cases illustrate, humans are most vulnerable to hyenas when they sleep. The hunter Peter Hathaway Capstick claimed that people who drink to excess are especially vulnerable, since they sometimes fall asleep outdoors and unguarded. Many people have awakened abruptly to discover some part of their anatomy—ear, nose, lips, hand, foot, genitals—excised by a passing hyena who was not hungry enough to make an entire meal of the person in question. Leakey recounted a case that sounds like something out of *Candide:* a fifteen-year-old girl was rescued from hyenas before they could kill her, but one of the carnivores had bitten a chunk from her buttocks, leaving what Leakey described as "a permanent hollow." Roger Caras mentions that "a native hunter working for Sir Alfred Pease" lost part of his face to a hyena. In *Man Is the Prey,* James Clarke described a man whose

> face ended below his cheekbones: his nose, palate, upper teeth,
> tongue, and almost his entire lower jaw were gone. Only his eyes
> and the upper part of his head remained intact and yet he was alive
> and moderately healthy and had taught himself to swallow food. He
> had received one bite, just one snap.

A 2005 report from an American doctor working in Nigeria mentioned the case of a woman who lost consciousness while giving birth and awoke to find a hyena eating her child. The woman herself was bitten on the thigh badly enough to leave a scar.

The tendency of spotted hyenas to take people varies by region and clan. Like lions and wolves, they develop cultural preferences for prey. Tanzania and Kenya have long suffered from hyena problems. For example, one Tanzanian village saw more than sixty people bitten in a brief span. In some of these cases, the hyenas invaded homes to attack people. In a separate incident, hyenas even killed a patient as he left a Tanzanian hospital.

Perhaps the most notorious series of hyena attacks occurred in the Mlanje District of Malawi between 1955 and 1962. A single clan killed at least three dozen people and injured many others. The attacks came frequently in the summers, when people slept outside. A six-year-old girl was devoured entirely except for the back of her head. Of a man described as "the village idiot," nothing was found but the bloody scraps of clothes. One woman suffered neck wounds and the amputation of her arm before people arrived to rescue her. The hyenas took the arm with them as they retreated into the bush. The woman died the next day.

Other devastating series of attacks occurred in two different regions of Ethiopia in the late 1990s and in Somalia in 2005 and 2006. In Eritrea, attacks occurred within the capital city of Asmara. In Malawi in 2005, authorities attributed nine deaths and fifteen other maulings in the span of a few days to a hyena that was said to be rabid. Authorities had the animal shot.

Many writers note that hyenas and other scavengers serve to dispose of corpses in several African cultures, and that this habit may encourage them to view humans as food. Peter Capstick, noting that hyenas formerly ranged across Europe and into wider stretches of Asia than they do now, went so far as to suggest that "more human flesh has gone down hyenas' throats than down those of any other animal."

IN HER ESSAY "Hyena," Joanna Greenfield, a former volunteer at an Israeli zoo, describes the immature striped hyena she was charged with feeding and watering:

> A mane trickled down sloped shoulders like a froth of leftover
> baby hair; he looked strangely helpless, as if weighted down by
> the tangled strands, and his back rounded to a dispirited slump.

Even though he had a hyena's posture, he was like a German shepherd. . . . His stripes twisted a bit at the ends and shimmered over the coat like feathers at rest. . . . [T]he hyena has callused skin on its throat, thick and rough, like eczema.

As a hand-reared cub, this hyena had bitten people before it took up life in a cage, though all these incidents had apparently been minor. One day, when Greenfield brought a dish of water into the cage, the hyena attacked, seizing her by the arm and chewing off chunks, which it swallowed without relinquishing its hold. Greenfield pounded and kicked at the animal without much effect. When she poked at its eyes, it let her loose. But she wasn't out of the cage yet, and as she tried to pass the hyena to make an exit, it attacked again, latching on to her right leg. "In three moves I didn't feel, he took out most of the calf," Greenfield wrote. She managed to escape the cage. So did the hyena. It appeared interested in pursuing its act of predation to a conclusion, but at this point other people arrived to help. Medical treatment saved Greenfield's life, despite massive tissue loss—parts of her leg had been stripped to the bone. The hyena was later killed, against Greenfield's wishes.

The striped hyena ranges from northern Africa through the Middle East and into India and Pakistan. It is mostly a scavenger on the kills of larger carnivores and a predator of small animals. It lives comfortably near humans, dining on garbage and taking livestock as large as cattle.

STRIPED HYENAS CAN DRIVE LEOPARDS AND CHEETAHS FROM THEIR KILLS.

Everywhere in its range, it is overshadowed by more dangerous predators—tigers, wolves, lions, spotted hyenas. Nonetheless, it is a formidable carnivore. Striped hyenas have been observed to drive leopards and cheetahs from their kills.

Most human victims are children. In 1974, for example, the Bihar district of India saw nineteen children killed by striped hyenas. Similar spates, in fact, seem to occur every few decades, perhaps corresponding to periods when other prey is scarce. These days they are mostly confined to poor areas of India, where children must tend livestock without adult supervision.

THE PET FERRET IS A SEMIDOMESTICATED FORM
OF THE EUROPEAN POLECAT.

5. OTHER CARNIVORIDS

AN UNUSUAL MARITAL DISPUTE arose in Benton, Louisiana, in 2006. The husband claimed, from his jail cell, that the couple's pit bull puppy was responsible for gnawing four toes off his infant daughter. His wife, from her separate cell, averred that the puppy was innocent and that their pet ferret must bear the blame. I'm with her. Pet ferrets take a special interest in infant humans.

Biting is typical play behavior for a young pet ferret, a more or less domesticated form of the European polecat. It's hard to define when such bites ought to be taken seriously. The City of New York reported seventeen ferret bites in 1999, presumably meaning bites annoying enough to prompt a report. Babies are special objects of attention because of their helplessness. It has been suggested that ferrets also find the scent of milk appealing. In 1998, a pet ferret inflicted more than fifty wounds on the face and chest of a five-week-old girl lying between her sleeping parents. She received more than a hundred stitches. The parents received unwelcome attention from the authorities. In 2000, a pair of ferrets inflicted more than a hundred wounds on the face of a ten-day-old girl while her mother slept. A pet dog rescued the baby.

The only members of the order Carnivoridae that prey on people are found among the bears, canids, cats, and hyenas. Smaller carnivorids like the ferret can still be dangerous because they're well equipped to bite and scratch, but they typically tangle with people only when they're kept captive. Eurasian badgers, for example, often hurt their keepers. In 2002, a pet raccoon mauled a two-month-old boy in Des Moines, Iowa. In August 2006, a nine-year-old girl reached into the meerkat enclosure at the Minnesota Zoo. One of the meerkats bit her on the hand. Though the bite itself was minor, officials slaughtered all the meerkats to test them for rabies. The results were negative.

In the wild, rabies really can prompt small carnivorids to attack people. Both skunks and raccoons are major vectors of rabies in parts of North America. In 2007, an outbreak of rabies among raccoons struck Connecticut. Several coons attacked dogs, and one woman was bitten. A skunklike carnivorid called the ratel or honey badger is the major vector of rabies in Kenya.

Speaking of skunks, I remember an autumnal day when I was a child. We were driving across a yellow field, my grandmother and I, to deliver lunch to my grandfather. The tall grass parted before the bumper of the pickup truck, and there in a clearing before us was a skunk. It did nothing in particular, merely milled as if waiting for a friend, but my grandmother sprang into action. She cranked madly at the steering wheel. Her right hand darted over to shift, but at first found only my knee; then we were reversing away. She screamed loud enough to make a tinny echo in the truck. It was the famously bad smell she feared—being inside a closed vehicle isn't adequate protection. On foot, we'd have had more to fear. The repugnatorial fluid sprayed from the anal glands of the skunk can burn the eyes and inflame the mucous membranes. The worst effects of this defensive attack are temporary blindness and choking. The ratel is similarly armed. Many other carnivorids in the weasel family also produce a nauseating stench, though they don't spray their scent at humans.

• • •

IN 2006, A PREGNANT woman swimming in Claytor Lake near Roanoke, Virginia, was bitten on the buttock, thigh, and arm by a river otter. It attempted to drag her underwater. Her sister helped her to shore, the otter still attached to her thigh. Here the sister punched at the otter's head until it retreated. Many reports of otter attacks come readily to hand, most of them describing a particular attack as an unprecedented occurrence. In another 2006 attack, a seventeen-year-old California girl swimming in Sugar Pine Lake suffered wounds to her arm, foot, and leg. The otter pursued her onto shore, where a friend scared it away with a rock. Otters have even climbed aboard boats to attack their occupants.

River otters typically reach body lengths of two or three feet, with another foot of tail, and weigh only about 25 pounds. Nonetheless, they seem capable of matching an adult human in the water. In some cases, the otters have been rabid. It may be that mother otters protecting their cubs, and males with territorial concerns, are involved in some attacks. In one case, an otter attacked a pet dog, then bit the foot of a man who tried to save the dog. The otter fled with the dog's body. This occurrence suggests at least the possibility of a predatory attack on the pet, though it was much larger than the otter's usual prey—crustaceans, insects, fish, and occasionally snakes and birds.

In 2003, near Billings, Montana, a runaway pet otter bit three men who tried to return it to its owner. So alarmed were the men that they counterattacked with a shovel and a pickup truck. To their discomfort, they left insufficient brain matter for a rabies test.

IN THE OCEANS, much larger and more formidable carnivorids live, and one of them may be willing to try people as prey. The Antarctic leopard seal reaches lengths of more than 13 feet and weights of almost a thousand pounds. Large leopard seals take seabirds and smaller seals. This largish, warm-blooded prey resembles us, though we might prefer to think otherwise. Leopard seals swim under ice, stalking the penguins and other birds that walk on it. When a bird comes close to the edge, the seal leaps out of the water and seizes it, then shakes it to death. This behavior generalizes easily enough to humans. On an Antarctic expedition in 1985 and '86, a man named Gareth Wood was walking on ice when a leopard seal emerged from a fissure and bit him on the leg. One of Wood's companions kicked the seal repeatedly with his cramponed boot, drawing blood from its head, until it let go. It came back for a second bite. This time two companions kicked the seal; it let go for good. In 2003, a scientist with the British Antarctic Survey was snorkeling when a leopard seal seized and drowned her.

Seals and walruses—the pinnipeds—evolved from land carnivores. All of them have retained the predatory lifestyle. The prey varies with the species, but usually includes fish, squid, crabs, and the like. Besides the leopard seal, none of them seem to regard people as prey. They attack mostly in defense of self or territory. In 2005, near George, South Africa, a woman tried to help an apparently stranded Cape fur seal into the water. It bit her nose off. Presumably it felt the woman was attacking it. The largest pinnipeds, including leopard seals, elephant seals, and walruses, have sunk rafts and even boats in defensive attacks.

The defensive responses of the seals known as sea lions don't necessarily match the intentions of the humans who provoke them. Often enough, people go along minding their own business, hardly aware of a sea lion, only to find themselves bitten smartly on the calf. The sea lion has the full complement of carnivore teeth, including sharp canines, and can bite as effectively as a dog. In 2005, sea lions were especially numerous and aggressive along the California coast. The *Los Angeles Times*

A LEOPARD SEAL ON ICE.

reported an incident in which eighteen lions climbed onto a 37-foot sailboat, causing it to sink. (The largest species of sea lion attains lengths of more than ten feet and weights of more than 2,400 pounds. Other species are much smaller, but still hefty enough to endanger a boat when they pile on in numbers.) Swimmers and surfers were bitten. People on boats were bitten and pulled into the water. In Monterey, people were bitten, and the creatures left abundant vomit and feces on the docks. The nuisance of their loud barking and their smells seemed to concern most residents more than any suspicion of danger. In 2006, a sea lion bit at least fourteen swimmers in a San Francisco lagoon. It harassed one swimmer out of the water, then followed her onto land and bit her again. In another case, it bit a woman repeatedly as she swam for shore, sending her to the emergency room with six minor wounds.

Fishermen sometimes get into trouble with sea lions because the animals want their catch. In 2004, a sea lion leaped out of the water in the port of King Cove, Alaska, and onto a boat where a professional fisherman was working. The lion bit him on his hind end and plunged back into the water with him. Once beneath the surface, it let him go. He bobbed to the top and was rescued. Though his clothes were torn, the man's only injury was a minor scrape on his buttock. All this happened in a few seconds. The boat was laden with cod, and was in fact docked at a seafood restaurant to unload its haul. Nearby, others were engaged in cleaning octopus. The man was standing two feet from the hold when he was snatched. The food-rich environment would seem to explain the attack, and the sudden loss of interest probably means that a human being was not the sort of food the sea lion was aiming for.

Surprisingly, this is not the only case of human buttock injury in the lore of sea lions. In 1987, a man was snatched from a dock at Kodiak, Alaska, in precisely this manner. In his case, the sea lion's intention seems even more obviously to have been hunger for fish. Sources report that the man had been feeding sea lions from the dock, and one source even claims he had put a fish in his back pocket and invited the sea lion to take it. There can hardly be a clearer instance of a victim's asking for it.

AQUATIC DANGERS

THE IDEA OF PREDATION IN
CONCENTRATED FORM.

6. SHARKS AND THEIR RELATIVES

CLASS CHONDRICHTHYES

IN THE SUMMER OF 1975, the water changed. Not the actual water: the water of the mind. Before that, the scariest thing in my mental waters was a six-foot frog called the Creature from the Black Lagoon. After that summer, and ever since, the scariest thing in the water has been the great white shark.

That was the year a movie called *Jaws* came out. It changed our cultural view of the shark, just as *The Exorcist* redefined the image of demonic possession and *The Texas Chain Saw Massacre* redefined our image of what we now call the serial killer. Before *Jaws*, the terrors of the water were centered in such science-fictional creations as the giant cephalopod from *Twenty Thousand Leagues Under the Sea.*

I remember that summer well. National Geographic specials had put me under the spell of Jane Goodall and her chimpanzee acquaintances.

Born Free, a "based on a true story" account of humans and lions living in harmony, had recently been converted to a weekly TV show. It was an era of conservation. It was well known, of course, that sharks bit people and even ate them; those were facts of life for many people in tropical places. But for most Americans, at least, it was possible not to be actively aware of this harsh reality. In fact it was bad taste, in that environmentalist era, to mention such behavior. But suddenly the brute fact of human-eating was back in the cultural conversation.

I mention *Jaws,* fictitious and unscientific as it was, because it neatly diagrams our odd history with anthropophagous sharks. Arriving as it did at a moment of cultural cuddliness, it was a rude reminder that, no matter how much we may love them, wild animals are not our friends. While the lions in *Born Free* looked comely enough to help us overlook their dangerous attributes, sharks were impossible to cuddle, even in fantasy. From the human view, they look like the idea of predation in concentrated form. A wave of gratuitous shark killing followed *Jaws,* so severe that the great white is now classed as a vulnerable species. (Perhaps it would have been anyway, since our habits have fouled the oceans for every living thing.) Peter Benchley, the author whose novel ignited this cultural moment, later deplored what his book had inadvertently started.

Strangely, this is not the first time we learned our place with the help of the shark. The lesson recurs frequently, and then we undergo a sort of collective amnesia, once again losing ourselves in delusions of superiority. *Jaws* was mere fiction, but, like other horror movies of its era, its power to scare derived partly from the notion that it, too, was "based on a true story."

The true story began on July 1, 1916, near Beach Haven, New Jersey. Charles Vansant, a twenty-two-year-old textile salesman, was swimming in the ocean late in the afternoon. Witnesses shouted warnings when they saw a dark fin approach him. As he tried to come ashore, he was seen to struggle in the shallows. Blood colored the water. Vansant had been bitten in the leg, but now he was free. A lifeguard grabbed him under the arms and pulled him toward shore, but the shark bit Vansant on the thigh and tried to pull him out to sea. As he struggled, other swimmers formed a chain to pull him in. It was a bizarre tug-of-war, with the shark pulled far enough in to scrape bottom before it let go.

One side of Vansant's left thigh was stripped to the bone. His right leg bore a lesser wound. He died at 6:45 that evening of "shock and blood loss," an hour after entering the water.

The event was widely reported in newspapers. It shocked American readers. Most of them had been taught that sharks are harmless. Biologists were on hand to claim that in fact, sharks had weak jaws incapable of hurting a person. The animal in question must have been some other sort of aquatic life (large turtles were mentioned), and the attack was branded a fluke. There was, of course, no genuinely scientific reason to doubt that a shark was involved. What made this idea hard to accept was the cultural idea that human beings are fundamentally different from other animals. If sharks made no distinction between us and the lesser animals, something was wrong with the natural order.

The sequel to the Vansant attack followed five days later in nearby Spring Lake, New Jersey. Charles Bruder was swimming a quarter mile from shore when witnesses saw "a massive spray of water." Two rescuers in a rowboat saw a circle of blood in the water. Bruder was then thrown or shaken above the surface. Sharks often throw or shake large prey to break its spine. The motion also serves to saw off edible chunks of flesh against the animal's serrated teeth.

Bruder went under, then stuck his head up and said he'd been bitten by a shark. Rescuers offered him an oar, which he used to pull himself to the boat. They lifted him in. His rescuers saw that his feet were missing, and much of the flesh had been stripped from his lower legs. A fist-sized bite was missing from the right side of his torso. He died of blood loss on the beach within fifteen minutes.

In the ensuing days, people reported many supposedly hostile sharks. The next injury occurred not in the ocean, but in nearby Matawan Creek, 17 miles inland from Asbury Park. On July 11, Rensselaer Cartan, sixteen, was brushed by a shark while swimming there. The skin of a shark is studded with knobs of bone called denticles; a mere touch can make human skin bleed. Cartan was left with a bloody chest. He might have been hurt worse, for sharks often bump objects in the water to see what they are, and bleeding shows them that the object is potentially edible.

The next morning, Thomas V. Cottrell, a retired sailor, saw a shark in the creek, headed for the town of Matawan. Residents ignored his warnings. They knew a big shark couldn't possibly swim that far inland; certainly they had never seen a shark of any kind there. In the afternoon, a certain stretch of the creek was filled with boys at play. A shark was seen streaking toward Lester Stilwell, ten, who lay floating. It rose out of the water with Stilwell's arm in its mouth, shook him, then pulled him under. In the struggle it hit Albert O'Hara, eleven, with its tail, knocking him into the pilings of the pier. Stilwell came to the surface and screamed, but was pulled back under.

Summoned by Stilwell's friends, townspeople came to look for his body. Most of them disbelieved the shark story. They expected to find the boy drowned. Stanley Fisher, twenty-four, and two other men dived repeatedly in the area where Stilwell had vanished, trying to recover the body. Fisher found it at the bottom. The shark was feeding on it. He tried to take the body and was attacked. Men in boats went to his rescue, but he was pulled under repeatedly. When he finally made it to shore, one leg was half stripped of flesh from hip to knee. The wound measured 14 inches. He died within a few hours.

Men in boats hurried down the river to warn others out of the water. Three-quarters of a mile downstream, three boys were swimming when they received the alarm. Two escaped, but Joseph Dunn, twelve, was bitten in the lower leg. With the help of the other boys, he struggled free. He was hospitalized for two months, but eventually learned to walk again.

Tradition has assigned this string of attacks, which killed four people and seriously injured another, to a single immature great white shark. At an estimated eight to ten feet, it was too small to be an adult. Circumstances make it clear that the three attacks in Matawan Creek were the work of a single shark. This shark can't be ruled out in the open-water attacks, but the only factor in favor of indicting it is its size, which fits many dangerous sharks common in the area. It seemed reasonable to people of the time to blame all the attacks on one shark because they considered preying on people abnormal. Two abnormal animals surely wouldn't turn up at the same time.

In a sense, it's true that humans are not normal prey for a shark. We simply aren't in the water that often. But the big sharks are generalists, and we now know that many species will take human beings when the opportunity and hunger coincide. Besides the great white, a number of

THE LEMON SHARK, A MEMBER OF THE REQUIEM FAMILY, OCCASIONALLY
ATTACKS PEOPLE AND EVEN BOATS.

other anthropophagous species occurred in the area, including tiger and
bull sharks. The latter often swim up rivers, even hundreds of miles into
fresh water. The Matawan Creek attacks occurred in merely brackish
water, which doesn't entirely rule out the various saltier species.

SHARKS ATTACK ABOUT a hundred people a year. Ten to fifteen of these
attacks are fatal. The species most often documented to attack and kill
individual people is the great white (or white pointer). The milky belly
of the great white makes it hard to see against the sky; its back is a
murky gray, brown, or blue, camouflaging it when seen from above. It
can reach 21 feet and two tons. That makes it the largest active predator
among the sharks. It's big enough to take people as prey, and any bite it
gives is likely to inflict grievous injury.

A typical attack occurred at Pringle Bay, South Africa, in 1997. By-
standers saw a three-foot-long fin jutting from the water. A diver was
standing in the water. The next moment, where he had stood, the water
was red. That was all. The man's wife and daughter were watching from
the beach; they never saw him, nor any part of him, again. But not all
great white attacks are invisible. A witness to a 2002 attack in Northern
California described it memorably for the *San Francisco Chronicle:* "I

looked over and this guy was about three or four feet out of the water in the shark's mouth. You could see its teeth, its gums. Its eyes were shut. Its gills were wide open, like shutters. The whole dorsal fin on its back was out of the water." The victim of that attack, though critically injured, lived. His wounds extended from shoulder to thigh and required more than a hundred stitches.

Surfers are among the most frequent victims. Some biologists believe the outline of a surfer on his board attracts great whites because they mistake it for a seal. Support for this theory came in 2003, when a great white fatally attacked a woman swimming with sea lions near Avila Beach, California. The woman was wearing a wet suit and flippers, which presumably increased her resemblance to a sea lion.

Often the shark bites, then releases a human victim, allowing him or her to escape. It has been suggested that the first taste of human flesh tells the shark it has bitten the "wrong" kind of prey, something other than a seal or walrus. I'm more persuaded by the strategic explanation: the first attack, which is sudden and devastating, is meant to induce massive trauma. The prey animal then bleeds to death, or at least to the point of weakness, allowing the shark to eat it without a fight. Great whites have been observed using this strategy on elephant seals.

In fact, people do not always manage to escape between the first strike and the follow-up. In 2000, a New Zealander honeymooning in South Africa managed to get back on his surfboard and start paddling for shore after a first hit. The second hit finished him, and nothing was ever found of his body. A surfer in South African waters experienced a similar attack the following year. The shark took a bite of leg and surfboard together, as if sampling pâté on a cracker. It dragged the man underwater, then released him. The man remounted his board and paddled toward shore. The shark struck him hard from beneath, knocking him into the air, but without capsizing the board. The man kept paddling and made it to safety. Because he was in only six feet of water when the attack began, the man was able to escape into the shallows.

There's also a theory that many shark "attacks" are merely exploratory—a case of the fish groping the human to see what it is. This theory explains why so many sharks simply lose interest and let an injured human go: they've satisfied their curiosity.

But some great white attacks are simply deliberate predation. For example, in December 2004, at Adelaide, South Australia, an eighteen-year-old man was riding a surfboard towed behind a dinghy when he was dismantled by a white shark at least 15 feet long. It may have been joined in the attack by a second shark. His friends struck at the sharks with oars, but could not dissuade them. In 1985, in Peake Bay, South Africa, a 20-foot great white bit a snorkeler in half, then circled back to eat her.

Great whites can poke their heads out of the water and look around in the air. Some have been observed to do so before attacking a boat. This does not seem to me the behavior of an animal confused about the identity of its prey. Large great whites have bitten holes in boats to get at the people inside. Some have sunk boats.

In other boat attacks, the motive seems doubtful. In 1977 a great white leaped out of the water in False Bay, South Africa, landing on a ski boat. A man was squashed beneath it, his bladder ruptured and his pelvis broken, but he lived. The noise or electrical emissions of the boat may have had something to do with this and similar incidents, or the shark may have been interested in the thrashing and bleeding of hooked fish.

The great white is classed among the mackerel sharks. Several smaller members of this family are dangerous to people, including the sand tiger and the short-fin mako, both documented human-killers.

SOMETIMES OUR COLLECTIVE amnesia about sharks is a function not merely of our cultural beliefs, but of propaganda. In World War II, the U.S. government suppressed stories of shark attacks on sailors and soldiers in the Pacific theater. It was feared that this subsidiary horror of war would ruin morale.

These wartime attacks hardly compare with the horrors humans inflicted directly on each other, but they rank as the greatest cases of mass predation on humans ever documented. Predatory attacks on a few people at a time are documented for American black bears, tigers (working singly and in mother-and-offspring groups), lions (singly and in prides), and spotted hyenas (in clans). Wolves seem to have descended on towns en masse during, for example, certain medieval episodes of plague. Saltwater crocodiles and Nile crocodiles have certainly killed more than one person on occasion, though a famous account of salties slaughtering more than nine hundred people at once turns out to be a gross exaggeration. Tales of mass predation by piranhas seem to be mere folklore. None of these animals can match the sharks.

Throughout history, shipwrecks have turned people into prey. In 1907, for example, two passenger steamers collided in the Straits of Rhio. Sharks took survivors who dived into the water. Incidents like this are especially likely during war, when ships sink in greater numbers and hostile humans interfere with rescue attempts. The most extreme example on record befell the crew of the USS *Indianapolis* in the South Pacific at the close of World War II. Having delivered the fuel for the atomic bomb soon to be dropped on Hiroshima, the *Indianapolis* fell victim to the torpedoes of a Japanese submarine. The crew comprised 1,196 men. Of these, 321 emerged from the water alive four and a half days later, having survived on rafts and floater nets and in life jackets.

It is impossible to know how many of the 875 men who died between the sinking and the rescue five days later were killed by sharks, but the number seems to be in the hundreds. Raymond B. Lech speculated, on the basis of what information the survivors could give, that about eight hundred men escaped the ship before it sank. (Other authors place the number closer to nine hundred.) Lech's count means about five hundred men died in the water. The causes of death included drowning, heat, thirst, the toxic effects of ingesting saltwater or fuel oil, and burns and other injuries from the explosions on the torpedoed ship. Some, under the duress of thirst, exposure, and fear, committed suicide. Some went into a frenzied delusional state and killed shipmates. Others killed intentionally for life jackets or food.

The rest were taken by sharks. Men sped across the face of the water, propelled by unseen sharks. Others bobbed in the water as if asleep; on closer inspection they were found to be missing their lower halves. Some were dragged down suddenly, never to reappear; their empty life jackets might float up moments later.

Sharks attacked human bodies soon after the sinking. At first the sharks concentrated on the bodies of the dead. As more sharks arrived, the competition among them became more fierce, and they began to take more living people. They preferred isolated men, but soon they grew bold enough to snatch men even from groups that tried to fight

TIGER SHARKS TAKE AN EXTRAORDINARY VARIETY OF PREY.

them. When men died of other causes and were released into the water by shipmates, the sharks instantly moved in to dismantle the bodies. Attacks on living men increased as the days passed. During the rescue, crews in the air witnessed about thirty sharks massacre sixty men in a single frenzy.

A few men had life rafts, but these were no guarantee of safety. A man named McCoy was in a flimsy raft with four others. They huddled together at one end of it as a shark poked its head through the floor. McCoy told author Doug Stanton the eyes were big as plums, the white teeth two inches each, and the jaw about two feet across. McCoy kicked at the shark in desperation. Its hide tore his foot.

Rescuers found eighty-eight corpses partly eaten. No one can say how many of these men died because of shark attacks and how many were scavenged after dying of other causes. Most bodies were not examined or recovered. Stanton estimates the sharks killed two hundred men. Most survivors suffered scrapes as the sharks bumped them investigatively. Some emerged missing limbs, or with chunks of flesh missing from thighs, torsos, or buttocks. Of the 317 survivors (excluding four men who died in the hospital after being rescued), 183 had lost some flesh to sharks.

Many other wartime shipwrecks led to mass predation. During the Guadalcanal campaign, sharks attacked Americans from the cruiser

Juneau and the destroyer *Duncan*. Attacks weren't limited to the Pacific theater. In 1942, the British steamship *Nova Scotia* was torpedoed and sunk by a German submarine off the coast of Natal. Sharks took many men. Of the more than nine hundred aboard, fewer than two hundred survived.

There need not be a great many bodies in the water to interest sharks. In 1982, a yacht called *Trashman* sank off the mid-Atlantic coast of the United States. Its crew of five escaped in an inflatable rubber dinghy. As thirst set in, two of them drank seawater, became delusional, and swam away from the dinghy. Sharks quickly killed them.

MOST OF THE sharks involved in the *Indianapolis* tragedy belonged to a family called requiem sharks. These sharks aren't as massive as the great white, but more than a dozen of the species have hurt people, and the larger kinds can easily kill humans. The largest of them, sometimes topping 20 feet and three thousand pounds, is the tiger shark. Young specimens have dark stripes on their gray hides, a trait that can help identify the species. (Otherwise, few laymen can distinguish between the requiem sharks.) Tiger sharks are aggressive feeders. They take an extraordinary variety of prey, from turtles and squids to birds and other sharks. What makes the tiger especially dangerous is its comfort in shallow waters frequented by people. Like the great white, it ranges much of the tropical and temperate waters of the world. But the tiger is especially common near Hawaii, where it has hurt surfers and swimmers. A twenty-nine-year-old man who went body-boarding in Waimea Bay off Oahu seems to have been killed by a tiger shark. He was never seen again, but his board washed up the next morning. A 16-inch bite had been taken out of it. Experts were able to diagnose the species of shark by the shape of the teeth marks. Tiger sharks have killed at least twenty-eight people in individual attacks and injured dozens of others.

Bull sharks are much smaller animals, rarely exceeding 11 feet, but they are thickly built and aggressive. They have killed at least twenty-three people. In 2005, a bull shark attacked a fourteen-year-old girl boogie-boarding in the ocean near Pensacola, Florida. A surfer who answered screams found her floating facedown. The shark pressed its attack, trying repeatedly to take the girl until rescuers got her to shallow water. In a 1997 case, a bull shark amputated the leg of a man swimming with his pet poodle. The man soon died. (Dogs, by their splashing, increase the odds of attracting sharks. Charles Vansant, the first victim in the 1916 Jersey Shore attacks, was also accompanied by a dog. The dogs themselves have often been eaten by sharks.)

The oceanic whitetip has probably killed more people than any other species of shark. It inhabits deep waters and rarely encounters surfers and swimmers. But in shipwrecks, it is often the first predator on the scene. This species killed many of the victims of the *Nova Scotia* disaster; along with the tiger, the blue, and the mako, it participated in the horrors of the *Indianapolis*.

In 1972, professional divers Rod Temple, Robbie McIlvain, and Bret Gilliam set out to adjust some scientific gear and take photos on a reef near St. Croix. As they worked, a pair of whitetips approached them. The divers often swam among sharks and didn't panic at the sight of these, but they did find it unusual to see whitetips only a few hundred yards from shore. They knew the species as aggressive, so they kept an eye on them.

When it was time to surface, the process had to be slow. The men had dived deep, and they needed to decompress. Gilliam and McIlvain came up to a depth of 175 feet and rested on a ledge of the reef, waiting for Temple. He took longer than expected. Then the two saw air bubbling up. They assumed Temple's equipment was giving him a problem. Gilliam went down to help him, sending McIlvain up.

Gilliam found Temple fighting for his life. One of the whitetips, a 12-footer, had torn a handful of flesh from Temple's leg. At that depth, his blood billowed out green. The second shark bit him on the same leg even as Gilliam tried to pull him free. Temple raked at the gills and eyes of his attackers. Gilliam punched them. They ate pieces of flesh even as the men fought them. Then both sharks let go, and Gilliam pulled his friend up the reef. McIlvain saw what was happening and came to help. But the sharks struck again, latching on to Temple and pulling him and Gilliam down into deep water. According to Gilliam's account, Temple had by this time "lost a huge amount of blood and tissue." He stopped fighting. Gilliam assumed he was dead, but after a moment he began to fight the sharks again. They backed off, circling. The men sought the meager shelter of the reef. As Gilliam watched the sharks, they ate the body parts floating in the water, including a recognizable portion of Temple's leg. Temple shook his head and pushed Gilliam away to signal his resignation. But Gilliam wasn't ready to abandon him. He tried to take hold of Temple's waist harness. That's when he discovered the sharks had already disemboweled his friend.

Gilliam clutched Temple and made a desperate surge for the surface. The sharks attacked again, wrestling Temple away from him. The water darkened with blood and specks of flesh. Gilliam's air supply was exhausted. The sharks had dragged him more than 125 feet deeper during the course of the attack. He saw them still at work on Temple's body. He kicked for safety alone. He arrived at the surface on the verge of oxygen starvation and suffering from decompression sickness. Strangers found him and saved his life. McIlvain, having seen both men dragged down "in a cloud of blood," had reported them dead. Gilliam soon returned to diving, though he had lost much of the sight in one eye.

A FEW OTHER sharks occasionally attack with predatory intent, and the large hammerheads have even killed people. More common, though, are attacks like the one that befell a sixteen-year-old scuba diver near Marathon, Florida. He saw a two-foot-long nurse shark swimming near him and seized it by the tail. It retaliated by clamping on to his chest. The boy was rushed to the hospital with the shark still attached. Doctors had to surgically remove it. The boy survived without serious injury.

From the cobbler wobbegong, a bottom dweller that looks like a deep-dish pizza, to the rarely hooked frilled shark, which looks like an evil sock puppet, dozens of sharks hurt people with minor bites. It most often happens in the course of fishing or wading. But biting isn't the only recourse sharks have. Some wear venomous spines or wield blade-like attachments to their fins.

Among the shark's relatives one finds an even broader assortment of weapons: the slashing rostrum of the sawfish; the jolt of the electric ray; the ridged butting gear on the head of the bowmouth guitarfish. More than 150 species of rays possess stingers—stiff spines that lie along their tails, ending in serrated barbs supplied by venom glands. Some species possess several spines, others only one. These generally disk-shaped rays range from one to six feet in diameter, with perhaps another two feet of tail.

The stinger is purely a weapon of defense. When attacked, the ray can whip its tail around, stabbing or raking an aggressor with its sting. The wound resembles what a clumsy person might inflict with a steak knife, and it may cause heavy blood loss. Because the barbs at the tip of the spines point back toward the ray's body, the victim may have trouble prying the stinger loose. The venom, which only sometimes makes its way into the wound, causes devastating pain at the site of the injury. It may also cause fainting, nausea, diarrhea, muscle cramps, sweats, twitching, pain in the gut, a drop in blood pressure, and seizures. Despite these frightening symptoms, the sting is usually not lethal. Infection is a further danger, especially when, as is frequently the case, the barb breaks off in the wound. The sting may force sand and other foreign matter into the human body, along with dangerous microbes of the staph, strep, and other varieties.

Humans rarely get stung. The typical scenario has the person stepping on a ray camouflaged in the sediment beneath shallow water; the ray stings a foot or leg by reflex. An occasional person gets stung while hauling in a netted specimen or teasing the animal. In 2006, a spotted eagle ray three feet across leaped out of the water and onto a boat near Lighthouse Point, Florida. When an eighty-one-year-old man tried to remove it, it drove its foot-long barb into his chest. He survived after open-heart surgery.

The performer Steve "Crocodile Hunter" Irwin is among the few people to die of mechanical injury from the barb of a ray. His TV crew was filming him as he swam with bull rays. Irwin's widow has declined to release the film, so the exact cause of the incident may never be known. His usual practice was to touch animals and even provoke them into defensive behaviors. It made for interesting TV, though the stress this sort of teasing places on some animals endangers their health. As for his own safety, Irwin depended on his reflexes and his ability to gauge an animal's tolerance for human presence and touching. This time, he must have judged wrong. The ray stabbed him through the heart.

THE MOUTH OF A GROUPER IS BUILT TO ENGULF ITS VICTIMS.

7. THE BONY FISH

SUPERCLASS OSTEICHTHYES

I KNEW I'D LOST THE POOL by the way my neighbor's pole bent under its load. Everybody aboard the boat had put five dollars into a gallon jar, and whoever took the biggest fish of the day would get the jar. The winner was a barrel of a man, half Hemingway and half Santa Claus. After his victory he glistened with sweat. Others crowded to shake his hand. The creature he'd landed lay beside him on the deck, flexing its scabby mouth as if it meant to say something. I gazed into that cavernous orifice and was impressed. You could lose your head in there. The thing was a grouper—not an especially large grouper, actually, but wide as a pony.

A really big grouper would go ten feet and 900 pounds. Several that size are on record, and one hears reports of the bigger ones that got away. But even specimens weighing 100 pounds are formidable. The mouth of a grouper is broad and built to engulf prey, not to nibble at it. A big one can easily accommodate the hand or foot of a diver—or, in at least one case, the head. The creature's teeth are small, but grinding plates in its throat can mangle a human appendage. According to Fishbase, the definitive ichthyological database, the goliath grouper has "been known to stalk and attempt to eat divers." There are scattered reports of groupers killing people.

In one bizarre incident, a man died after attacking a goliath grouper with a spear gun. The speared grouper rushed away, looping the man's arm in the line attached to the spear. The man was towed behind the fish until it sought refuge in a cave. There it wedged itself so tightly the man could not pull it out. Nor could he loosen the line. Both were found dead, the fish still wedged, the man drowned.

There are more than twenty thousand species in the superclass Osteichthyes, which comprises fish with skeletons made of bone rather than mere cartilage. That includes most of the familiar fish, barring sharks and rays. None of these twenty thousand regularly succeeds in preying on people, but the failures cause us plenty of trouble.

An underbite full of sharp teeth makes a barracuda one of the scariest things you can meet in the water, but, at hardly a hundred pounds, even the largest are too small to find us feasible prey. Biting is another matter. Barracudas snap at shiny objects like watches or jewelry, especially in murky water. Their attacks are typically quick, single bites, following which they retreat, having found diving suit or human flesh unpalatable. Fishbase reports that their attacks are "rarely fatal." In 2006, a fisherman near Fort Lauderdale, Florida, hooked a barracuda estimated at 20 to 25 pounds, which bit him badly enough to require an emergency room visit.

Then there are the piranhas. Myths and old movies portray them swarming to strip human beings to the bone in seconds. A few of the meat-eating kinds, which have sharp, triangular teeth, really can overwhelm animals this way. The capybara, the four-foot-long aquatic rodent of the Amazon, sometimes dies a toothy death. But humans have little trouble escaping after the first nibble. In fact, people often swim in piranha-infested streams without danger. Trouble happens when a person wades near a nest. The defending parent bites a piece of flesh from the invader, leaving a cratered wound, then swims away. A piranha may also mistake a toe or finger for manageable prey, an error that occasionally leads to amputation. In 2002, piranhas bit at least thirty-eight people in a single town on the Rio Mogi Guacu in Brazil.

In the United States, virtually every big lake or reservoir is the setting for legends of giant catfish ("as big as a Volkswagen," went a version of the story I once heard about Lake Tenkiller in Oklahoma) that have eaten divers. These stories bear all the signs of folklore, such as the "friend of a friend" source and the lack of traceable names and dates. Although it is true that catfish sometimes bite people in North America, tearing the hide off a finger with ease, the stories of predation are bogus. Throughout the world, large catfish bite people without provocation. A Vietnamese species, *Wallago attu,* bites when handled, causing substantial injury. Another Southeast Asian species, the Mekong giant catfish, holds the record for largest freshwater fish, at nine feet and 646 pounds, but scientists consider it harmless. Theodore Roosevelt wrote of South American catfish that eat children and monkeys, but he could personally attest only to the monkeys.

That peculiar literary genre, the shipwreck survival narrative, offers many cases of people nibbled by triggerfish. These fish are not large enough to seriously threaten a person under normal circumstances—the ocean triggerfish runs about two feet and five pounds—but they have teeth like tiny ice picks, designed for breaking the shells of coral and crustaceans. They wound people, contributing to deaths from exposure. The bleeding may help attract sharks.

But we need not venture into the ocean to find a fish willing to wound. In the lakes near my current home in Wisconsin, for example, are muskies. These members of the pike family grow up to six feet long. Their jaws, which project like the bill of a duck, are equipped with long teeth. The roofs of their mouths are lined with short teeth that curve back toward the throat. They are generalist predators, taking fish, frogs, crayfish, ducklings, snakes, and small mammals. They even lunge out of the water to attack birds and mammals visible on the shore. A muskie can swallow prey almost half the length of its own slender body. Some choke to death from ambitious feeding. Once in a while a muskie takes a bite out of a fisherman or swimmer.

The tiger or Wisconsin muskie is a hybrid of muskie and northern pike. It, too, is known to bite people without obvious provocation. In

1998, a Wisconsin man was fishing from a boat, dangling his foot over-board, when a 36-inch tiger muskie bit his toe. He hauled the fish aboard and captured it. The man required sixty stitches. In a 1995 case, a tiger muskie bit a fourteen-year-old Minnesota boy on the hand and wrist as he swam in a lake. It's likely these fish mistook a human body part for some more manageable prey item.

Also amazing for its voracity is the bluefish. Groups of bluefish some-times feed in a shark-style frenzy. They are cannibals when opportunity presents, and it is said they will vomit what they've eaten so they can eat more. Their prey is mostly small fish. A surfer whose feet dangled into a frenzied mass of bluefish attacking a school of prey lost two toes. They bite fishermen on occasion. Their teeth are blunt cones mounted on ex-travagantly muscled jaws. A 25-pound bluefish is considered large, so the danger to people is usually minor.

Moray eels are built like aquatic pythons. They may reach 13 feet. In his book *Shark Trouble,* Peter Benchley describes a specimen half that length as having the girth of "a large honeydew or small watermelon." They rush out of crags in reefs or rocks to attack prey. Occasionally they attack people, though they never seem to follow through on the first bite by killing and eating the person. According to Benchley, the bite of a moray is "ragged (thus difficult to suture), exceedingly painful, and quick to become infected." Their bites have put some divers in the hos-pital. A common scenario has divers bitten by morays conditioned to as-sociate people with food. This happens when tourist outfits repeatedly feed the morays to draw them out for viewing. But Benchley also men-tions cases in which no such conditioning was apparent.

These are only the most formidable bony fish to bite humans. But fish do other nasty things to people. The most surprising danger, at least to an individual human victim, is collision. In 2002, on the Suwanee River in Florida, a woman handed her baby to her husband, then no-ticed a sturgeon leaping in front of the vessel. "Look at—" she said, her remark cut off by another sturgeon that slammed into her, collapsing her lung, breaking five ribs, and knocking her out. A sturgeon big enough to leap onto a boat is typically four to six feet long and more than a hundred pounds. The reason for the jumping is unknown.

Similar incidents in the American Midwest have involved bighead carp and silver (or flying) carp. Both of these species were imported

SWORDFISH USE THEIR
BONY BILLS TO SLASH
PREY.

from Asia because they devour plankton in great quantities. That habit made them useful in, for example, sewage treatment plants, where plankton grow out of control. But the carp escaped into the Mississippi basin. When startled, as by the sound of a boat engine, they leap. At sea, flying fish have been known to strike sailors. These fish are much smaller than the sturgeons and carp, with maximum lengths of about 18 inches, so most collisions with them are minor affairs. The tarpon, a game fish prized for its fight, sometimes leaps into a boat when hooked and injures people, either by collision or by thrashing.

A COLLISION BECOMES even more serious when the fish is well armed. Swordfish are aggressive and energetic predators found in all the warm oceans of the world. They use their bony bills to slash prey, killing it and cutting it into chunks small enough to swallow. At 15 feet and 1,200 pounds, large ones were a danger to the old wooden ships. They hunted smaller fish that sheltered under the ships and boats. A swordfish lunging for prey could build considerable momentum, giving its five-foot bill penetrating power. In *A Furnace Afloat,* Joe Jackson documents several nineteenth-century ships damaged by swordfish. A whaler called the *Fawn* was pierced through "the copper shielding, the felt, the deal, and the hard oak timbers to a depth of 14 inches." Jackson also mentions South Seas natives impaled when swordfish damaged their fishing boats. The Western fishing industry hunted swordfish by harpoon, and thus its sailors faced many of the dangers whalers did. In 1886, a Captain F. D. Langford, having launched a rowboat from his schooner in pursuit of swordfish, was fatally impaled through the floor of the boat. Modern steel ships and submarines also get attacked, but they're too sturdy for the swordfish to do real damage.

Swordfish occasionally hurt divers. A swimmer was fatally gored in the belly off the coast of Massachusetts in 1813. In 2003, a cetacean biologist named Mark Ferrari was diving with a pod of false killer whales near West Maui, Hawaii, to observe their predatory behavior when their prey—a swordfish—impaled him through the shoulder as it tried to escape. Ferrari eventually recovered the use of his arm after rehab.

Marlins and sailfish, both similarly armed with bills, rarely hurt anyone except an occasional unlucky fishermen. However, in 2006, near Bermuda, a charter fishing guide named Ian Card was standing on deck when a blue marlin leaped from the water, impaling him and driving him overboard and beneath the water. He wrestled free and was rescued.

A family of smaller predators called needlefish don't try to stab or slash people, but their narrow, pointed jaws happen to make them effective projectiles when they leap out of the water in pursuit of smaller fish. One species, the garfish, is hazardous prey for night fishermen in Papua New Guinea. The fishermen use lights to attract them. In one case, a leaping garfish fatally severed a man's carotid artery. In 2000, another member of the family called a houndfish leaped from the water off the Florida Keys, impaling a teenaged snorkeler. Two chunks of the fish's beak remained in her neck and had to be removed surgically.

I WAS ON my first fishing expedition in the Gulf of Mexico. The pole began to resist me. I reeled in line, and a flashing shape emerged from the blur of blue water. When I pulled it into the air someone called out that it was a red snapper, though it looked like a gigantic goldfish to me. On the deck I relieved it of the hook. It lay gasping. Every few seconds it would twist spastically, as if it had just remembered it was obligated to move. On the advice of my companion, an elderly relative who seemed to know what he was talking about, I strung it on an 18-inch bit of rope for safekeeping. I managed this by a sort of sewing. The rope was threaded through the eye of a thick bronze skewer. I had only to plunge the skewer into one of the fish's eyes and bring it out through the other one. It was surprisingly easy. The fish flexed its fins a bit, but otherwise lay still.

As I baited my hooks, each with part of a quartered squid, I marveled that no one got hurt doing this. There was the slightly undulant deck to cope with, and the thin tapering knife of the crewman hacking through another batch of bait, and the hooks, and the bronze skewers. And there was the snapper, now gasping and flexing again despite being impaled through the head; its fins were spread on spines like fabric on the frame of a kite. They looked sharp, those spines.

Later that day, as I seized my third or fourth catch preparatory to skewering it through the eye, I found out how right I'd been about the spines. Two of them stabbed into the meat between my forefinger and thumb, and the sticky brine of the bait bucket stung the wounds. By evening, the sting had softened, but I still noticed it as I bit into the fish's battered flesh.

The world of fish is rich with such weapons. The blue tang bears a scalpel near its tail and will slice the flesh of meddlers. Others have spines to impale the unwary foot or the grasping hand. Like any wound received in the water, these present a special risk of infection.

Thousands of fish around the world enhance this mechanical defense with toxin. Most of the 2,400 species of catfish, including such familiar kinds as the madtom, have at least mildly venomous spines. A few, like the eeltail catfish, can send people to the hospital. Their stings cause inflammation and severe pain. The stinging catfish *Heteropneustes fossilis* attacks people even when there is, to our eyes, no need for defense.

Many fish with venomous spines hide on the bottom in shallow water, waiting to ambush crustaceans and smaller fish. Among the ones people are mostly likely to regret stepping on are certain toadfishes, stargazers, weevers, and scorpionfish. But the scorpionfish and their relatives are diverse. Some, like the beautiful lionfish commonly kept in aquariums, are active predators. People who handle them can find themselves stricken with terrible pain, vomiting, and headache. Some scorpionfish, like the Australian fortescue, get caught in fishing nets and injure the fishermen who must remove them.

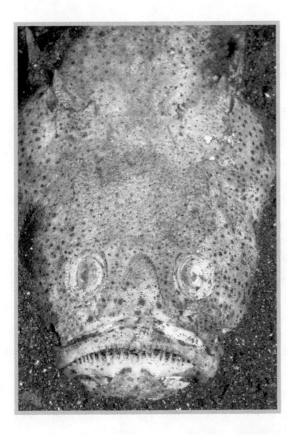

A VENOMOUS
STARGAZER
CAMOUFLAGED
IN SAND.

The most dangerous scorpionfish, and perhaps the most dangerous venomous fish in the world, are the stonefish. These denizens of the Indian and Pacific oceans are said to bear the largest venom glands of any fish. The wounds they cause are described as "excruciating." Victims experience neurological problems, including paralysis and permanent loss of feeling in the wounded limb. Some have died.

LESS DANGEROUS, BUT perhaps far more disconcerting to read about, are certain pencil catfish. They feed by swimming into the gill openings of other fish, where they lock themselves in place by extending the spines on their own gills. Then they bite into an artery and engorge themselves with blood. The entire process takes only a minute or two. Some members of this family, notably the wormlike and translucent candiru of the Amazon, invade the orifices of people, particularly the urethras of people urinating in the water. The fish is typically only a few inches long and less than 14 millimeters in circumference. Once inside, it locks itself in place as usual. But its invasion is a mistake, for it doesn't thrive there. The candiru can't withdraw from the human body, nor can the victim extract it. Surgery is the only answer; otherwise, the person must eventually die from shock or the inability to pass urine. Though the complete amputation of the penis has fallen out of favor in the medical profession, it was, in less surgically advanced times, the only solution. In a 1997 case, endoscopic removal proved effective.

Fish have also been known to invade the human body in freak accidents. In 2002, one such occurrence killed a seventeen-year-old boy near Phnom Penh, Cambodia. The boy caught a fish called a kantrorb by hand, but it escaped his clutch and leaped into his mouth. Its backward-pointing spines prevented its being dislodged, and the boy choked.

IN THE EARLY days of the literary form that came to be called the novel, market-savvy writers presented their inventions as truth. Aphra Behn was one of these writers. Her 1688 book *Oroonoko* artfully mixes fancy with genuine observations of the New World. Her most startling claim concerned a fish:

> [I]t has a quality of cold, that those who are angling . . . shall, in the same minute the bait is touched by this eel, seize him or her that holds the rod with benumbedness, that shall deprive 'em of sense for a while; some have fallen into the water, and others dropped as dead on the banks of the rivers where they stood.

While much of her book now strains credibility, Behn's account of the creature she called the numb fish remains accurate. We know it better these days, of course, as the electric eel.

Several bony fish, including various kinds of knifefish and elephant fish, generate electricity. They use it as a sensory tool to help with navigation in murky water and for communication. Most don't develop a big enough charge to harm other animals. The few that do use their power to stun prey or to defend themselves. It is these few that occasionally hurt fishermen and swimmers. Catfish of the genus *Malapterurus* offer enough jolt to knock a person down. The electric eel packs even more power—perhaps 600 volts. It really has rendered people unconscious.

RIGHT WHALES HAVE SUNK BOATS IN SELF-DEFENSE.

8. THE WHALES

ORDER CETARTIODACTYLA

IN 2002, A WHALE leaped out of the waters of Morro Bay, California, and landed on a 22-foot fishing boat. The boat's owner, a fifty-one-year-old man, was killed. The boat was damaged but stayed afloat. The whale slid back into the water, scraping a few yards of its wrinkled hide onto the gunwale as it went. This was probably an accident; the whale must not have noticed the boat when it breached.

Genetic evidence shows that whales evolved from land-dwelling hoofed mammals, their closest kin being the hippopotamus. Aquatic life has allowed some whales to achieve massive size. The blue whale, which can reach lengths of 100 feet and weights of 100 tons, is generally ranked the largest of all animals, including even the prehistoric ones. Life in the water has also altered cetacean feeding habits. While their hoofed kinsmen eat plants, the whales have evolved into two distinct lines, the baleen and the toothed. Baleen whales feed by filtering small organisms from ocean water. They do this with rows of baleen—big bristling slats made of material like human toenails. They don't prey on people or other largish animals, but like their relatives on land, they may find occasion to harm us. Accidents like the one in Morro Bay are devastating simply because the creature is massive. Gray whales show aggressive behavior, such as bluff charges and threatening sounds, toward boats that come near their calves. Humpback whales have actively attacked boats. Each of these species approaches 40 tons and is powerful enough to destroy small vessels. The whale that killed the man in Morro Bay was probably a gray or a humpback. Right whales and grays have battered whaling ships and sunk boats in self-defense.

Toothed whales are all active hunters. The sperm whale, also known as the spermaceti or cachalot, is the largest active predator on earth. Its usual prey includes fish and squid. In the nineteenth century, specimens almost a hundred feet long were recorded; perhaps such giants still exist somewhere. The spermaceti is a denizen of the deep seas and rarely encounters human beings. In the eighteenth and nineteenth centuries, hunting these formidable mammals was a high-dollar industry. They were prized for the clean-burning oil that could be rendered from their blubber, for the even finer oil found in their heads (the sperm or spermaceti), and for the ambergris found in their guts, which was used as a base for perfume. A whaling ship would launch several small boats, each crewed by eight or ten men. In the bow of each boat stood a harpooner whose job was to plant his weapon in the mountain of flesh before him. Thus anchored, a boat might approach close enough for the sailors to hack into a vital spot with spadelike weapons. The whales often reacted to attacks by slamming the boats with their massive flukes. It was not unusual for men in the boats to die in such encounters, bludgeoned by the whale or drowned in the general wrack.

On a few occasions, a sperm whale managed to destroy not just the boats sent to dispatch it, but also the ship itself. The first clear record of a ship sunk by a sperm whale concerns a mere accident: the *Union* ran into a resting whale in 1807. But later cases provide examples of genuine offense by the whale. In 1820, the crew of the ship *Essex* was in the process of wounding three different whales from three different boats when a fourth whale, a bull estimated at 85 feet long and 80 tons, deliberately rammed the ship, then turned and rammed it again. The *Essex* went down in minutes. It has been speculated that the hammering noise made by the first mate as he attempted to repair one of the whale boats communicated some inadvertent challenge to the big bull, but I find defense of his fellows a more plausible explanation. We now know that sperm whales are intelligent animals. The big bull probably understood what was happening and tried to stop it.

The crew of the *Essex* escaped in three boats and went drifting. Some of the men eventually resorted to cannibalism. One was, after a drawing of lots, killed by his comrades for food; others were simply eaten after they had died of thirst. Eight of the twenty men were eventually rescued.

Other ships counterattacked by sperm whales include the *Pusie Hall* in 1835, the *Lydia* and the *Two Generals* in 1836, the *Pocahontas* in 1850, and the *Ann Alexander* in 1851. The latter two vessels were sunk. In 1896 the steamer *Seminole,* a passenger vessel, accidentally ran into a resting whale. The whale's podmates attacked the ship, ramming it four times and wreaking serious damage even on its steel hull.

Some whales, having survived an attack, apparently developed a distaste for human beings generally, or at least for our seafaring artifacts. A prominent case was Mocha Dick, a scar-faced 70-foot bull so named be-

PERILOUS SITUATION OF WHALEMEN.

IT WAS NOT UNUSUAL FOR MEN TO DIE WHILE ATTACKING THE SPERM WHALE.

cause he was encountered, among other places, near the South American island of Mocha. From about 1810, Mocha Dick attacked whaling ships and their boats, and also other kinds of vessels, at various sites in the Pacific Ocean. It's difficult to sort folklore from fact in this case. Certainly much fiction, under the guise of memoir or journalism, has been attached to his name. Marine biologist Richard Ellis considered the following exploits of this semilegendary figure legitimate:

- 1840, some 200 miles from Valparaiso, Chile: Mocha Dick successfully repelled an attack by the *Desmond,* smashing two boats and killing two men.
- 1840, some 500 miles south of the previous incident: Mocha Dick rescued the carcass of a dead comrade from the boats of the *Serepta.* He destroyed one of the boats, forcing the other to abandon the carcass. He then stood guard over the carcass.
- 1841, near the Falkland Islands: The *John Day* launched three boats to attack Mocha Dick, but he demolished two of them and sent the third scurrying for safety.
- 1842, near Japan: Mocha Dick destroyed a schooner. Three whaling ships came to the rescue. Six boats were launched; Mocha Dick dismantled two of them, damaged one of the ships, and supposedly swallowed two men.

Probably the exploits of several different whales have been attributed to this one. It may be that, once educated to the danger of ships, many bulls made a point of destroying these menaces. In any event, Mocha Dick is best known to us in his overtly fictionalized form, Herman Melville's Moby-Dick.

Sailors' accounts of whaling expeditions provide many dubious tales of sperm whales committing extravagant violence against human beings. One piece of folklore, often recounted as fact even today, has a sailor swallowed and later rescued when his shipmates kill and carve up the whale. He suffers amnesia and something that sounds like heat stroke, and the whale's gastric juices bleach him, hair and hide, a permanent white.

Another story concerns a sailor attached to a seal hunt. He finds himself alone on an ice floe, from which he topples into the water. He's snatched up by a sperm whale. His shipmates shoot the whale with a cannon. The whale escapes, but its wounds prove mortal, and the ship catches up with it three miles out. The sailors hack through the blubber to excise the whale's forestomach (a sperm whale has multiple stomach compartments, like a cow). They hope to recover the body of their shipmate. Once this massive organ is on board, the ship's doctor saws it open with a galley knife and exposes the human body within. He finds that the gastric juices, far from bleaching the exposed skin, have simply digested it, turning the man's face and hands and part of a leg into soup. His clothing has largely protected the rest of his body, and the doctor reports some lice still alive on the man's head. Despite its vivid details— I particularly like the lice—this story, too, is false. In fact, though biting is a plausible means for a sperm whale to dispatch a man, the narrow gauge of its throat makes actually swallowing humans improbable.

Now that we recognize whales as intelligent animals, many people (and many governments) disapprove of hunting them. Ironically, this fellow feeling toward whales leads to dangers of its own. In 2007, for example, a sperm whale was stranded in a bay of the Japanese island of Shikoku. Three fishermen put out in a boat to guide the whale to freedom. It reacted with what witnesses described as panic. A swat of its tail demolished the boat. Two men were rescued; the third died.

OF THE DOLPHINS, porpoises, and other toothed whales, none is particularly aggressive toward people. Mostly we run into trouble when we seek them out—by hunting them, by capturing them for aquariums, by swimming with them. Even then, they hurt surprisingly few people, considering their power and their predatory disposition. There are reports of at least some minor aggression by bottlenose dolphins, pygmy killer whales, and rough-toothed dolphins.

The pilot whales have proved moderately dangerous. These predators of squid reach maximum sizes of around 22 feet and three and a half tons. They travel in pods of ten or more. They are black; their foreheads protrude distinctively. People have often dived with them safely, but occasionally they become aggressive. In 1992, a diver named Lisa Costello was in Hawaiian waters, along with her cameraman, to film her interactions with pilot whales. She petted one whale. It seemed to look her in the eye, then seized her leg and plunged downward, dragging her to a depth of about 40 feet before she could escape. Her cuts were minor. This behavior has been explained in many ways—as play, as aggression, as a defensive reaction against the human intrusion.

Pilot whales often seem curious about ships. In 1989, a pod of pilot whales surrounded and repeatedly rammed a 39-foot cutter. The couple aboard were attempting to circumnavigate the globe and were hundreds of miles from land. A particularly powerful strike breached the hull; the ship went down within an hour. The couple drifted on a raft for sixty-six days. They were rescued, close to starvation, near Costa Rica.

PEOPLE OFTEN ASK me what the most formidable predator in the world is. On the Web you can find message boards where people speculate about which animal would win if there were some way to establish a "fair" fight between them. There have even been computer simulations of fights between, say, a lion and a Nile crocodile. These exercises can be fascinating, though ultimately they say more about the views of the human beings who engage in them than about the animals themselves.

As it happens, though, there is a clear answer to this perennial question, and the answer is orca.

Orcas, also known as killer whales, reach 30 feet and seven tons. They hunt either in pods, as their groups are called, or singly, and are deadly either way. For example, at least half a dozen cases of orcas preying on sperm whales are on record. In one case, twenty-five orcas dismantled five spermaceti, using hit-and-run tactics, biting out chunks of hide and flesh until the larger whales were exhausted and bloody. The spermaceti tried to defend themselves by forming a circle, heads inward, tails out, and swatting the orcas with their flukes. The spermaceti has more than enough power to demolish an orca in this way, but the orcas were too fast and, as far as human observers could tell, suffered no damage. The formidable alpha bull spermaceti was a special target of the orcas, and they eventually devoured him.

Orcas also attack the blue whale. The orcas invariably win, sometimes ripping out the tongue of the blue to eat it and leaving the giant to bleed to death, food for the sharks. This sort of attack is common;

orcas practice it on other whale species as well. Some orca attacks seem designed to feed the orca without necessarily killing the prey. In attacking a large whale, each of several orcas in a pod might slice off and swallow a few hundred pounds of meat without killing the victim. After a few hours, when they've eaten their fill, the orcas simply leave. In such cases, the attack is not technically predatory; it's the largest example of parasitism found on earth.

The largest of all fish, the whale shark, possesses perhaps the toughest hide of any animal, a six-inch layer of leather. This shark is a filter feeder, not an active predator like most of its relatives. It can reach a length of 50 feet, and because of its size and tough hide, has no enemies except people—and orcas. Circumstantial evidence shows that orcas attack whale sharks, ripping out great mouthfuls of flesh and leaving divots in the mottled hide.

Of the noncetacean marine mammals, the most formidable— walruses, leopard seals, and sea elephants—are all among the orca's regular prey items. Even land animals occasionally fall victim to the orca when crossing the water or when standing too close to the edge of the ice. Polar bears and a moose have been discovered in the stomachs of orcas. These may have been scavenged, but orcas have been seen circling polar bears on ice floes, which is a typical prelude to predation. There is one eyewitness report of a black bear killed by orcas as it swam across a small body of water. Other finds from orca stomachs include fish, squid, sea turtles, birds, otters, a pig, and a dog.

The great white shark is occasionally a victim of orcas. In one case, a great white approached two orcas that were eating a seal. One orca attacked, striking the shark underwater, then seized it in his jaws and pulled it to the surface. While the first orca held the shark there, the other disemboweled it, feasting on its liver. Though the great white is an awe-inspiring predator in its own right, all the well-documented accounts I have come across (there are only a few) have the orcas winning their battles easily. The orca, though small as whales go, holds a considerable size advantage over the shark.

Besides simple biting, orcas also kill by ramming and by forcing victims down in the water so that they drown. The tactic of pulling sharks up out of the water is a standard part of their arsenal, perhaps meant to drown the gill breathers in air. Some orcas leap out onto land to take seals and penguins. They have been observed to ram through ice in order to dislodge and eat animals standing on top of it. They can crack ice at least a meter thick, an astounding display of power.

This latter habit accounts for a rare instance of a wild orca attacking a human being with what may have been predatory intent. The man in question was Herbert Ponting, a member of Robert Scott's 1911 expedition to Antarctica, and he escaped without injury. Whether the orcas meant to eat him or the dogs standing nearby no one can say; probably they were simply interested to sample any animal they could knock into the water.

In 1972, a family named Robertson was attempting to circumnavigate the planet when their venture ran afoul of a pod of orcas. The whales rammed the Robertsons' 43-foot yacht, sinking it. The family and their crewman managed to stay afloat with the help of a dinghy and an inflatable raft. Once the yacht went down, the whales apparently lost interest, for they troubled the crew no further, though they could easily have finished them off if they had wanted to eat them. The Robertsons and their crewman drifted for thirty-eight days before they were rescued.

In fact, despite their long-standing reputation as man-eaters, there are no clear-cut cases of orcas preying on people. There are, however, many cases of captive orcas hurting their trainers. Many of these cases involve simple accidents. One trainer who was smashed under an orca survived the shattering of his thoracic vertebrae, pelvis, ribs, and femur, though he required six operations and three pounds of implanted hardware. Purposeful attacks happen on occasion. Trainers have been bitten, pinned against walls, chased out of pools, rammed, and dragged to the bottom. One man was seized and dragged across a pool; he suffered internal injuries. In 1991, a twenty-year-old trainer in British Columbia fell into a pool. One orca seized her in his mouth and raced around the pool underwater. Two other orcas joined in foiling her attempts to escape. Her colleagues threw in a life ring, but the whales prevented them from pulling the young woman out. She reached the side of the pool, but was dragged back down. The whales played a macabre game of catch with her body; they may have regarded her as a toy tossed in for their amusement. It was only hours later that they allowed the other trainers to remove her corpse.

STINGING JELLYFISH ARE A HAZARD OF AUSTRALIAN WATERS.

9. AN ASSORTMENT OF AQUATIC DANGERS

A FISHING CREW HAULS UP a net from the deep. It looks like a good haul at first, but then someone notices the motionless eyes of one fish, then another. Many of them are dead. Their scales have already begun to lose their protective mucus, to flake away.

But then a dead fish begins to wiggle. Its flank bulges and retracts, as if with the motion of a monstrous breath. One crewman steps forward and prods the plump grouper with a gaff. It bursts. Suddenly the deck is writhing with snaky creatures. A few of them thrash in the net, smearing it with astounding quantities of slime. Each two-foot-long creature flexes a mouth surrounded by tentacles. The deflated grouper flattens against the net, a mere bag of bones.

The hagfish, sometimes called the most repulsive of all animals, scavenges anything it finds on the ocean floor. It slithers in through the mouth, gills, or anus. Once inside, it begins to devour the organs and tissues, leaving only the skin and skeleton intact. It is not especially concerned whether a meal is dead or merely immobilized, so a fish held in a net may be alive when the feeding starts.

Surprisingly, not all crews are disappointed to find their catches riddled with hagfish, for the scavenger itself can be sold in Japanese and Korean markets. What makes this fact even more surprising is that the copious slime of some hagfish is toxic. So is the blood, and sometimes the meat. Cooking fails to break the toxin down. It irritates the lining of the human gut. Hags can, like puffer fish, be prepared safely. Danger lies in the occasional culinary mistake.

Other primitive fish called lampreys carry similar toxins, both in their blood and in an anticoagulant they spit into bite wounds. Most of the forty-one species spend their youth as larvae that feed by filtering organic particles from the water. Once they metamorphose into adults, their lifestyles vary. Some become parasites. Each of these possesses a disk-shaped sucker with which it adheres to a fish. Then it burrows in with its rasping tongue. It drinks the blood and sometimes chews the muscle of the host. This is a more injurious style of parasitism than the kind we humans typically endure from insects and arachnids, and it may kill the host. When that happens, the lamprey swims off to find another.

Lampreys attack a variety of fish, and they have also been seen attached to sperm whales. Rarely, they latch on to human swimmers. But it can be worse to eat than to be eaten, for a lamprey, like a hagfish, sometimes carries its toxin in its muscle tissue, to the gastric distress of the predatory human. England's King Henry I died with a fever and a disordered belly after overindulging in lamprey.

People have tried to eat almost every kind of aquatic animal, and in the process have discovered a great many poisons. Even fish and shellfish well established as edible sometimes prove poisonous if they've shared a food chain with the wrong kind of algae, or if their meat has been improperly stored. But some aquatic animals cultivate poison as a defense. Take the sponges, for example. A great many of the more than five thousand sponge species feed on toxic matter to envenom their own flesh and thus discourage predators.

. . .

SEA SLUGS LICK THE FLESH FROM THEIR
PREY WITH TOOTHED TONGUES.

THE EFFECTS OF eating poisonous sponges vary. One troublesome species produces tingling of the lips, followed by paralysis. Some are potentially fatal. Some of them also exude toxins to protect themselves from predators, but in open water, these are unlikely to hurt people. In aquariums, however, a venom can become concentrated. One specialist in reef aquariums reports that, even with ocean water constantly circulating through its container, a specimen of the fire sponge *Tedania ignis* kept the water toxic enough to enkindle human skin to a sunburn red within minutes.

Another animal that never looked especially edible to me is the nudibranch, or sea slug. Nudibranchs are hermaphrodites, the biggest about a foot long, and many are brilliantly colored. They are all carnivorous, licking the flesh from their prey with a toothed tongue. Some of them take a special diet of poisonous sponges. The nudibranch may simply absorb the sponge toxin and perhaps modify it slightly, creating its own toxic defense. Some nudibranchs literally ooze poison. People have fallen seriously ill after eating them. Another group of nudibranchs eats stinging sea creatures like jellyfish and Portuguese men-of-war. The nudibranch swallows the stinging cells whole, somehow managing not to get stung itself, and transports them into its own outer layer, where they protrude as white bulbs. An Australian swimmer who touches a bulb gets stung just as effectually as if he had wrestled a jellyfish.

The sea cucumbers at least sound as if they ought to be eaten. Some look like lacy versions of their cousins, the starfish. Others look like knobbed, bristly incarnations of their namesake vegetable. The harmless kinds are considered good food in China and the South Seas. When people eat the wrong species, the poison can blind or kill them.

But we need not venture into the sea to eat unwisely. The local creek provides danger enough. Most of the world's four thousand amphibians secrete at least a mild toxin to protect themselves from predators. In the many parts of the world where frogs and salamanders are considered good food, the toxin rarely causes problems, for people eat the leg muscles, not the toxic skin. But accidents happen. In Oregon, a child died after eating the tail of a Western newt. People have also died from eating the cane toad or its eggs.

The venoms of amphibians can be absorbed through the skin, causing rash or even systemic effects. People sometimes take a dose of venom by rubbing their eyes or licking their fingers after an otherwise uneventful handling of an amphibian. These events are not likely to be significant, though they may cause considerable irritation of the eyes. Some species, such as the banded rubber frog, have sent people to the hospital. The Japanese spiny newt possesses sharp ribs that it can extrude through its hide. The ribs pierce the bodies of attackers, injecting the venom produced by the skin. People have fallen ill from handling these newts. The fire salamander, a notoriously testy European species, squirts venom from an orifice in its back. It can hit people three or four feet away, causing momentary blindness. Similar effects result from the expelled venom of the cane toad.

Toad venoms have been known as pharmacologically active substances for millennia. People obtained them by boiling live toads of various species and reducing or drying the exudate. Some venoms were used in traditional Chinese medicine to treat colds and various other common complaints. Ancient Roman wives supposedly knew toad venom as an expedient for resolving unhappy marriages. The venoms of various toads are reputed to have hallucinogenic effects. People have developed several methods for exploiting this property. One is to dry the toad's skin, grind it to powder, and smoke it. Another is simply to lick a live toad. Among the toads used in this way are various members of the genus *Bufo,* including the cane and Colorado River toads. Doctors consider this a dangerous undertaking. Some South American cultures may have used toad venoms in mind-altering rituals as well as in medicine. In Haiti, the cane toad and others have been used as ingredients in the so-called zombie rituals designed to intimidate and enslave people through a combination of psychological manipulation and drugs.

The most dangerous amphibian venoms are found among the so-called poison dart frogs, only a few of which are actually used by hunters to envenom darts. The skin of *Phyllobates terribilis* can envenom a dart with a mere dip. The dart can then bring down monkeys and other fleet prey quickly—an advantage in the jungle, where prey can be lost if allowed a few extra seconds of flight.

WHEN I TAKE my family out for seafood, we order crab legs, then fight over the claws. Everyone wants a claw, because if you're careful to dig out the meat and leave the right piece of cartilage as a lever, you can work it like a marionette, making it pinch your brothers. I almost regret teaching my boys about this, because their little fingers fit inside the claws better than mine and make them much more effective pinchers than I am.

No matter how tightly we pinch, however, we can't match the pinching power of a live lobster or crab. Of particular note among the pinching crustaceans are the mantis shrimp (or squilla), some of which grow to more than a foot long. These aggressive predators possess folding claws like jackknives. They are a hazard for divers, slicing toes and fingers.

The robber crab of the Indian and Pacific oceans climbs trees to cut

MANY CRABS SCAVENGE HUMAN BODIES WHEN THE CHANCE ARISES.

down coconuts, and its pincers are strong enough to tear off the husks of the coconuts so it can eat the insides. It grows to the size of a human torso and can be found scuttling with spidery motions across roads and onto porches and even into houses. Legends claim the robber crab kills and eats people. One such story tells of a tragic shipwreck, with dozens of castaways devoured by the mighty crabs. There's no hard evidence to support this story, but it's often repeated as true. It may seem credible because many crabs do scavenge human bodies when the chance arises.

Such legends inspired the filmmaker Robert Flaherty to explore the Pacific isles. Flaherty had already had great success with his protodocumentary film, *Nanook of the North,* which told a vivid story of man triumphant against the unrelenting forces of nature. Flaherty hoped to film a similar story of primitive man versus nature in the tropics. He was disappointed to find the living in southern latitudes easy. The robber crabs he had hoped would provide a sequence of epic struggle turned out to be less formidable than he had been led to believe. In fact, he saw children baiting the giant crabs out of their craggy retreats, catching them, and cooking them for lunch.

THE DANGERS OF the water are many and varied, but the robber crab will not be our only disappointment in the search for man-eaters. In

fact, sharks and crocodilians are the only aquatic animals that unequiv-
ocally take people as prey. Perhaps the most disappointing aquatic dangers are the cephalopods. No creatures are more disturbing in their
gelatinous otherness than the cephalopods—the squid, the cuttlefish,
the octopus. Their motions are strange, their eyes enormous and staring
(the largest eyes on earth belong to squids). Perhaps these qualities explain why the cephalopods so often figure in legendary attacks.

In the folklore of the sea, we find many monsters with a multiplic-
ity of tentacles or snaky necks. The Scylla that menaced Odysseus is
perhaps the earliest example. Renaissance writers such as Archbishop
Olaus Magnus wrote of such creatures "drown[ing] easily many great
ships." It seems dubious that any real squid ever possessed both the
size and the inclination to take down a ship. The largest scientifically
attested cephalopods are the giant squid, which reaches 43 feet and
more than 600 pounds, and the colossal squid, which reaches 46 feet
and more than half a ton. These predators dwell "Below the thunders
of the upper deep; / Far, far beneath in the abysmal sea," as Tennyson
put it, and appear to human witnesses rarely. The presence of a huge
squid at the surface implies that something is amiss, that it's dying or
perhaps stunned by the sonic attack of a sperm whale. Richard Ellis's
The Search for the Giant Squid reports only one incident that could be
called an attack on people, and the people in question, two boys in a
rowboat, had to smack the creature with an oar to provoke it to (ineffectual) action.

Other cephalopods have done more damage, though usually in self-
defense. The Humboldt squid grows to six feet and more than 25
pounds. Because it lives mostly below 600 feet, it rarely encounters people by accident. Japanese diners prize them, and fishermen in various
parts of the world take them by hook to supply this market. They bite
fishermen and divers with their powerful beaks. There are reports,
probably apocryphal, of fishermen who have fallen overboard and been
devoured by them. Octopuses of similar size have wrestled and bitten
people, too, and there's one credible report of an octopus crawling out
of the water to attack a man on shore.

Certain other cephalopods, including the flying squid, possess venoms potentially dangerous to people. The most dangerous of these are
the blue-ringed octopuses of the Pacific. In its relaxed state, a blue-

OCTOPUSES HAVE WRESTLED AND BITTEN PEOPLE.

ringed octopus is about the size of a baseball. Stretched, it is less than ten inches long. It paralyzes its prey—small crustaceans and mollusks— with a neurotoxic venom, which it sprays into the water. The components of the venom include tetrodotoxin. This substance is made by bacteria that grow in and on the octopus's body, particularly in its salivary glands.

Like many other cephalopods, this octopus can change colors as a form of communication. Its particular variation on this habit is to flash blue rings on a yellow background when threatened. The trouble for humans is that this threat display doesn't look especially threatening to us. Some people find it so delightful they pick the octopus up to play with it. When that happens, the octopus's only recourse is to bite, jabbing its assailant with the same venom it uses for hunting. This, too, is a hint likely to be lost on the human, for the bite is not especially painful. But if the bite has given a good dose of venom, matters soon change. The symptoms begin with a tingling in the tongue and lips. They may quickly progress to near total paralysis. Victims who later recovered reported that they were able to see and hear as they lay motionless and terrified, their friends trying to help them. One victim was still able to move his eyes after most of his body had ceased to respond to his commands—doctors could see him watching them. The paralysis may extend to the respiratory system, and in this case, the venom is fatal unless CPR or a ventilator is available within minutes. Within twelve hours, the body has dealt with the worst of the venom, and victims begin to breathe on their own. Within twenty-four hours, most people make a complete recovery. But a handful of victims have died minutes after the bite. Besides deliberate handling, people may get bitten by stepping on the octopus or even by putting on a boot in which it has taken shelter.

THE WATER IS full of things it's better not to step on or handle. Sea urchins, for example, are equipped with stiff spines. Many of them look like headless, tailless porcupines. Scattered among the 750 species are a few dangerous kinds. The unwary wader in Pacific waters may, for instance, find the three-inch spines of the giant red urchin protruding through the top of his foot. The long-spined urchin (*Diadema antillarum*) has injected people with a life-threatening venom through its spines. Some sea urchins have tentacles ending in jawlike pinchers. These pedicellariae, as they are called, can wound people. A species called *Toxopneustes pileolus* has inflicted life-threatening bites with its pedicellariae.

Closely related to the urchins are the starfish, or sea stars, which range in appearance from the pale pink five-armed kind many of us dissected in high school biology to those with two dozen arms and elaborate bristles and knobs. A number of kinds produce venom, which they inject through their bristles, much like the urchins. Most of these starfish bring only a rash to human victims. The crown-of-thorns starfish has a more severe venom, which has caused fever, vomiting, and temporary paralysis in people.

Then there are the cone shells, a group of beautifully patterned aquatic snails that hunt other mollusks, fish, and worms with a harpoonlike apparatus fired from the proboscis. This gear injects a potent venom. People run into trouble with some large tropical species not only by stepping on the snails, but also by trying to collect their shells. The most dangerous species include the geographer cone and the textile cone, each of which has caused people to die within a few minutes of the sting. The death rate for human victims of some cone shells is an extraordinary 20 percent. That puts them among the most effective of all our venomous enemies.

ANOTHER SURPRISING AQUATIC danger is the snapping turtle—surprising, at least, to those who haven't encountered it. I often think it looks like an irritable dinosaur struggling to escape from beneath a decorative plate. A friend tells me he has occasionally managed to provoke a snapping turtle into breaking a thick stick with its bite.

Most turtles are harmless, or else they inflict only minor bites. But snapping turtles bite more powerfully than most, and they have attacked people with little or no provocation. In 1999, six boys were swimming in the shallow water of Turnkey Creek in Ohio when a snapping turtle launched itself from the bank and swam toward them. It bit a nine-year-old and, after a long struggle, severed his big toe. A local newspaper story refers to an ongoing "turtle problem" in the creek, with law enforcement agencies warning swimmers of danger. Attacks like these are probably cases of the reptile defending its territory.

JANUARY 30, 2002, in northern Australia, was the height of summer. Richard Jordan was on the beach near Hamilton Island. He'd come there on vacation from his home in England. He was fifty-eight. Six years before, he'd had surgery to replace the valve between his heart and aorta. He was still taking medicine every day to keep his blood from clotting. But he was living an active life, and in fact had come to snorkel that morning in the jeweled blue water.

Jordan and his wife stepped into the ocean shortly after eleven. They were still in the shallows when he told her, "Something has got me." He didn't see what it was, but he felt a lashing pain on the skin of his face and chest. They walked out of the water. Within twenty minutes, Jordan felt the muscles all over his body begin to cramp. He was sweaty and nauseous and scared. The hotel doctor took his blood pressure and found it dangerously high at 260/160. His heart was racing. His pulse was 142. About thirty-five minutes after the stings, the doctor gave him several drugs to control the symptoms. Ten minutes later Jordan suddenly passed out. His breathing was labored.

The doctor feared he'd had a stroke. He fed oxygen to Jordan through a tube; he found a vein for an IV; he hooked him up to an EKG. Word went out that a patient urgently needed to get to a fully equipped hospital on the mainland.

When a rescue team arrived by air, they found Jordan unconscious, his pupils fixed and dilated. His breathing was still strained and he was sweating to the point of dehydration. He was drooling abundantly, and blood had begun to leak from his nose. His face, neck, and chest had reddened. The rescue team did what they could with medication, but Jordan's blood pressure went back up to 210/134 before they reached Mackay Base Hospital at 4:20 in the afternoon.

An X-ray showed Jordan's aorta inflamed, his heart enlarged. The heart was twitching, its electrical impulses limping out of synch. A CT scan confirmed the hotel doctor's suspicion: a massive hemorrhage had flooded the brain. The neurosurgeon saw no point in operating.

Throughout the night, Jordan's skin remained flushed. He continued to have bouts of sweating. By three in the morning, doctors could hear a crackling in his chest. His lungs were beginning to fill with fluid. He lingered. At 5:10 the following day, the doctors declared him brain-dead.

It was clear in the first half hour or so that a box jellyfish had stung Jordan. Such accidents are common in these waters, though usually they are no more dangerous than sunburn or bee stings. (Of victims who turn up at emergency rooms, only about half are admitted to the hospital for extended treatment.) On certain Australian beaches, the lifeguards wear nylon leggings to protect them from stings, and bottles of vinegar, which neutralizes any uninjected venom lingering in the embedded stingers, are left at stations for public use. The nylons, though effective against larger jellyfish, don't seem to help against the small kinds of box jellies like the one that killed Jordan.

Jordan died of Irukandji syndrome, a reaction to the stings of certain kinds of box jellyfish. (The name Irukandji refers not to a specific jellyfish, but to the people of the region.) The one box jelly so far proved to cause the syndrome is *Carukia barnesi,* a transparent creature whose bell is less than an inch across. Half a dozen other small box jellies, all related, probably cause the syndrome as well. It's hard to prove because, like Jordan, most victims never see the tiny, transparent creatures that sting them. The usual symptom is soaring blood pressure, and a blood test will show high levels of a certain protein complex that causes the heart to contract. Often the symptoms include extravagant cramping pain in the belly, chest, lower back, arms, legs, and lower jaw. Men may get painful erections that won't go away. The nerves may stop working, shut down by the pressure of swelling arteries. The victim vomits; he has headaches; he feels restless and panicky; he has trouble breathing. His heart palpitates and may fail. Jordan's past heart troubles put him at higher risk for a stroke, but he's not the only one to have died this way during an episode of Irukandji syndrome. For example, a forty-four-year-old man from Columbus, Ohio, was killed in the same manner, and in the same area, two and a half months after Jordan died. There is no particularly useful first aid for Irukandji syndrome, and no antidote.

The largest jellyfish measure seven and a half feet across the bell and trail tentacles 120 feet long, making them the longest known animals, though they weigh only a few pounds. All jellyfish possess cellular structures called nematocysts. A nematocyst is a sort of threaded projectile

MANY JELLYFISH GIVE PAINFUL STINGS TO SWIMMERS WHO BRUSH AGAINST THEM.

that explodes from a cell when it is stimulated by touch or by certain chemicals. In some animals, the nematocyst may be tipped with glue or a tangle of threads for various purposes. The kind of nematocyst that interests us here, though, is the most common type, a stinging harpoon often laden with venom. The jellyfish reflexively fires several, or even several million, of its nematocysts to stun prey or fight off attackers. We humans accidentally fall into the latter category when we brush against a jellyfish. We also happen to emit some of the same chemical triggers fish do, which marks us as prey and causes us to get stung, though none of the jellyfish actually eats people.

Many of the jellyfish present no serious danger, their stings causing either no damage at all or some minor pain and skin irritation. Still, there are dozens of species with painful stings. *Stomolophus nomurai,* a creature of East Asian waters with a bell better than six feet across, has killed at least eight people near Qingdao, China. The spectacular lion's mane jellyfish, best known to many readers as the improbable killer in a particularly knotty Sherlock Holmes mystery, can leave a human in pain for hours.

Of special note are the thimble jellyfish. The larvae of this jellyfish are popularly called sea lice, but they are not related to the tiny crustaceans of that name. Though microscopic, thimble larvae cause a rash that sometimes endures for weeks and brings on secondary infections. The larvae generally sting only when trapped by clothing, a habit that concentrates the stings in the areas of the body covered by the swimsuit. (I pause a moment to let you take in the implications.) The larvae can survive dried out for months. Some people have found themselves attacked all over again when they put on the swimming gear they peeled off and hung to dry the summer before.

The jellyfish have many similarly armed relatives that occasionally hurt people—true corals and fire corals, sea anemones and fire weeds, Portuguese men-of-war. But the most dangerous members of the phylum are box jellies like the one that killed Richard Jordan. They look roughly cubic from above, as their name suggests. Their tentacles hang from the four lower corners of the cube. They have complexly structured eyes, an unusual accoutrement in an animal without a brain. There are about twenty species, many of them dangerously venomous. They prey on crustaceans, fish, and worms that swim into their dangling tentacles. Once stung, the paralyzed victim is drawn up inside the bell for digestion. The box jellies are faster and more maneuverable than other jellyfish, which are mostly servants to the whims of the water. The notably dangerous box jellies include *Chiropsalmus quadrigatus.* Found near the Philippines, this creature kills twenty to fifty people annually. A similar species, *C. quadrumanus,* has killed at least one person in U.S. waters.

The world is full of creatures whose venom supposedly causes one to drop dead on the spot. There are, for example, assorted snakes slangily referred to as "five-steppers" or even "two-steppers," because that's how far you can walk between getting bitten and falling dead. In fact, there is nothing in the world that predictably kills people on the spot, but there are a great many creatures that manage to do so on occasion. Sudden deaths are on record for spiders, snakes, jellyfish, and insects. People who die suddenly sometimes prove to have histories of sensitivity or allergy, or else other medical problems (such as heart trouble) that made them especially susceptible. Envenomation is such a tricky process, with so many factors, that no creature can be said to be absolutely deadly.

Chironex fleckeri, often called the sea wasp (a confusing name, since it is also applied to the entire class of box jellies), has been responsible for a number of drop-dead incidents. For decades, scientists were aware of the Australian phenomenon of swimmers and divers coming out of the water, announcing they'd felt themselves bitten by something they hadn't seen, and expiring. In the 1950s, scientists finally were able to tie many of these deaths to the sea wasp. It is a large box jelly, with a bell the size of a head of iceberg lettuce and tentacles up to ten feet long, and its stings have killed people within three minutes. A more common scenario is complete recovery after some painful symptoms. The sea wasp must make contact with at least eight feet of tentacle to kill a person—the greater the stretch of tentacle touching human skin, the greater the number of nematocysts injecting venom. It is uncommon for this much contact to occur before the victim notices his predicament and defends himself. Still, about a hundred people have died of sea wasp stings in the last century.

THE REPTILES
AND BIRDS

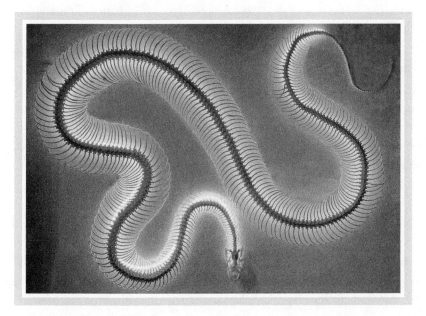

THE SKELETON OF A PYTHON.

10. THE SNAKES

SUBORDER SERPENTES

VENOMOUS SNAKES

IN ARKANSAS AT THE TURN of the twentieth century, it was the custom for children to go about their chores and their play barefoot whenever it was warm. One day a boy named Jeff stepped in a bright pile of autumn leaves that lay, red and rust and dirty yellow, along the trail. A ridge of leaves reared to bite him on the foot. It might have been an illusion, a breeze momentarily catching a few leaves by their edges and lifting them, except for the pinprick of pain in his big toe. The air was suddenly full of a smell like cucumbers. Then a short thick snake, rust-red and rawhide, was visible, but only just, speeding away over the leaves into the under-growth. It made no sound, even in that crisp medium. The older boys with Jeff knew it for a copperhead, and they also knew the remedy. They made a sedan chair of their arms and carried him to the nearest farm, for it was important not to let him exercise. That might carry the venom to his heart. Once home, they poured kerosene into a basin and made Jeff sit with his foot soaking. He suffered no symptoms.

Jeff, who was later known to me as Grampa, told me this story often—the last time when he was nearly a hundred. To the end, he believed his friends had saved his life with the kerosene. In fact the folk remedy had no effect. The truth is that snakes don't always inject their venom. Venom is a precious resource; it takes time and energy to make. It is often more economical for a snake to warn away the careless foot or hand with a dry bite. If that doesn't work, the second bite is likely to serve a solid dose of venom.

The kinds of snakes vary in their readiness to inject. Factors like this make it impossible to say exactly how deadly a particular snake is. Each kind has its own peculiarities. There are, for example, two major groups of venomous snakes that almost never kill people. The African burrowing snakes burrow in search of centipedes, rodents, and other prey. Some of them have special adaptations for this subterranean lifestyle: their fangs protrude to the sides of their closed mouths and can be used by swinging the head to the side. Because they spend most of their time underground, they rarely encounter humans. Occasionally a person rolls over onto one in his sleep. Accidents like that have led to pain, blistering, bellyache, and even, on rare occasions, death.

It's even harder to get bitten by a sea snake. About fifty snakes are grouped in this family (except when they are grouped elsewhere; snake systematics is notoriously changeable). They show various adaptations to sea life: a flattened, rudderlike tail, nostrils that close against water, the ability to hold the breath for eight hours. All of the sea snakes are venomous, and some of the venoms are among the most powerful known. But sea snakes rarely meet people, and they aren't very aggressive. More important, they are poorly equipped to injure; the fangs of most species are slender and meant for fish, not the hide of a diving mammal. Some species can penetrate human skin only at its thin points, as between the toes. People run into trouble rarely even when they harass the snakes. Divers collecting them for the restaurant market in Japan face some slight risk. Sea snakes may also turn up, unwanted, in fishing nets, creating danger for fishermen.

. . .

AMONG PEOPLE WHO handle venomous snakes routinely—zookeepers, herpetologists, amateur enthusiasts—bites are inevitable. Some experts have been bitten more than a hundred times by various dangerous snakes and lived to tell. It becomes, for some, almost routine; they keep medical supplies and even a few antivenins around the lab or the house. Another fact of the herpetological life is that a substantial fraction of this snake handling club die by the fang. You get a little older, your reflexes slow, and one day the snake you used to handle with impunity demonstrates he's in a bad mood and never really liked being milked anyway.

Case in point: Karl Schmidt, a zoologist with the Field Museum in Chicago. He has been dead for half a century, but his name is still known to many of us who grew up playing with animals and reading about the exploits of others who got to work with exotic species we couldn't hope to meet. Schmidt collided with the laws of probability when he was sixty-seven. He took hold of a little boomslang, as he had done many times before. This time his grip landed a fraction too far back, and the boomslang planted one fang in his thumb. The blood ran freely from this puncture. Schmidt sucked out what he could of the venom. It hardly seemed a problem; he'd been bitten before, full bites by bigger reptiles with more firepower.

The boomslang was then regarded as only mildly venomous. It belongs to the family Colubridae, which contains most of the world's snakes. Among its 1,600 species are racers, garter snakes, king snakes, and other mostly harmless kinds. About four hundred species are venomous. They typically chew their venoms into prey with their hind teeth. These back teeth don't usually serve well for defensive biting, and that fact, along with the mild venoms most of them use, means that only a few of the venomous four hundred are really dangerous to us. Among these dangerous few are the African twig snake, which lives in the trees and threatens attackers by hissing and inflating its neck, and the East Asian yamakagashi, which tries to repel human advances by spewing a smelly fluid from the back of its neck.

Schmidt knew he could expect an emphatically swollen thumb, an arm tender for a week or two, perhaps some nightmares and nausea. The nausea hit him on the bus ride home. That evening he bled from his

COBRAS KILL TEN TO TWENTY THOUSAND PEOPLE A YEAR IN INDIA ALONE.

gums. He should have gone to the hospital then—he knew as much about snakes as anyone, and must have realized the venom was breaking down his blood. He behaved as if he meant to recover. In the night he vomited, but late in the morning he called work to say he'd be back the next day. That afternoon there was more vomiting, and then he felt he couldn't breathe. His wife called for help. He arrived at the hospital dead two hours after he'd told colleagues he was getting better.

THE BOOMSLANG AND its kin play a minor role in human suffering compared to the really dangerous snakes, all of which fall into three groups—the elapids, the vipers, and the pit vipers. Together, the venomous snakes kill more people than any other group of nonhuman animals except disease transmitters like mosquitoes. The most conservative estimates put the annual death toll worldwide at forty thousand, but recent reports suggest that snakebite fatalities are grossly underreported.

Let's start with the elapids, a family that contains such notorious snakes as the mambas and the cobras. There are more than two hundred species of elapids, all venomous. They are mostly slender, fast-moving snakes. An elapid injects venom through fangs in the front of its mouth.

These fangs stay in position at all times, so they have to be fairly short. Elapid toxins generally operate on the central nervous system, causing paralysis and sometimes stopping the heart or lungs.

Among the elapids, the cobras and kraits are the most important for us. They kill tens of thousands of people each year. My grandfather could have predicted the reason: bare feet. In places like India, large numbers of barefooted people cohabit with large numbers of snakes.

The kraits are Asian snakes of retiring demeanor. Some of them are unobtrusive; others are more than two yards long. Their bites generally result in little pain for some hours, after which intense abdominal pain sets in. The death rate is an unusually high 50 percent in those who receive antivenin, and of course much higher in those who don't.

One morning in 2001, an American herpetologist was on a scientific expedition to Myanmar when, in a careless moment, he allowed a krait collected by his party to bite his finger. He briefed his followers on what to expect. He would, he said, be conscious through the entire forty-eight hours it would take for his body to process the toxin, though he would soon be unable to speak. His colleagues watched him carefully. Before long, he couldn't open his eyes except with his fingers. His breath began to labor. As predicted, he lost the power of speech and could communicate with his colleagues only by writing notes. In the afternoon his friends kept him alive by blowing air into his lungs. "Blow harder," he advised them in a note. They tried. But a few moments later he changed his mind. "Let me di," he wrote, and reluctantly they did.

Among the thirty or more species of cobra found in Asia and Africa, the Indian spectacled cobra and its close kin deserve special mention. Though they do not rank especially high among the venomous snakes for either aggression or potency of venom, they are abundant in the most heavily populated region of the earth, and they often enter houses in pursuit of rodent prey. Because of their significance in the Hindu faith, their human countrymen don't often kill them. Karl Kauffeld of the Staten Island Zoo caught a glancing bite from an Asiatic cobra, only one fang penetrating his flesh. He described the ensuing sensation thus: "I felt no anxiety; I felt no pain; it did not even occur to me as strange that the darkness was closing in on the light." He survived. Some have died within fifteen minutes. The herpetologist Grace Olive Wiley, a popular media figure in the first half of the twentieth century, died within two hours of being struck by a cobra. These snakes are estimated to kill ten to twenty thousand people in India annually.

Death doesn't tell the whole story, however. The people most likely to get bitten are farmworkers with little access to modern medicine. Those who survive are often scarred for life, physically and otherwise. For example, one case in the medical literature involves a man bitten on the back of the hand. In photos, his hand might be a freshly bitten pomegranate, for much of the tissue has died and sloughed. Two clean bones lie bare within the wound. Another case in the literature involves a teenaged boy bitten on the left leg. In the photos, it hangs useless beside his good leg. It is blackened and withered, like a tree branch twisted by persistent wind.

Some cobras deserve mention for their specialized tactics. The rinkhals (or spitting cobra) and a few others can propel jets of venom through forward-facing holes in the fangs. The snake aims these jets at the eyes of intruders. The pain the venom causes has been compared to that of car battery acid. It can cause temporary or permanent blindness. Also of note is the king cobra, a predator of other snakes. It is the longest venomous snake, sometimes reaching 20 feet. It doesn't often encounter people, but because of its size, it packs a large dose of venom and thus causes high mortality among people it bites.

Another elapid, the black mamba, is sometimes called the most dangerous snake in the world. The factors in favor of its candidacy include its speed, its ability to travel through trees and along the tops of tall grass (so that it often meets people at eye level), its aggression, and even its disconcerting habit of turning up in toilets. There are three other mamba species, all dangerous. The bite of the Western green mamba, for example, may kill a person within half an hour. The mambas are closely related to the cobras, but their habits differ in important ways. The pioneering snake collector C.J.P. Ionides reported that cobras typically bite once, then hang on to chew the venom in. But the mambas tend to bite and release several times in quick succession, injecting double or triple doses of venom.

The corals are mostly banded in bright colors that advertise their venom. More than ninety species of these elapids occur in Asia, North

America, and Australia. Many are small and unlikely to penetrate human skin, but the venom is potent. In 2000, a fifteen-year-old Florida boy captured a snake ringed in red, yellow, and black. He identified it, incorrectly, as a king snake. He stuck out his tongue in imitation of his captive's air-tasting ways. The snake bit the boy's tongue. He raced home on his bicycle. There he began to sweat, drool uncontrollably, and vomit. At the hospital, doctors put a ventilator tube down his throat, a measure that saved his life as his tongue and throat swelled. For the next two days, his appearance was strangely altered. "He looked like the Pillsbury Doughboy," his mother told a newspaper, in one of those family moments teenagers particularly enjoy. The boy proclaimed his intention to continue collecting snakes.

IN 1950, KEVIN BUDDEN, a twenty-year-old amateur herpetologist from Sydney, set out on a long expedition to collect a taipan. He had the misfortune to succeed.

Budden collected snakes to sell to museums, but his dream was to catch a taipan for research. Australia is home to eighty-five related species of elapids—brown snakes and black snakes, rough-scaled snakes and death adders and others. It's not always easy to sort them. The taipan, up to four yards long and highly aggressive, had recently come to public notice because several people had died spectacular deaths under its ministrations. Workers cutting cane and even people walking near hidden nests drew attacks. Nobody who received a firm bite had survived. Budden hoped a live specimen would help scientists develop an antivenin.

In the northern Queensland city of Cairns, Budden heard several encouraging reports of sightings. He even photographed a dead specimen. As he explored a bushy area near a main road one morning, turning over stones and rubbish, he bagged a small nonvenomous snake, a few lizards, and a dozen cane toads. Then he heard the shrill distress call of an animal. He turned over a slab of building material and found the source of the cry: a mother bush rat, ambushed in her nest. Her attacker, a six-foot-five-inch copper cable, was just beginning to swallow her. Budden put his boot on the snake's neck. It frantically vomited out the rat to defend itself, but it was too late. Budden had a grip on it. It rotated in his hand, but could not escape or bite.

Budden couldn't manage his specimen bag with his one free hand, so he abandoned it and went to the road. Soon a man named Harris stopped to offer him a ride. Budden was already in the truck before Harris realized what he'd taken in. He wanted no part of the taipan, but Budden explained its importance for lifesaving research. He convinced Harris to drive him to the home of an expert who could definitively identify the specimen.

The expert assured Budden he was indeed holding a taipan. He provided a specimen bag. By this time, Budden's hand was covered in the snake's saliva and his grip was growing stiff and uncertain. As he tried to thrust the taipan into the bag, it slipped loose and stabbed its fangs deep into the meat of his hand. It struck deeply again before Budden could force it into the bag.

Harris wanted to kill the taipan, but Budden forbade it. He made the other men promise the snake would reach the hands of responsible researchers. Then he went to the hospital. For many hours, he kept faith that he'd eventually recover. But soon he was blind, and then, despite the efforts of his doctors, he had to be placed in an iron lung because his own lungs were paralyzed. By the following afternoon, even that wasn't enough.

The taipan Budden died for was the first live specimen scientists had ever been able to milk for venom. It was a key element in research that led, some five years later, to the development of an antivenin.

The taipan's close cousin, the fierce snake or inland taipan, lives in desert regions and is unlikely to encounter people. In animal tests, the venom of this species has proved fifty times as deadly as that of the Indian cobra, drop for drop. This is the most potent venom yet discovered in a snake.

But the reptiles most likely to kill somebody in Australia are the tiger snakes. These variably colored snakes, which can exceed six feet, often turn up in yards and garages, so they're more likely than other venomous snakes to get stepped on or handled. Because the bite wounds they inflict may cause little pain or swelling, they sometimes go unnoticed. In one case, a seven-year-old boy rolled down a hill and

THE EYELASH VIPER,
ONE OF THE
VENOMOUS
LANCEHEADS OF
CENTRAL AND
SOUTH AMERICA.

cut his foot. He was taken to the emergency room, where doctors noticed scratches on the back of his thigh but didn't recognize them as bite wounds. He was found dead beside his bed twelve hours after the bite.

VIPERS POSSESS a more advanced system for injecting venom: their fangs are hinged, so that they lie flat along the upper jaw when not in use, but sweep into the upright position for action. One benefit of this space-saving system is that vipers may develop very long fangs, with which they can inject venom deep into the flesh of a victim. Many vipers have spade-shaped heads much broader than their necks. They tend to have thin necks and tails, with the main stretch of body between noticeably thicker.

The venoms of vipers are usually full of hemotoxins that not only kill prey but also begin to digest it before the snake has even swallowed it. Similarly, the venom partially digests the foot or hand of a human being who receives a defensive bite, and in the process causes swelling, pain, and bleeding. Doctors advise victims to remove the rings from a bitten hand; otherwise they will cut into the swelling fingers. Things can get worse: nausea, fever, shock, gangrene, paralysis, death.

The current count lists about 122 species of vipers, all venomous to some degree. Some scientists rank Russell's viper the most frequent human-killer of any snake. It's a beautiful animal, typically with a chain of chocolate ovals running along its back on a ground of gray or tan. Like the cobra, it lives in areas well populated with barefoot people—Indonesia, India, and parts of China. It's also very aggressive. What sets it apart from most snakes, however, is its habit of injecting a large and lethal dose of venom with each strike. Unlike the American copperhead that bit my grampa Jeff, the Russell's viper knows no restraint.

Even more aggressive are the saw-scaled and carpet vipers. They are abundant in populous areas of India, the Middle East, and North Africa. In the latter region, they kill more people than any other kind of snake. All of them are under three feet long, but their aggression and potent venom make them perhaps the most dangerous of all snakes. A saw-scaled viper rubs the loops of its body together to make a rasping sound of warning. It is quick to follow up this threat with an attack. The herpetologist Sherman Minton reported that one saw-scale pursued him for 40 feet. It struck at his feet as he retreated. Minton's boots probably saved his life. The bite of the saw-scale causes internal bleeding. Blood seeps from every orifice of the seriously bitten victim. His urine and saliva are tinged red. His death may be quick, or it may take weeks.

In sub-Saharan Africa, a viper called the puff adder is probably the most frequent ophidian killer of humans. It is a thick-bodied snake that bites readily. Its patterned hide camouflages it in soil or leaf litter. The painful swelling caused by its bite has in some cases been so severe that doctors cut the flesh to the bone to provide some relief. One survivor found the entire right side of his body swollen for weeks afterward.

More than a dozen other snakes of this genus occur throughout Africa and the Middle East. Notable among them is the Gaboon viper. It has the longest fangs of any snake, sometimes two inches long. These allow it to inject venom deep into the muscles of a victim.

The way one handles a snakebite often determines its danger. The case that reminds me of this principle, recounted by Ionides, involves a mildly venomous viper called the night adder and a misguided attempt to help. Night adders live in the savannas and jungles of Africa. Their staple food is frogs. Their venom does not usually kill a human being. An exception happened when one man was bitten and his friend, fearing for his life, sucked the venom out. It is the sort of thing that always works in old jungle movies and Westerns, but in this case the friend paid for his solicitude. His throat swelled shut and he died. Possibly he had some minor sore in his mouth, a point of entry for the venom. The man who was bitten suffered no ill effects.

A WESTERN
DIAMONDBACK
RATTLESNAKE
EATING A MOUSE.

. . .

IN THE COUNTRYSIDE one is surrounded by invisible life. My father implied as much one day when he told about a pasture where industrial scrap iron had been dumped. Dad's job was to cut the iron into small chunks for recycling. Prairie grass had grown up among the rusted frames and panels and tanks. As Dad moved among this mélange sizing up the job, he heard a rattlesnake buzz before him. It sounded like autumn leaves scraping pavement, but impossibly faster. (Richard Henry Dana described it as "the letting off of the steam from the small pipe of a steamboat.") The rattle is a series of dry segments formed of a material that resembles human fingernails. When the rattler shakes its tail, the result is a distinctive buzz that affects the human nervous system strangely, causing a sense of alarm even in people who have no idea what they're hearing. Scientists think this noisemaker evolved as a way for the snake to warn off bison and other large animals that might trample it.

The vibration of Dad's steps must have disturbed the reptile. He couldn't see it in the tall grass, but as long as it made its warning noise, he could avoid it. He changed course, only to hear a second snake joining in chorus with the first. Then there was a third, and a fourth. None of them were visible. The snakes could not hear each other—they are poorly equipped for airborne sound. It was the vibration of the trodden ground that moved them to protest. At times like this, one could wish nature indifferent to man. Dad climbed straight over a mountain of iron to make his escape.

Like my grampa's copperhead, rattlesnakes are pit vipers. The pits that give them the name are openings on the face, about halfway between nostril and eye, which lead to heat-sensing organs. They register temperature differences down to thousandths of a degree. This sense is so acute that it probably maps the landscape for pit vipers the way vision does for us.

Human behavior is at least as important as snake behavior in making danger. For example, certain Hindu festivals involve the adoration of cobras. People get bitten at these ceremonies because their own beliefs have brought them into contact with the snakes. In the United States, certain Christian groups, such as the Church of God with Signs Following, handle rattlesnakes and copperheads as a celebration of their own faith. About a hundred people died from this practice in the twentieth century. Many still practice it. At a church near Jonesville, Virginia, on Easter Sunday 2004, a preacher named Dwayne Long handled a rattlesnake and was bitten on the finger. He declined medical treatment, as his faith dictated, and died the next day.

It's fairly difficult to get bitten by a rattlesnake. At roundups in the Southwest, I have seen men step on them in stockinged feet, drape them across their shoulders, and even kiss them on what passes for their lips without consequence. Even though it's not particularly likely to draw a bite, intentional provocation like this accounts for most of the dozen or so snakebite deaths that occur in the United States each year. But I've also known people who were bitten while minding their own business. In the Oklahoma Panhandle, the culprit was usually an irritable little snake called the prairie rattler. Its bite led, after a few hours of increasing discomfort, to a hand or calf so swollen that the plasma seemed to ooze out of it under pressure. Red lines radiated from the wound like the spokes of a wheel. After a hospital stay, the victim would tell of his restless nightmares, from which he woke to an itching that seemed to go all the way down to the bone.

Western diamondback rattlesnakes grow to more than seven feet long and 30 pounds, and they kill more human beings than any other snake in North America. I vividly recall a biologist acquaintance describing a diamondback victim whose leg had "busted just like a ripe tomato." In severe cases, the bitten flesh turns purple, then black. The victim may vomit, lose his balance, and perceive nonexistent smells and tastes. One woman, whose petite arm swelled to 14 inches in circumference, described the pain as worse than childbirth.

The venom of the Mojave rattler contains a stronger neurotoxic component than is usual for a rattlesnake. In lab tests it looks extremely dangerous, but it rarely bites people. Similarly neurotoxic venom is found in the South American rattlesnake known as the cascabel. It encounters people far more often. Its bite causes peculiar neurological symptoms—blindness, disturbed hearing, paralysis of the skeletal muscles so profound that the victim's head may droop like that of a hanged man. In the manner of many elapid venoms, that of the cascabel may kill by stilling the power to breathe.

The other pit viper in the United States, besides the copperhead and the many species of rattlesnake, is the water moccasin or cottonmouth. Adult moccasins come in the dark colors of moss and mud. They may reach six feet in length. They live in water and are so adapted to the aquatic lifestyle that hatchling moccasins use their tails as fishing lures. Moccasins are as viable in saltwater as in fresh, and an agricultural drainage ditch will serve almost as well as a lake or river. They bask on floating logs and brush, on the bank, and on rocky ledges uphill from the water. Bites to people most often occur when the moccasin gets stepped on, though occasionally a swimmer is bitten. It may frighten attackers (and even people who accidentally come close) by yawning wide to show the inside of its pinkish-white mouth. It may, on the other hand, simply bite—in the air or underwater. One victim who was bitten near the spine while swimming spent the rest of his life in a wheelchair. Researchers say half of all moccasin bites result in fingers or toes crippled by gangrene. But deaths are rare.

South America is rich with pit vipers. Besides the cascabel, there are the bushmasters—at nearly 12 feet, the longest venomous snake in the Americas. The bushmasters vibrate their tails in leaves to make a warning sound like that of the rattlesnakes. They generally retreat from trouble, but have killed people on occasion.

The most lethal pit vipers belong to a genus called the lanceheads, which includes the massive barba amarilla and the snakes known to outsiders as fer-de-lances. In Brazil alone, lanceheads bite about sixteen thousand people per year. They kill far more people in the Americas than any other genus of snakes. The common lancehead is the champion human-killer among American snakes. As the snake venoms of the world go, the lancehead's is not particularly potent. It kills only about 7 percent of its victims, and almost none of the lucky few who have quick access to modern medicine. The problem is a familiar one: abundant snakes, abundant people working outdoors, and lack of funds for antivenin. Because of these circumstances, the lanceheads rank with the cobras and kraits and saw-scaled vipers as major killers of people.

The venom of a lancehead digests the flesh, causing a ripple of systemic symptoms. The specific mechanism of death is usually circulatory failure as the plasma seeps into tissues or leaks from the mucous membranes, or else bleeding into the brain, or overload of the kidneys as they try to clean the by-products of digested flesh from the blood. For the observer, the most memorable symptoms are the visible ones—blood blisters big as knuckles, blood oozing from gums and eyes.

BIG CONSTRICTORS

IN COMMERCE CITY, COLORADO, in 1993, a fifteen-year-old boy was found dead in his bed. His face, arms, hands, and feet were smeared with blood. His torso had been bruised, clearly by the coils of a snake. At autopsy, a bite wound was found on his foot; other wounds on his palms and fingers showed he had tried to pry the snake off. Ruptured vessels had flooded his eyes and brain with blood. The culprit was a relative's pet named Sally. She was a Burmese python of modest dimensions—11 feet 2 inches long, 15 inches at her greatest circumference, and weighing 53 pounds. The boy had weighed 95 pounds.

The Burmese python is popular in the pet trade because of its immense size, its generally docile demeanor, and its great beauty. One Burmese I saw had a ground color like mossy water; on this its irregular inky patches seemed to float. A record specimen weighed more than 400 pounds, and some exceed 27 feet. Their numbers in human homes may be vaguely suggested by the fact that a breeding population exists in the Florida Everglades, apparently the result of a great many pet owners having released their pets once they became intractable or inconvenient. Some three hundred specimens have been recovered there. The combination of size and frequent proximity to humans puts the Burmese python in first place as a human-killing constrictor.

In the Bronx, New York, in 1996, a neighbor discovered a nineteen-year-old man in the corridor of his apartment building. He lay in a puddle of blood, wrapped in his 13-foot pet Burmese python, and he was already dead. Nearby, still in its box, was the live chicken he had meant to feed to the snake. In Irwin, Pennsylvania, in 2001, an eight-year-old girl was home alone when a ten-foot Burmese python, one of five pet snakes in the house, escaped from its cage. Her mother found her unconscious, the reptile still coiled around her neck. Two days later, doctors declared her brain-dead.

Like a disproportionate number of pet pythons, Richard Barber's was named Monty—though his was female. Barber, forty-three, of Aurora, Colorado, was showing his pet to two roommates when it tightened its hold on his neck. He fell to the floor. The python wrapped his head and shoulders and squeezed him to death. His roommates couldn't unwind the snake. Police and firefighters had trouble, too; a newspaper account claims it took five of them, using nightsticks as pry bars, to unwind the snake, after which it became aggressive with a firefighter.

A SOUTH AMERICAN
BOA CONSTRICTOR.

THE LARGEST SNAKES are all constrictors. When taking prey, a big constrictor typically starts with a bite, which is not venomous but serves to hold the victim. The teeth curve backward, so the prey can't easily disengage itself. Next, the snake wraps its body around the prey and squeezes. The pressure quickly interferes with the circulation, so that the victim may faint or become disoriented. At the same time, it cuts off the breathing, either by strangulation or by squeezing the torso so tightly that the prey can't get a decent gulp of air. Once the victim is dead, the snake may examine it more closely, flicking its tongue over the entire body for a thorough smelling. Then, if it finds the prey suitable, it swallows it headfirst.

Big constrictors take prey as large as goats, midsized pigs, and young crocodilians. This range puts children and even small adults within their theoretical capacity. Some of them habitually take our close kin the monkeys. Wild chimps show great alarm at the sight of a python, which may suggest that they have reason to fear predation. The world is deeply awash in folklore and faked photos of big snakes eating people. Yet there's no firm evidence that this ever happens. If it does, the event must be extraordinarily rare.

But killing people without eating them is another matter. The key is in that interval between the killing and the eating. Some snakes are not especially good at estimating what they can swallow. They may kill when the opportunity presents, then decide the prey is too large, or else unpalatable for some other reason we don't understand. It seems likely that we are unpalatable; in a number of cases, constrictors have killed but left unconsumed even very small children. The most likely site for such an error is not the wilderness, where snakes are free to move about and choose among diverse prey, but a comfortable home in the West.

Nothing in my experience feels quite like a live snake. It's great fun to handle one and let it move on your body. At first touch, it's dry and startlingly alive, like an electric cable. Then, as it moves on your flesh, it is deeply relaxing, like the hands of an especially sensitive masseuse. But I've often met herpetologists and exotic pet enthusiasts who have had close calls. The hobbyist is sitting with a snake draped on his shoulders. He's done it a hundred times without incident. Suddenly he feels a pressure at his throat and a rising panic. Most such incidents end quickly with the snake getting removed before any harm is done. But occasionally people get hurt. Some pass out and are only rescued by friends. I have even heard of this happening to a powerful man who weighed 250 pounds. The snakes are remarkably strong. Sometimes there is no one nearby to help, and the snake kills.

No other snake can match the Burmese python's lethal combination of size and popularity as a pet, but five other big constrictors have proved dangerous to people. The reticulated python of Southeast Asia may reach 32 feet. A much smaller specimen, less than 13 feet long, killed its owner in Port Orange, Florida, in 1999. It seized the man by his forehead, then wrapped him in its killing embrace.

The African rock python also reaches astounding lengths—a maximum of about 28 feet—but it is relatively slender, topping out at 250 pounds. In Centralia, Illinois, in 1999, a small pet rock python escaped from its aquarium. Four adults were sleeping in the room. Between two of them, the python found a three-year-old boy, whom it bit and asphyxiated, apparently without rousing anyone else.

The boa constrictor of South America is smaller still, with a big specimen measuring 14 feet. In Cincinnati in 2006, a forty-eight-year-old pet owner was found dead with his 13-foot boa around his neck.

The largest snake in Australia is the amethystine, or scrub, python. It grows to lengths of more than 27 feet, though it, too, is slender compared to the Burmese. A few people have been attacked by wild ones. In 1999, a man and his seven-year-old son were camping on Morton Island, Queensland, Australia. As they slept, a large snake, probably an amethystine python, crawled into the tent. It bit the boy on the face and wrapped around his neck. The father was able to detach it and throw it out of the tent. The boy suffered about twenty wounds on his face, upper body, and hands. In another case from Queensland, a woman investigating the screams of her five-year-old daughter found the girl in the yard with an amethystine python attached to her lip. After her rescue, the girl explained that she had herself attacked the snake in an attempt to rescue her kitten from its predatory attack. The girl recovered with some scars. The kitten was not seriously injured.

The heaviest of all the snakes is the green anaconda, which can weigh up to 500 pounds. One reasonably convincing report mentions a specimen 34 feet long. The four species of anaconda are reputedly aggressive, both in the wild and in captivity. An exotic pet dealer I interviewed told me the anacondas are fit only for the most experienced herpers, because they bite frequently. He declined to let me handle the thigh-thick monster he kept in a wood and glass enclosure, or even to handle it himself for my edification. This aggressive temperament, ironically, is the reason why so few hobbyists have been hurt by anacondas. The Burmese python can be placid enough to fool owners into treating it carelessly. Few make that mistake with anacondas.

THE EYE OF A YOUNG
CROCODILIAN.

11. THE CROCODILIANS

ORDER CROCODYLIA

IN 2006, A DEPUTY SHERIFF in Lakeland, Florida, responded to reports of screams for help at Lake Parker. It was about 4:00 A.M. The
deputy heard a man calling and peered into the dark water. The sight
that greeted him was described in the *Orlando Sentinel:* "a naked man
slumped over, caught in the jaws of a huge alligator amidst thick cattails
in bloodied water." With the help of three other officers, the deputy rescued the man, playing what he called a tug-of-war with the alligator.
The reptile eventually gave up. The forty-five-year-old victim had two
broken arms, one of them almost severed. He had lost tissue from his
thigh and buttocks. He told the officers he had been smoking crack co-
caine, then had fallen asleep on the shore, where the gator seized him.

Drugs, including alcohol, often play a role in crocodilian attacks; at
least two fatal alligator attacks have been linked to illegal drug use. In

2008, an eighteen-year-old man was drinking with friends in the wilds of Florida when he declared that he would swim across a slough. Others tried to dissuade him, but he undertook the stunt. Halfway across, an 11-foot alligator latched on to his left arm. He fought and eventually managed to poke the gator in the eye. It let him go, but kept the arm. Wildlife officials shot the alligator and verified its identity by extracting a human arm from its stomach. The young man was fitted with a robotic arm. He told reporters he'd prefer to see the state ease restrictions on gator hunting.

WHEN THE COLONIAL naturalist William Bartram explored what is now Florida, he reported the alligators eager to take him—and his boat. "Very large ones attacked," he wrote, "rushing up with their heads and part of their bodies above the water, roaring terribly and belching floods of water over me. They struck their jaws together so close to my ears, as almost to stun me, and I expected every moment to be dragged out of the boat and instantly devoured."

AMERICAN ALLIGATORS HAVE ATTACKED MORE THAN
FOUR HUNDRED PEOPLE IN FLORIDA SINCE 1948.

But the American alligator, hunted near to extinction once well-armed European Americans seized the area, was by the mid-twentieth century regarded as almost harmless. Like the cougar, it revealed its dangerous nature afresh as the policy of extermination fell out of favor. American alligators have attacked more than four hundred people in Florida since the state began to keep records in 1948. Twenty people have died in these attacks. So far in this century, American alligators have killed thirteen people.

The alligator gauges its prey by height. A six-foot-long alligator once killed a toddler; a large gator of 13 to 16 feet will occasionally take even a full-sized adult. But for most alligators, a person five or six feet tall, when standing upright, looks too large. However, the gator's perception of prey size is one-dimensional; a person that looks too large while standing may be attacked when he bends to tie his shoes or tend his garden, or when he sits down to fish. People don't look as large when they swim, snorkel, or wade. All these situations have provoked attacks. Most dogs look small enough, and gators often prey on them. People have been attacked while defending their pets. In July 2004, on Sanibel Island, Florida, an alligator later measured at 12 feet 3 inches seized a fifty-four-year-old woman by the arm and dragged her into a pond in her backyard. A struggle ensued, with several people coming to her aid. The battle lasted five minutes. When the gator finally let go and the rescuers dragged the woman out of the water, she was found to have bite wounds on her buttocks and legs. Doctors amputated the mangled arm below the elbow, but the woman succumbed to infection.

Alligators are road hazards in Louisiana and Florida. In one case, a woman struck an alligator with her Honda Accord, then loaded it into her backseat, apparently in an attempt to find medical help for it. She wrecked her car when the gator began to thrash. A report in *The Tampa Tribune* does not mention any injuries.

THE ORDER CROCODYLIA comprises twenty-three species of alligators, crocodiles, caimans, and gharials. All of them are theoretically capable of injuring people. Several kinds, such as the freshwater or Johnston's crocodile of Australia, specialize in fish and other aquatic prey. Their snouts have evolved a narrow shape suitable for fast slashes

A CAIMAN ON THE BANKS OF A BRAZILIAN RIVER.

through water. These species tend not to hurt people, because their equipment is poorly suited for taking large animals. Australian authorities report only two attacks by "freshies" on humans. An extreme example of this fish catching adaptation is the Indian gharial. Its snout is so long and thin as to resemble the handle of a pan, its teeth regular and fine, and its limbs so adapted for aquatic use that they are weak and ineffectual on land. It grows to about 23 feet, making it one of the largest reptiles on earth. Besides fish, it eats carrion, including human corpses sent down the Ganges River in funerary rites. But its rare attacks on live humans are defensive.

Many crocodilian species are too small to prey on humans. Cuvier's dwarf caiman, for example, rarely exceeds five feet in length. But even these small species can inflict impressive lacerations on zookeepers, exotic pet owners, and others who interfere with them. Edward Ricciuti reports two cases of people whose hands were bitten by captive spectacled caimans about three feet long. (Ricciuti adds that when he handled it, one of these caimans also resorted to the classic reptilian defense: it urinated on him.)

Among the crocodilians with both the size and the jaw structure to harm people, the species vary. The alligators, which are distinguished by wide, rounded snouts and other minor anatomical differences, tend to be less aggressive than the crocodiles. Zookeepers sometimes walk across the backs of gators to reach the far side of a pool; they don't even fantasize about trying this stunt with crocodiles.

Several factors can prompt a crocodilian to attack. All of them defend their territories against members of their own species, but some extend this defense to any large invader, including a person. Adult crocodilians defend their eggs and their young. The young of many species make distinctive distress calls that may draw help even from adults other than their parents. And of course crocodilians defend themselves against people who deliberately provoke them. In cases like that, machismo and alcohol are usually involved; almost all the victims are male. Sometimes, though, the humans are motivated by less frivolous concerns. In 1997, a group of scientists ventured to a place called Umuya Lagoon in Ecuador to collect the hatchlings of a black caiman. They used a canoe to search for nests, then picked the hatchlings up by hand. The hatchlings beeped with distress. One night the expedition's leader, Pablo Evans, was bending over in the canoe to look at a captured hatchling when a large adult caiman, probably the mother, leaped a yard out of the water and seized Evans by his buttock and his raincoat. She dragged him underwater. He surfaced four yards away from the canoe. As he swam desperately for the vessel, a colleague smacked the returning caiman on the head with an oar. She vanished; Evans was rescued with a minor puncture wound, some torn skin, and "a large bruise in the shape of a caiman's lower jaw."

But the most important factor, accounting for 90 percent of attacks, is predation. It's not that any of the crocodilians particularly seek us out. Rather, they are generalists who take a great many kinds of prey. The old myth of humanity having some special power of inducing fear does not hold up consistently across any group of animals, but it collapses completely with the crocodilians, who treat us the same as gazelles and cattle. They are interested in eating any animal that seems small enough to overcome without undue risk. They may strike in the water, at its edge, or on land. In a couple of cases, they have tried to take sleeping campers from their tents. They are intelligent—in fact, they have the most complex brains among the reptiles—so they can learn the habits of people and anticipate them at favorite watering spots. They are similarly clever at evading hunters.

They most often strike from ambush, disguising their presence either by floating mostly submerged in the water or by lying in tall grass at the water's edge. The attack proceeds by a quick lunge, with the predator typically securing a powerful hold that it does not release without considerable urging. It may roll in the water, disorienting its prey and even wrenching off pieces of it. It may shake its head, rattling the victim to pieces and shattering the spine. Or it may hold its victim underwater to drown.

Human victims get injured not only from the penetrating teeth wounds and the shaking and rolling motions, but also from the crushing force of the bite. The force of the crocodilian bite has been measured at around 1,000 kg, which is enough power to lift a small truck. That's for a largish crocodile of about 13 feet; genuinely huge ones exert far more power.

IN AUSTRALIA'S NORTHERN TERRITORY in 2003, the Finniss River was rising, fed by the rains that accompanied Cyclone Debbie. Three young men rode four-wheelers in a deserted area. Eventually they repaired to the river to wash. The current was running faster than they expected. It swept twenty-two-year-old Brett Mann away from the shore. His two nineteen-year-old friends, Ashley McGough and Shaun Blowers, dived in to help him. They caught him, and the three started toward the bank together. Then McGough saw a 12-foot saltwater crocodile and shouted a warning. They made for a tree overhanging the water. Blowers and McGough clambered up. They looked for Mann, but he was nowhere in sight. They had heard neither screams nor splashing.

Soon the crocodile surfaced with Mann's corpse in its mouth. Blowers described the croc as intentionally showing them the body. Probably it had merely held him underwater long enough to drown him before rising to survey the other available prey. It vanished again, presumably caching Mann's body, as salties often do, then returned within minutes to circle the tree. McGough and Blowers stayed put. The crocodile waited beneath the tree through the evening. The night was too dark for the men to see each other. They huddled together against the cold and tried to keep each other awake. They assumed the croc was still beneath them in the rising water. The morning light proved them right. The patience of a crocodile can last for weeks; it can even slow its metabolism so it doesn't starve while waiting to ambush a particular prey item.

Meanwhile, the men had been missed and the authorities summoned. Officers in a police helicopter spotted Blowers and McGough clinging to the tree in heavy rain. As the copter hovered to rescue them, its draft nearly knocked them from their perch. They were brought aboard after twenty-two hours in the tree, the crocodile having waited below for them through the morning. At a hospital, they were treated for hypothermia and shock. Police searched the flooded area for ten days before they found and killed a likely suspect.

The saltwater crocodile is the largest crocodilian on earth, and the largest animal that habitually preys on humans. It occurs in northern Australia, India, and Southeast Asia. It can cross stretches of ocean and is thus spread among the islands adjacent to these areas. It may reach lengths of 21 feet and weights of more than a ton. Some scientists estimate that salties kill a thousand people per year. Statistics on attacks by salties are hard to come by except in Australia, where careful records are kept. There, salties launch an average of two fatal and three nonfatal attacks per year. Virtually all attacks in the wild are fatal unless other humans come to the rescue.

A 1987 attack illustrates the destructive power of the saltie. At a crossing in Kakadu, Northern Territory, a fisherman slipped and fell into the East Alligator River. As he struggled toward the bank, a big crocodile cruised toward him. The man hurled a beer can at his pursuer. He reached the bank and began to pull himself out with an overhanging branch. The crocodile leaped out of the water and, with a single bite, decapitated him. Then it seized his body and swam upstream. Rangers pursued and found the crocodile still holding the body in its mouth. They shot the croc, which released the body, sank into the water, and was never seen again.

That case was unusually spectacular. A more typical attack, from the same area, was witnessed as a young woman's scream from the water; a pair of vermilion eyes revealed in a flashlight beam; and a reptilian silhouette sliding away in the dark.

Despite incidents like these, the death rate in Australia remains low, partly because authorities in that wealthy nation are well armed and prompt to destroy man-eaters. In the less prosperous nations that occupy most of its range, the saltie seems a greater danger. But the reporting from most countries is sketchy, so it's hard to be certain. The claims for the saltie as earth's premier predator of humanity rest largely on inference: they are aggressive animals known to take humans, they occur in heavily populated parts of the world, and throughout much of their range, medical care is poor. The bite of a crocodilian is rich with bacteria, and many who initially survive the attack soon die of infection. The crocs themselves have considerable immunity.

It's obligatory in any discussion of crocodile attacks to mention a famous incident that took place on Ramree Island near Burma during a World War II battle between Japanese and British forces. About a thousand Japanese soldiers retreated into a mangrove swamp, attempting to cross ten miles of swamp in order to connect with a larger force. British soldiers heard screams throughout the night as the Japanese were attacked by crocodiles. Twenty men emerged alive to surrender in the morning. Many authors have repeated this tale uncritically (including me, in an earlier book). But the circumstances hardly allowed clear observation, and recent investigation suggests that many of the Japanese soldiers escaped. Still, this incident may qualify as the greatest recorded instance of mass predation of humans by any animal except sharks.

Serial predation by salties has also been described; one 19-foot croc killed thirteen people in Sarawak, and other instances of a single saltie taking at least two or three people have occurred. In 2006, Indonesian citizens killed a saltwater crocodile suspected of killing several people. In its stomach they found fragments of human skull, two hands, a leg, some hair, and a pair of shorts.

OTHER MEMBERS OF the family take people on occasion, including the Orinoco crocodile of South America; the mugger crocodile of India; and the American crocodile of the Caribbean, Central and South America, and a bit of Florida. But the saltie's only competition as the most frequent killer of humans among crocodilians, and perhaps among all predators, is the Nile crocodile.

In 2005, a party under the auspices of the Ugandan government arrived in the town of Lugaga on Lake Victoria. Their mission was to capture a particular Nile crocodile. It was reported to have taken at least eighty-three people in twenty years—a span representing perhaps a quarter of its life. Mostly the victims were taken while fishing or filling water vessels. The five men captured the croc with nets and ropes, then recruited dozens of local fishermen to help them lift it into a truck. It was more than 16 feet long and weighed more than a ton. It ended up as a stud in a reptilian breeding farm, destined to sire generations of boots and bags.

People have known the Nile crocodile as a predator of man at least since ancient Egypt. "When a person, either Egyptian or stranger, is killed by a crocodile or by the river itself," wrote the Greek historian Herodotus, "the people of any city where he is cast up must embalm him and lay him out fairly and bury him in a sacred place. His friends and family may not touch him. The priests of the Nile handle the corpse and bury it as that of one who was something more than man."

Like other crocodiles, the Nile model progresses from a youth dining on insects and little fish to an adulthood full of bigger game. When it reaches about ten feet in length, a Nile croc is big enough to take large mammals like wildebeest—or human beings. The females slow their growth at about this size, but the males find size an advantage in their battles for territory and mates. They continue to grow for the rest of their lives, with very old males attaining a maximum of about 20 feet. A crocodile of that size can take almost any animal except an elephant or hippopotamus. One big croc seized a rhinoceros by the nose as it drank and, after a long tug-of-war, pulled it down to its death.

When Europeans first became familiar with the habits of Africans, they were often shocked at how readily the "savages" accepted the deaths of their comrades by crocodile. J. H. Patterson, who wrote about African wildlife in the early twentieth century, reported that one of his employees "went down to the river's edge to fill his calabash with water, when a crocodile suddenly rose up out of the stream, seized the poor fellow and in a moment had dragged him in." The man's friends calmly (as it seemed to Patterson) appropriated his weapons and food and went on. But Patterson soon learned that "accidents of this kind are of fairly frequent occurrence."

Patterson's contemporary Arthur Neumann witnessed a similar incident. He had just finished bathing in Lake Rudolf. His cook, Shebane, had moved down the shore a few yards to do the same. "I heard a cry of alarm," Newman wrote. "There was the head of a huge crocodile out of the water, just swinging over toward the deep with poor Shebane in its awful jaws, held across the middle of his body like a fish in the beak of a heron. He had ceased to cry out, and with one horrible wriggle, a swirl and a splash, all disappeared."

Often, victims simply disappear without even a noise. That was the case when a Peace Corps volunteer named Bill Olsen vanished in Ethiopia in 1966. When last seen, he'd been wading waist-high in the Baro River. "He was nowhere to be seen and I never saw him alive again," wrote a hunter named Karl Luthy, quoted in Alistair Graham and Peter Beard's book *Eyelids of Morning,* "although we were to meet face to face much later when I fished his head out of the croc's belly." Luthy and his comrades found, in addition to Olsen's crushed head, "his legs, intact from the knees down, still joined together at the pelvis," and "other chunks of unidentifiable tissue." A photograph showing these items in a cardboard box ran in *Time* magazine.

The Lugaga crocodile is not the only one to have taken many people serially. In the Shabeelaha Hoose region of Somalia in 2000, for example, a single croc apparently took three people. On Lake Victoria in 2002, the Uganda Wildlife Authority killed four crocodiles that it said were collectively responsible for at least forty deaths. The most notorious serial predator of humans in the species is an enormous male one researcher has named Gustave, whose territory lies in Burundi. This 20-foot croc, made famous by coverage on the website and TV shows of National Geographic, was blamed for the deaths of five people near the town of Magara in an eight-day span. He's also been blamed for hundreds of other deaths. While Gustave may indeed have taken many people, it seems to me that mythology has leached deep into his tale. It makes a good story—and a better TV show—to have a single, seemingly supernatural character at work. The simpler and more unsettling fact is that almost any large Nile crocodile will eat people when the chance arises.

The Nile crocodile currently eats about a thousand people a year. For it, as for other crocodilians, humans only occasionally appear in a diet of whatever's available. One survey found human remains in fewer than one percent of Nile crocodile stomachs. Still, the present day may be the most likely point in history for a person to die this way. Turmoil in human affairs is the cause. Political refugees are vulnerable to animal attacks. For example, people fleeing the Mugabe regime in Zimbabwe find the most likely shelter in South Africa. What separates the two countries is the Limpopo River, a prime piece of habitat for crocodiles. About a dozen people a year are reported killed by crocs in South Africa, but that number doesn't include refugees traveling in secret. Michael Garlock's book *Killer Gators and Crocs* reports that an Apostolic preacher led his flock into the Limpopo in 1988, promising them divine protection. Thirty-six of them were killed by crocodiles.

Similarly, government protection of crocs can put people at risk. In 1982, the government of Malawi accepted the CITES treaty, which regulates trade in endangered species. In fact, it regulates some species that aren't endangered, including the Nile crocodile. As a result, the nation culls about one-quarter as many crocodiles as it used to. By 2000, crocs were taking an average of two Malawians per day in the nation's Lower Shire River Valley. In the district of Nkhotakota alone, crocs took eight people in one month. For the entire nation of Malawi, crocodiles reportedly killed or maimed 250 people in 2001; but the reports from individual districts show that this number is probably low. In the ensuing years, Malawi has continued to struggle with the problem, with local officials sometimes arranging limited culls. Local people typically don't own weapons adequate to dealing with crocs; when they do take action, they may be prosecuted for poaching. The problem isn't the conservation effort itself, but the government's failure to adapt it to local conditions. Many people in Malawi depend on the rivers and lakes for food, drink, and livelihood. They don't have the option of staying away from the water.

High levels of predation on humans have also been documented in Tanzania, Namibia, Zambia, and Madagascar. But the worst trouble spot in the world may be Burundi, where civil war has boiled for decades. Genocidal mass murders have repeatedly left waterways littered with corpses. In this environment, crocodiles have had ample opportunity to eat human beings—the dead, the injured, and the dispossessed.

THE KOMODO DRAGON, LARGEST OF ALL LIZARDS.

12. THE LIZARDS

SUBORDER LACERTILIA

In 2002, police in Newark, Delaware, called at the apartment of a forty-two-year-old man to make sure he was all right. The man had not been seen for a few days, and his friends were concerned. Of course, the officers knew that calls like this can lead to gruesome discoveries. But they couldn't possibly have been prepared for what they found: seven lizards feeding on the man's corpse. They were slender reptiles, the largest about six feet long. Each had been at work on the body with blunt, shearing teeth and wicked claws. Their forked tongues slithered out periodically to taste the air.

The man had meant to keep these Nile monitor lizards as pets. Even after an autopsy, no one was sure whether they had overcome him. Possibly he had died of some other cause. Maybe the lizards had only scavenged his body. Maybe not.

There are about sixty species of monitor lizards scattered through Asia, Africa, and the islands of the Pacific and Indian oceans. They have long tails and necks; many of them look like thick snakes with legs. They all eat meat. Some of them carry venom. No one is sure how big a role the venom plays in subduing prey (except in the case of the Komodo dragon, which I'll discuss in a moment). People bitten by monitors often bleed profusely, which may be evidence of a venomous effect.

The larger monitors put one in mind of a predatory dinosaur; some can even stand on their hind legs like little T. rexes. Many of them find human flesh palatable. In Bali, people traditionally disposed of corpses by allowing water monitors to eat them. Elsewhere, monitors sniff out and dig up corpses to eat; in some parts of the world, people find it necessary to cover graves with stones to prevent such scavengings. As for live people, few monitors are large enough to prey on adults, though many injure people who handle them. The water monitor, certain Australian goannas, and the Nile monitor are all prone to hurt the unwise. The Nile monitor—the species that may have killed the man in New Jersey—is the largest lizard in Africa. It is extremely aggressive when interfered with and has inflicted nasty bites on keepers. While it may reach lengths of seven feet, it is too slender, at barely 40 pounds, to kill an adult human by itself in ordinary surroundings.

THE KOMODO DRAGON, largest of all lizards, is found on four Indonesian islands. It is the only lizard proved to prey on people in the wild. It may reach ten feet and 250 pounds and is abundantly armed with serrated teeth up to an inch long. Its yellow forked tongue laps out continually as it swings its head from side to side. The tongue brings airborne particles to an olfactory organ in the roof of its mouth. It detects prey with this sense and by sight. Once it has located a likely candidate, it stalks in close, then ambushes the prey with a bite to the throat or belly.

The dragon often overcomes even large animals like horses and water buffalo. For decades, scientists believed the dragon could do this because its bite was septic. It would ambush large prey, then retreat to let the victim die of fast-moving infection. Biologists have found fifty-four dangerous species of bacteria in the dragon's mouth, including varieties of staph and strep. The eating of carrion and feces, along with the bleeding of its own gums, helps to maintain this infectious stew. The lizard itself seems to have considerable immunity.

However, field studies failed to find dragons actually using the bite-and-retreat strategy. Instead, they showed that the dragons manage to kill even their largest victims quickly. In 2006, biologists discovered that dragons possess venom glands. The venom turns out to be a key factor in their successes. As the dragon bites, it yanks its head backward, tearing the victim's flesh. Venom oozing from the lower jaw enters the wound with the teeth. The venom acts quickly, tranquilizing the victim even as the dragon inflicts further wounds. Often there is no real resistance.

Once the prey is dead, or at least incapacitated, the dragon swallows it whole if it's small enough. Animals as large as pigs and goats have been swallowed. The dragon's copious bloody saliva lubricates the meal for easier swallowing. Larger prey must first be torn apart. After digesting its meal, the dragon vomits a neat bundle of indigestible parts: teeth, hooves, hair, horns.

Among the notable attacks on humans found in the literature are the 1974 death of a Swiss baron who lagged behind his tour group in Komodo country. Nothing was ever seen of him again except his camera, hat, and bloody shoe. A fourteen-year-old boy bled to death after a

THE DRAGON'S BLOODY SALIVA LUBRICATES THE MEAL FOR EASIER SWALLOWING.

dragon tore flesh from his buttocks. The corpse of another child had to be extracted from the maw of a dragon that had half-swallowed him before adults could kill it. In 2007, a dragon ambushed an eight-year-old boy in the scrubland of a national park on the Indonesian isle of Komodo. It seized him by the waist and wagged its head side to side in a predator's typical spine-breaking shake. The boy's uncle drove the dragon off by pelting it with stones, but the boy was already dead. In 2009, a man stealing sugar apples from a wildlife preserve on Komodo Island fell from a tree. Two dragons tore into him. Fishermen rescued him, but he died before reaching the hospital.

Dragons only rarely manage to kill people, but they don't hesitate to try. People have been ambushed by dragons hiding beneath their houses or behind vegetation. In 2009, a park ranger on the island of Rinca was doing paperwork in a hut when he was attacked. The elevated hut was accessible only by a ladder, which the dragon climbed before lunging at the man behind his desk. He held the dragon by the neck for a moment, then leaped out a window, escaping with injuries to his foot and hand.

In 2001, Phil Bronstein, editor of the *San Francisco Chronicle,* was on a private tour of the Los Angeles Zoo when a Komodo dragon bit into his foot and held him. His then wife, actor Sharon Stone, described the attack: "There's that moment of stillness where you just stare in disbelief. Then Phil screamed and we heard this crunching sound." Bronstein pried the dragon's jaws open and extricated himself, losing a strip of flesh in the process. He scrambled out of the cage as it clawed his thigh. Once they were separated by a locked door, the dragon slammed its body against the cage, trying to continue the attack. Bronstein underwent reconstructive surgery to repair his severed tendons, after which he was expected to spend four weeks in a cast and three more months in rehab, recovering his ability to walk.

VENOM OCCURS IN at least three other families of lizards, but only one of them is known to harm people: the beaded lizards. There are two species in the family. The Gila monster of the southwestern United States and northern Mexico grows as long as two feet. The Mexican beaded lizard of Mexico and Guatemala sometimes achieves three. Both are slow, stout-bodied lizards with skin strongly patterned, the usual

THE SCALES OF THE GILA MONSTER ARE LOADED WITH BITS OF BONE.

colors being black and some variation on orange, pink, or yellow. The scales on the body of a beaded lizard enclose tiny spheres of bone. The bony hide provides some protection from predators.

The Gila monster preys mostly on small mammals, birds, and eggs. The Mexican beaded lizard prefers the eggs of other lizards and birds, only occasionally taking a small mammal. When they bite people, both lizards chew the venom into the wound. They have no fangs, but an abundance of small teeth grooved to carry the venom, which issues from glands at the rear of the jaw. As this venom floods the lizard's mouth, the chewing works it into the bite wounds. This slow delivery works because once it bites, the lizard does not easily relinquish its grip. About 70 percent of bites succeed in injecting venom. That's a remarkably high rate for a venomous animal.

Historically, one was most likely to get bitten when sleeping outdoors. The lizard, prowling by twilight or dark for prey, might get trapped when a person accidentally rolled onto it. These days, the most likely victims are herpetologists. In one case, a twenty-three-year-old herper captured a Gila monster near Lake Mead, Nevada, and was bitten on the forearm. It took him a minute and a half to free himself from the lizard's grip—he had to pry its mouth open with pieces of iron. His arm soon swelled and became enormously painful. Then the systemic symptoms set in: low blood pressure, rapid pulse, dizziness, vomiting, and, within two hours, a heart attack. By that time the man had reached a hospital. He recovered, though his heart was permanently damaged. Others have been less fortunate.

THE TALONS OF THE GREAT
HORNED OWL CAN CRUSH
THE SKULLS OF SMALL
CARNIVORES.

13. THE BIRDS

CLASS AVES

WHEN I WAS NINE, I got a new puppy, a black mongrel with tan patches on her face and feet. She was rambunctious, and several times in her adult years knocked me over with a torpedo attack, charging full speed and flooring me with a head-butt.

It was an autumnal dusk; the puppy and I were in the backyard, me on all fours to give her playful cuffs as she charged and feinted. The sensation of being watched hit me suddenly. I have felt it several times since, always in the presence of large predators, but then it was new to me, that cold weight in the belly, that urge to look around. I'm no mystic; I believe this sensation has some material cause, probably subliminally received data from one of the usual senses.

At the time, though, I knew nothing but the fear. The puppy kept playing, oblivious. One flop ear cocked slightly, as if to ask why I had stopped. I gathered her under my windbreaker, and as I did, something drew my attention up. A great horned owl moved silently over my head, close enough for me to see the pattern of its feathers even in the dusk. It stopped on the CB radio antenna that jutted from our roof. I had no awareness of its finding its footing or orienting itself; it was just suddenly at rest, upright, and it looked back at us on the lawn. It seemed simultaneously to be staring me in the eye and gazing disdainfully over my head, ignoring me.

All this must have taken only a few seconds. I rushed into the house, the puppy squirming against my embrace. I went out the front door to see if I could get a better look, leaving the puppy safe inside. On the front walk I was perhaps 20 feet from the owl. It no longer seemed to be looking at me. There was a sound like the snapping of a heavy blanket, and the owl was suddenly in flight, making me sidestep involuntarily as it cruised over my head. It was a good thing I moved. The air was suddenly full of a hideous smell. The owl had left a splatter of white, like leftover gravy, on the walk. By the next day the smell had vanished, and I poked at the mess with an elm twig. It was crusty now. Inside, it was like ashes, and there were little clotted masses, which might have been bones.

The great horned owl achieves a wingspan of more than four and a half feet. Along with less formidable prey, it takes skunks, minks, weasels, hawks, and domestic cats. A skunk was observed to struggle futilely for fifteen minutes while a horned owl gripped it unrelentingly with its talons, gradually crushing its skull and spine. (For a rough comparison, try crushing a Brazil nut with your bare hand.) Owls typically tenderize snakes, including rattlesnakes, by breaking their spines at intervals, so that they resemble a helping of rigatoni in a hide bag, before swallowing them headfirst.

These owls are unlikely to attack humans except in defense of a nest. A few attacks have occurred in areas where no nest was visible; possibly these are cases of the birds defending hidden caches of meat. When they do attack people, their usual strategy is to dive-bomb with the talons. One biologist named Errington, quoted in Bernd Heinrich's *One Man's Owl*, rates such a strike as the equivalent of "a blow by spiked brass knuckles." Errington claims that an owl's talon strike could blind or even kill a person. One man who meddled with a nest found himself bloodied and torn, one talon penetrating the muscle of his arm. Heinrich also reports the case of Charles R. Keyes: the strike of an owl slashed him across the cheek and ear and numbed one side of his head. He called the wound "rather ugly but not dangerous."

A scientist named Arthur Cleveland Bent once climbed a tree to investigate an owl's nest. The mother owl lit on a nearby tree and began a threat display, complete with puffed plumage, open wings, and the snapping of her beak. The father, too, arrived to protest Bent's presence. Bent nearly lost his grip on the tree when one of them swooped to hit him on the shoulder. In the cause of science, he persisted. Higher up the tree, he "felt a stunning blow behind my ear, which dazed me . . . her sharp talons had struck into my scalp, making two ugly wounds, from which the blood flowed freely." At this point, Bent began to value the sanctity of the nuclear family above the cause of science. He retreated.

Folklore has long claimed that the biggest raptors not only launch such defensive attacks, but also take children as prey. Legends tell, for example, of mountain climbers finding human skeletons in aeries and of ten-year-old shepherds snatched from their duties. Large eagles take fairly heavy prey, such as lambs and fawns. But the most powerful eagles, such as the harpy eagle of South America, the Philippine sea eagle, Steller's sea eagle of Russia, and the crowned hawk-eagle of Africa, rarely exceed 20 pounds. Some reports claim these giants, particularly the harpy eagle, can briefly lift even prey slightly heavier than themselves. Even so, this puts all but the smallest humans outside their range for snatching. At nine, I was certainly beyond the range of the owl that so unsettled me. Clearly my puppy was the target.

But a bird of prey need not carry off its victim. The crowned hawk-eagle has been observed to kill and partly eat animals on the ground, including in one case a 66-pound bushbuck. In *Man the Hunted*, Donna Hart and Robert W. Sussman propose that these eagles may attempt to take children because of their resemblance to the monkeys that form part of their diet. They further propose that recent human ancestors, smaller than the current model, probably fell to eagles often enough, and that the eagles have not entirely abandoned this ancestral relationship. They adduce the case of a seven-year-old Zambian boy who weighed 44 pounds. As he walked to school, a crowned hawk-eagle swooped on him, lacerating his head, chest, and arms. A woman with a garden hoe came to the rescue and killed the eagle. The boy recovered. The bird attacks monkeys in a similar way, driving its talons through their hearts.

In December 1969, the U.S. Merchant Marine ship *Badger State,* laden with bombs for use in the Vietnam War, went down in stormy seas, a victim of its own explosive cargo. As survivors floated in the water, they were attacked by albatrosses. These huge sea birds sometimes have wingspans of 12 feet. They struck the men on their heads, gouging with their beaks. The men were at pains to protect their eyes. Albatrosses normally feed on fish, carrion, and garbage. They may follow ships to eat their garbage. Probably in this case they made no distinction between the living men and the other kinds of food the ship produced.

THE BLACK-CHESTED
BUZZARD EAGLE WILL
HURT PEOPLE WHO
APPROACH ITS NEST.

No other birds show any interest in us as prey, but many birds, like the parent owls I mentioned, swoop to strike or gouge people in protection of nest or territory. In Europe, buzzards sometimes claw at pedestrians who accidentally pass near their nests. In 2004, a buzzard attacked twenty-two people engaged in a bicycle race in Devon, England, damaging either the helmet or the person proper in all cases. One man received a three-inch gash. The related red-tailed hawk has been charged with similar crimes. One redtail that nested near a golf course in Woodridge, Illinois, attacked at least sixty golfers over a period of four years.

Birds of prey aren't the only energetic defenders. Among the birds known to defend their nests with dive-bombing attacks are blue jays, barn owls, robins, swallows, and mockingbirds. It's not necessary for a human to actually attack the nest; birds often decide to make preemptive strikes. They are not especially good at judging human motives, and it is easy to find oneself under attack simply by walking near a nest, even if the nest is high in a tree and the human trespasser unaware of it until the attack is launched. It is not, of course, humans alone who experience such attacks. Anything large enough to look like a threat to the parent birds may suffer, including dogs, cats, and larger birds. The "attack" typically consists of shriekings and dive-bombings that stop short of the target; actual contact is rare, but it does happen on occasion. Species vary in their willingness to carry the assault to actual contact.

Crows are frequently implicated in dive-bombing attacks. In Tokyo, where the urban crow population is about thirty thousand, the birds have knocked people from their bikes. In Britain, a certain apartment building found itself assaulted by crows, which continually visited the place in search of food. They had been fed by the construction workers who erected the building, and afterward, when people lived in the apartments, they would find crows knocking at their windows for favors. The birds intimidated children and old people. In Germany, a single crow with the habit of knocking people in the head drew police to a park where, after one or two stratagems failed, they finally got the bird drunk on schnapps and arrested it.

Other corvid birds are similarly unimpressed by people and willing to slap us around. I have seen many such attacks by blue jays, who seem to launch preemptive strikes against any animal that passes near their nests. When I was eight or so, playing in what I thought of as my yard, a jay fetched me a smart blow on the head, drawing a drop of blood and leaving me a scab to prove my story to incredulous kin.

Magpies are similarly aggressive during their mating season, when territorial matters trouble them more than usually. In 1999, the city of Canberra, Australia, recorded 254 magpie attacks, which included scratches and pecks. An article in *The Independent* remarked, "Among their favourite targets, for reasons unclear, are cyclists, red-haired women and mothers with baby strollers."

Some of these attacks may be examples of a cooperative defense called mobbing. When one bird is under attack, or perceives its nest to be in danger, its neighbors join it in harassing the attacker. I observed an instance of mobbing in my own yard recently. The snow came late this year, announced by a late flight of Canada geese calling in the night. In the November morning the snow was too warm to hold its shape until

CROWS MOB LARGER
PREDATORS—AND
PEOPLE.

it hit the ground. The light seemed at once golden and soaked. As I passed by my kitchen window, an interesting movement snagged my eye. It was a great horned owl, a species I've continued to take a special interest in since my childhood encounter. It had been on the roof of the garage. The movement was its swooping hop onto the lowest branch of a box elder tree. Within a minute or so, a big glistening crow landed nearby, higher and to the side. An untidy mass in the tree the size of a football might have been a crow's nest. I had called to my wife, Tracy, at first sight of the owl, and we watched, knowing what would come next. We didn't hear the crow speak, but within seconds his friends had joined him in the tree. I didn't think to count them; Tracy guessed there were twenty. They set up a racket. Tracy wanted to open the window, but I wouldn't let her for fear of scaring the birds away before they'd played out their drama.

"I've never heard them sound like that before," she said.

The tree was bare, and the crows adorned it like notes on a treble clef. The tree next to it was also a box elder, but had somehow held on to a few of its jaundiced leaves longer. They hung down heavily in the damp, like scraps of drenched leather.

The owl looked over his right shoulder, his head turning 120 degrees and then looking forward again, toward us. To me he seemed unconcerned; Tracy said he seemed worried. After a moment of racket during which he didn't take the hint, a crow hopped down to a closer branch, about three feet from the owl. It seemed to me this was the big crow that had first called for help, though the crows looked too similar to let me feel sure.

The owl opened his wings with a rapid gesture so graceful it seemed slow. He soared over our patio with no visible effort. The crows were prompt to follow; they might as well have been attached to him with wires. They gabbled at him in voices like bedsprings. We ran barefoot, Tracy and I, out the back door to see the rest. As I stood on the porch steps looking up, the owl landed in a neighbor's cottonwood tree. A dollop of slushy snow slid from my roof to pelt me in the eye, somehow missing the lens of my glasses. I staggered out to my yard, my good eye on the birds. My neighbor burst from his house to demand answers.

"Oh, it's an owl," he said, and stood watching. The crows had taken up stations above the owl in the cottonwood and had not abated their cries. After a few seconds he once again took flight, and I lost sight of him beyond my neighbor's house. At that point I noticed how cold my feet were. Tracy and I went back inside, already telling each other the story, comparing the details we'd noticed.

Mobbing is a way for small, relatively weak animals to survive in a world of predators. Just as individual threat behavior tends to stop short of contact, so does mobbing. Mobbing has been observed to work not only against birds of prey but against bigger animals such as dogs. Even crows, those masters of the technique, may be driven off by smaller birds in a mob. Sometimes birds of different species mob collectively, improving their power to intimidate. Almost any predator will give way to a mob of birds. In theory it would be possible for the predator to take one of the smaller birds as prey when he's being mobbed, but this outcome is rare. One impediment to the predator's turning the tables is its inability to deal with multiple stimuli. A hawk seems unable to focus on and kill an individual bird in a mob. One might expect more sophisticated behavior from human beings, many of whom exhibit fine math skills, but the same sensory whelming seems to occur in most cases of human-mobbing. People panic and retreat.

Many bird species will mob the most dangerous predators on sight, even when no nest is threatened or even nearby. This behavior is often directed at birds of prey. Certain bird populations acquire the habit of treating people as threats worth mobbing.

Another scenario that can result in human injury is belligerent feeding. Anyone who has fed seagulls will know what I mean. You toss a few scraps of bread on the ground; the gulls swoop down and eat them, then swirl around you screeching in hopes you'll yield more. I've often fed gulls from my hand without harm, but occasionally people get bitten or scratched. Gulls accustomed to seeing humans as a source of food may pester even those who have never offered to feed them. Entire towns have been harassed in this way. On Australia's Fraser Island, kookaburras habituated to being fed by humans began to peck and dive-bomb tourists.

One more type of flying "attack" worth mentioning is the mass invasion. For example, one foggy night in 1961, hundreds of sooty shearwaters invaded the town of Santa Cruz, California, slamming into houses, breaking streetlights and headlamps, vomiting fish onto lawns and streets, and pecking at people. Such incidents invariably put people in mind of the fictional mass attacks in Daphne du Maurier's story "The Birds" or the film adaptation of it by Alfred Hitchcock. The real cases, however, seem less like hostility than mass confusion. It has been suggested that the shearwaters of Santa Cruz suffered from poisoning with domoic acid, which is produced by certain algae under environmental stress. People sometimes encounter this toxin in shellfish. In us it causes a kind of poisoning that includes amnesia and other signs of mental disturbance. But perhaps the fog is a more elegant explanation.

As ANY PARROT owner will tell you, pet birds can give serious bites. The nut-cracking beak of the African gray parrot, for example, can sever fingers. In 1998, the Labour Party's John Prescott, deputy prime minister of the United Kingdom, was engaged in a publicity event for environmental issues when a captive macaw, clearly a Tory, fetched him a bruising bite on the finger.

The greatest danger from flying birds is not attack, but collision. In 1960, a passenger flight took off from Boston's Logan Airport and immediately crashed into Winthrop Bay. Sixty-two people died; the other ten aboard were injured. The cause of the crash was a flock of starlings.

Airplanes have been colliding with birds since the Wright brothers. It is an extremely common occurrence. The U.S. government recorded thirty-eight thousand such incidents from 1990 to 2001, not including military flights. About 85 percent of collisions are negligible events for the aircraft, though fatal for the bird. Even in the not so negligible cases, crashes are rare. But because of serious accidents like the one in Boston, the government required manufacturers to design planes resistant to birds. The result was that smaller birds cause less damage than they used to. Engines can now withstand the ingestion of a bird up to four pounds. This doesn't mean that small birds pose no threat; when an entire flock collides with a plane, serious damage is possible. In 1997, a flight from the Dallas–Fort Worth airport was aborted after it encountered 437 blackbirds.

Larger birds, even when encountered singly, can destroy an engine. Swans, geese, ducks, gulls, crows, and raptors have all caused serious damage. In 2009, birds, apparently Canada geese, forced the landing of a US Airways jet in the Hudson River near Manhattan. Since 1988, at least 195 people have died in bird-related air accidents.

Collisions with birds can also cause car accidents. Large birds such as pelicans, turkeys, and pheasants are frequently involved. In 2004, a turkey vulture actively attacked a New Jersey man riding a motorcycle. As he tried to fight the bird, he collided with a car and was hurled to his death.

BIRDS ENCOUNTER US on the ground as well as in the air. The largest of them are in a group called ratites—flightless, fast-running birds with loose, shaggy feathers. Their usual diet is plant matter supplemented with an occasional insect, lizard, snake, rodent, or small bird, or perhaps the manure of some other animal.

Three ratites—emus, rheas, and ostriches—thrive in the United States, where people have tried to ranch them for their hides, meat, eggs, and oils. (The oil supposedly relieves the pain of arthritis and leaves one's hair shiny and manageable.) An occasional feral example turns up, escaped from a ranch or abandoned by an owner disillusioned with his financial returns. Ranching operations have increased the number of tussles between human and ratite.

My friend Jack raised rheas, and had the scars to prove it. "They'll bite your arm and then twist their heads," he explained. "They try to tear a piece out of you." Rheas are five feet high or occasionally even six, with a maximum weight of about 90 pounds. Their feathers are gray. Their wings, surprisingly large for an earthbound bird, help with direction and balance, allowing them to lean at seemingly dangerous angles as they run.

One Sunday evening in Arkansas, Tracy and I watched Jack feed the rheas. He had Tracy guard him with a high-powered squirt gun while he went in. The gun, he explained, was loaded with soapy water. When a rhea got a squirt in the eyes, it irritated him enough to distract him from his intended victim, which was anybody standing near the feed trough.

Tracy had to use her weapon several times. She would squirt; the rheas would shake their heads, back off for a minute, and then move in on Jack again.

"Watch your ammo!" Jack hollered. He was a combat veteran. "Cover my flank!"

In the wild, rheas live in the scrub forests and lightly wooded grasslands of South America, especially along rivers. The males attack mounted gauchos who come too close to their nests. The gauchos have learned to bring dogs along as a countermeasure. I had occasion to learn of the nest guarding skills of rheas on Jack's ranch. After we got to know the farm a little better, Jack and his wife would hire Tracy and me to tend the place when they took vacations. One morning I went with a farmhand named Pete to gather the rhea eggs. Our mission was to put the eggs in an incubator, increasing the survival rate. Pete looked for the eggs, which were hidden in tall grass. He could carry only two at a time, because each yellow egg was about the size of a cantaloupe. He was quickly laden, unable to defend himself. My job was to guard him.

AN OSTRICH MAY STAND
NINE FEET TALL AND
WEIGH 330 POUNDS.

When you're stealing their eggs, it takes more than a squirt gun to stop them. I used a six-foot pole.

"You have to grand-slam him," Pete said. "Otherwise, he'll get you." The birds would come at us silently, their heads bobbing on snaky necks. When I grand-slammed one, he would shake his head exactly the way characters in Warner Bros. cartoons do when they get smacked. Then he'd keep coming.

Jack also raised emus. The emu can reach heights of six feet and weights of 100 pounds. It's found in most of Australia outside the cities, an area that includes a great diversity of habitats, but it prefers forest and wooded grassland. With its mass of gray-brown feathers and its meaty drumsticks, an emu looks like a cross between a tyrannosaurus and a dust mop.

"They don't bite," said Jack. "They kick. It only takes one kick to split you open from your pelvis to your throat." He thought a minute, then added, "Don't ever let your cat near an emu pen. We used to have a cat."

I asked Jack why he didn't raise ostriches. He paused to light a cigarette before he answered: "Too dangerous."

The ostrich is the largest living bird. A big male may stand nine feet tall and weigh 330 pounds. The skin is a cyanotic blue. The male has black feathers and white; the female is dressed in drab gray. Their natural range is a belt across the widest part of Africa—mostly in the Sahara—and another patch in the south of that continent. Besides desert, they are comfortable in savanna country. They fluff and fold their feathers as necessary to regulate their body heat and moisture. The ostrich is said to be the favorite food of the lion; in one case a trio of lions invaded an ostrich ranch in Kenya and killed thirty-nine of the birds in a single night. Occasionally matters turn out differently, and ostriches have been said to slay lions with a single well-placed kick.

These kicks are even more effective against humans, who expose their soft bellies by standing upright. It's rare for a wild ostrich to attack a person, but captive ostriches are another matter. In 1997, near Joostenbergvlakte, South Africa, a couple walking to meet friends cut through an ostrich farm. An ostrich kicked the sixty-five-year-old husband into submission, then attacked the sixty-three-year-old wife, kicking and stomping her for what the husband said was an hour. Finally the bird left and the husband managed to drag the wife under the shelter of a bush and flag down help. The wife died in the hospital. In Washington State in 1998, a farmer took a kick from a captive ostrich that knocked her ten and a half feet. The following year, the same ostrich broke the neck of the farmer's eighty-one-year-old father, killing him.

But the most aggressive ratites are the cassowaries, which are closely related to emus. Their feathers are typically black, their heads bright blue patched with red or yellow. A bony ridge juts from the top of the head. Their three-toed feet possess sharp nails as long as five inches. The maximum size of these birds is about six feet and 150 pounds. The cassowaries prefer rain forests, which is one reason they were never introduced for breeding in the United States. Their range includes New Guinea and the suitably forested parts of New Zealand and Australia.

Cassowaries normally hide when they sense humans. In New Guinea, the native people hunt them for food, and a cornered cassowary defends itself with leaping kicks. Occasionally a person is disemboweled. Similar attacks occur when the males defend their territories in the mating season. In Australia and New Zealand, wild cassowaries seem to attack people about half a dozen times in a decade, often because nature enthusiasts offer to feed them. A captive cassowary tore into a keeper's leg at the San Francisco Zoo in 2001.

Gallinaceous birds—chickens and their kin—can be far more aggressive than the ratites, though their size limits their effect. An ordinary barnyard rooster will attack people by flogging with its wings and scratching with its talons and spurs. Fighting cocks—roosters bred for combat—are especially formidable. An acquaintance of mine whose family was involved in cockfighting told me she saw a cock easily dispatch a domestic cat. Often, a rooster flies in the face of a child, lacerating the skin and endangering the eyes. At the farm of some friends, a red rooster struck a five-year-old girl, drawing blood from her cheek. The victim was only slightly taller than her attacker. Her father took umbrage, then took the rooster's head. Adults get attacked, too, but greater height helps protect their faces.

A news report from 2001 describes a large wild turkey harassing a postal carrier. "He's really scary," the carrier said. "He's got feet bigger than my hands." Wild turkeys may weigh 25 pounds and have wingspans of six feet. They are armed with spurs more than an inch

long. Despite the silly image conjured by their overweight domestic
brethren, they can injure people. Peacocks, too, are fairly aggressive and
have scratched many people.

Swans and geese are far more aggressive than the gallinaceous birds,
both in defending territory and in demanding food. Almost every child
who grew up on a farm with geese has a tale of terror to relate. One
kinsman of mine was, at age five, battered about the head by a goose so
badly that his grandfather had to run to the rescue. He stopped the bird
by decapitating it with a swing of the pitchfork he happened to be
holding.

A zoo Tracy and I used to visit when we lived in Kansas provided a
good sample of swan aggression. It was a modest zoo, with emus gal-
loping through a pasture and a crippled eagle on an iron perch inside a
huge sagging cage. A cement wall surrounded a flat and grassless yard
that, a sign explained, was home to a badger; but badgers are nocturnal,
and the zoo was open only in the day, so I never saw him. There were
bighorn sheep, a reclusive bobcat, and a half-dozen shaggy bison whose
hair peeled off in great sheets in the summer.

Tracy and I came mostly for the pond, a little landscaped affair with a
wooden bridge over it. We were young and in love, and this was the sort
of backdrop we wanted. There were irises, cattails, gravel, even a few lily
pads in the water. The fowl were the usual sort—a variety of ducks,
some with iridescent green heads, some mousily brown. As we stood on
the bridge, a strange ritual would unfold. The zoo's resident black swan
issued forth from his coop, cruising the pond to bully every duck within
his reach. He would seize their heads in his bill and shake them. They
learned to run onto land at sight of him. Once he had cleared the water
of fowl, he made for the bridge, where he snaked his head between the
slats of the railing and bit my toes. He couldn't hurt me through my
shoes, but he tried, hissing like an asthmatic cat. We experimented. If I
wasn't available, the swan—Darth, as we called him—would readily bite
Tracy's toes, but if given a choice, he always preferred me. Tracy suggested a gender bias. We tested that by bringing friends along. It turned
out that any man was an equally agreeable target. I suspect size was
Darth's criterion—the height of a man, or else the size of manly feet,
which the bridge put at his eye level as he cruised the pond. Sometimes

Darth would lunge out of the water to attack people on land. A fence kept him from following up on these threats, but he was convincing enough to send some visitors running.

When a swan or goose is unfettered, it flogs its enemy with the bony knobs on its wings. The attacks are usually not serious, but swans have broken human arms with a particularly well-aimed blow. The largest swans reach 50 pounds, making them formidable attackers. They have killed at least two children.

Some birds defend themselves not by fighting, but by stinking. Of special note are the fulmars of the widely distributed genus *Fulmarus*. These seabirds, which look like gulls, can squirt a noxious oil from the mouth or nostrils. Both the nestlings and their attendant parents are likely to do so when an intruder interferes with the nest. The fluid can strike with precision from six feet, so that humans of innocent intentions may be preemptively befouled. The attack sometimes kills other birds by matting their feathers so thoroughly that they can't fly. For humans, the result is a lingering unpleasant smell. The least tern is similarly protective of its nest, dive-bombing and defecating on humans who come too close.

The pitohuis of New Guinea secrete toxins that can affect people who handle them. A biologist named Jack Dumbacher discovered this fact in 1989 when, after handling a hooded pitohui, he somehow licked his finger and found himself growing numb in the mouth and dizzy. He suffered no lasting effects. The toxin, since confirmed in other members of the genus, was found to be the same as that of certain poison dart frogs, though the frogs possess it in greater and more dangerous quantities. Probably bird and amphibian both acquire it by eating certain poisonous beetles. The bird seems to present only a minor danger; indigenous people know how to prepare it for safe eating.

BIRDS ARE IMPORTANT vectors of disease. Influenza, for example, may have originated in birds. People can get flu from a great many animals, but the important vectors are pigs and domestic birds such as chickens and ducks—hence the many references in news articles to "swine flu" and "bird flu." When flu (or any other disease) crosses a species boundary, it may become temporarily more virulent as it adapts to its new home. This has been the case with type A influenza many times, because it crosses among species rather freely and is constantly evolving anyway. Because of its shifting genetic structure, we never develop full immunity to it.

Flu kills far more people than almost any of the newsmaking diseases, yet gets little press except when it can be packaged under some new label like "swine flu." And in fact the mortality rate is generally low—perhaps a tenth of one percent. But because it infects so many people, and infects them repeatedly over a lifetime, it takes many lives. Flu is on hand to finish off people when they are old or sick with something else. It often ravages the linings of the respiratory system, leaving a victim open to the ministrations of bacterial pneumonia or other opportunistic infections. And a particularly large outbreak can be devastating: the Spanish flu pandemic of 1918 killed an estimated 20 million people.

Flu is only one of many important infections birds help spread, from psittacosis to *Salmonella*. In the terror-obsessed United States of the twenty-first century, West Nile virus has grown notorious out of proportion to its actual danger. Some people have come to fear the sight of dead birds in their yards. West Nile fever afflicts only about 20 percent of those who contract the virus; of that 20 percent, two-thirds of one percent develop encephalitis—inflammation of the brain. The symptoms can include tremors, stupor, disorientation, paralysis, and even death. In the United States, robins and crows are among the most commonly infected birds. The virus passes from birds to people through the bite of a mosquito.

THE MOST IMPORTANT danger birds pose is competition. The red-billed quelea, an African member of the weaver family, is probably the most numerous wild bird on earth. Perhaps one and a half billion individuals exist. Flocks sometimes contain millions. A single tree may contain five hundred nests, and tree branches sometimes break under crowds of queleas. It is these dense congregations that make the quelea dangerous to people. The birds eat grass seeds, including grains cultivated by humans. They feed en masse, sometimes devastating entire fields in a few hours. People have tried many control methods, including napalm. It is estimated that such human abuse kills one billion queleas per year. So great is the bird's reproductive capacity that these losses have not made lasting dents in its population.

Rodents, grasshoppers, and queleas form a select cohort. When their numbers swell, human beings suffer. Vast areas feel the touch of famine and death.

THE ARTHROPODS
AND WORMS

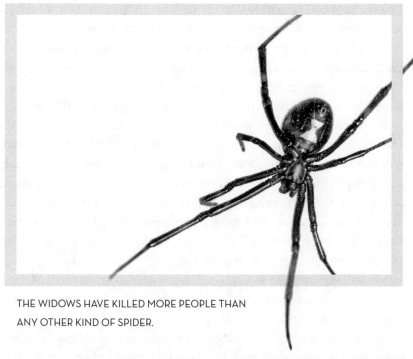

THE WIDOWS HAVE KILLED MORE PEOPLE THAN
ANY OTHER KIND OF SPIDER.

14. THE ARACHNIDS AND MYRIAPODS
SPIDERS AND THEIR KIN, PLUS CENTIPEDES AND MILLIPEDES

THE ARACHNIDS

SPIDERS
ORDER ARANEAE

HER LEGS ARE A TRANSLUCENT GREEN, like a clear straw through which lime Kool-Aid has recently passed. Her body partakes of this same green, but might at a glance be called gray or brown or yellow, so dull and indeterminate does it seem. Outside her kind, I have seen this color only on certain fungi.

She came into my life last night, descending on a strand from the ceiling, busy with her legs all the way down, as if impatient to be running again. Her line, billowing like laundry in a breeze, touched the top of my computer monitor, and then the spider herself was in motion, streaming down the screen. I put my hand out for her to run on, and then she dropped smoothly into the jar I put in her way. Her footsteps on my skin were soft as mist. In the jar, she runs the surfaces, vertical and otherwise, without a pause, as if she had a special dispensation to ignore gravity.

She's a sac spider, and I have met her kind many times without accident—in my house, where they scamper along the floorboards or come rappelling into the middle of conversations, and in my yard, where I have seen them speeding over the leaves of the lilac bush. Probably you have seen them, too, considering what a wide stretch of the world they live in. If you did, and you have no special interest in spiders, perhaps you thought of them as generic, as spiders so lacking in distinctive characteristics that no further name need apply. In fact, the (unlikely) bite of one might give you occasion to think harder about its identity. That bite, a minor affair at first, might leave you feeling fluish for a few days. Later, the wound itself might deepen into a patch of dead tissue—a necrotic lesion. This lesion would eventually slough, leaving an ugly little crater.

So it is with spiders. The ones that provoke awe rarely hurt anyone; of the harmful few, many look so bland they hardly alarm anyone but the most ardent arachnophobes.

My SON DROPPED a goldfish into the cage. The lamp bulb used to heat the cage glared on its dirty glass side like a humid sunset. The fish shuddered, propelling itself several inches into the air, then fell back to the dirt. The lamplight looked oily on its scales. That first flop was enough to draw the interest of the tarantula that lived in the cage, a creature big enough to fill my open hand. It advanced two steps, then stood listening with its feet—for the vibration of the ground is what draws it to its prey. The fish lay still a pregnant moment, as if aware of its danger; then it jerked into the air again. The tarantula rushed forward and closed like a hairy fist on the fish. The fish shivered, then lay still in the spider's fangs. We could see those two great fangs working alternately, like the arms of a baker kneading dough. A few moments later, long after we thought the fish dead, it gave a sudden spasm. The spider only contin-

THE QUIETEST MEMBER OF MY HOUSEHOLD: A CHILEAN ROSE TARANTULA.

ued its kneading, lost in its feeding trance. Now that it was fully in the light, its brown hairs gleamed with burgundy highlights. By morning we could find only a webbed pile of debris, perhaps a quarter of the fish's original size.

When my son decided he wanted a pet tarantula, we chose this particular species because, despite its size and its centimeter-long fangs, it rarely bites people who treat it gently. The tarantulas (family Theraphosidae) are mostly large, hairy spiders that actively hunt prey or else, like this one, ambush it from hiding. The biggest of them has a legspan of 12 inches. For a quick visual, shut this book and lay it on a table. Now imagine a spider straddling it, its legs touching the table on every side. The fang of a tarantula looks much like the claw of a cat, though some of them are an inch long. They can punch through clothing and even fingernails. Mere mechanical damage can make the bite of a tarantula painful.

But reports vary. Some victims have said the bite is barely noticeable. Others mention severe pain. One factor in this discrepancy is that a spider doesn't always inject its venom. It may rely on mechanical injury alone to deter a handsy human. But how dangerous is a good dose of the venom? People in the pet trade have told me many anecdotes of painful bites, and a few of systemic symptoms such as dizziness and confusion resulting from the bites of certain types of tarantula. Assorted species from South America, New Guinea, Australia, and Africa are claimed to be dangerous. Arachnologists acknowledge that among the many untested species and the probably even more numerous undiscovered ones, there may be lethal venoms.

Bites aside, tarantulas present other dangers to people who trouble them. The first is a defensive weapon: the hairs on the spider's hind end. When harassed, the tarantula uses its hind legs to kick these hairs loose. They flutter briefly in a cloud. A microscope reveals each hair as a sort of harpoon with spirals to keep it from coming loose once it lodges in an assailant's skin or mucous membranes. The hairs thus embedded irritate the attacker both mechanically and with a mild toxin. On our rambles around the farm, I sometimes saw our old dog Mr. Peck stand within a few inches of a frantically kicking tarantula, unaware of the biological weapons being launched against him. On the other hand, it is possible for predators to get such a snootful of irritation that they are effectively crippled, their eyes and noses swollen shut.

People are susceptible to the loose hair in varying degrees. The arachnologist William Baerg tested it on himself by rubbing a tarantula directly on his forearm, producing only a mild itching. In search of a larger sample, Baerg convinced his wife to submit to the same treatment. Her arm broke out in an itchy rash that vanished in half an hour. Some people develop an allergy to the urticating hairs, which may result in anaphylactic shock. Since a person has to be exposed repeatedly to develop this allergy, only those who keep tarantulas as pets or lab specimens run the risk.

The tarantulas have many large relatives with big fangs, and people have contrived to get bitten by many of them. For example, there are the trap-door spiders (family Ctenizidae), which plug their burrows with doors made of silk and debris. They rarely venture out of their burrows. They will even hold the door shut with mighty force if you are lucky enough to find it. As a last resort, they employ their fangs. The bites hurt, but aren't really dangerous.

The funnelweb spiders are similarly large and heavily fanged; they look like naked black tarantulas. They may be the only spiders that look awesomely dangerous—and really are. They build tubelike homes out of silk, charging from these to take passing prey, which they detect by vibration. Their venoms interfere with the chemical processes of nerve impulses, causing tingling sensations, nausea, shortness of breath, changes in blood pressure, mental disturbances, and, as the blood pressure plunges, even coma or death. Small children have died within minutes of a bite. They are more vulnerable because the dose of venom is spread over a much lesser mass. Adults usually suffer only mild symptoms. Various species occur in New Zealand and South America, but those proved dangerous occur mostly in Australia and Asia.

Probably all spiders bite only in defense, but the species vary in their understanding of what constitutes a threat. Male funnelwebs attack with what seems to us no provocation at all. They spend part of their lives wandering in search of mates, and in this condition they will pursue humans who come too close to them. Possibly they are acting on some sort of territorial instinct.

The funnelwebs are closely related to a wicked-looking group called the mouse spiders. These spiders, mostly found in Australia, were named for their supposed habit of digging deep burrows like rodents. They pack a venom similar to that of the Australasian funnelwebs, but they are far less aggressive. Their bites have caused sweating and strange tactile sensations near the wound.

Huntsman spiders aren't closely related to the tarantulas, but some of them are huge. The largest have legs spanning almost 12 inches, though they are built on a lighter scale than the biggest tarantulas. Studies have not found their bites significant, but they may cause bleeding and brief pain. Many spiders have spines on their legs. In the case of huntsmen, the spines can stab an attacker, including a human who tries to pick the spider up or puts on clothes in which the spider has taken shelter. The spines splinter as they pierce human skin, causing an irritation.

MANY PEOPLE, ON finding an unexplained bump or red patch on their bodies, assume they have been bitten by a spider. They are usually wrong. It's been estimated that 80 percent of the so-called spider bites physicians treat are really something else entirely—the bites of lice, fleas, or ticks; the symptoms of diseases like Lyme disease and tularemia; strep or staph infections developing around minor scratches. Even eczema or a too vigorously scratched mosquito bite may cast aspersions on some innocent arachnid. When several Americans came down with skin lesions in 2001, symptoms eventually traced to anthrax spread by terrorists, doctors first suspected brown recluse spiders.

Why do spiders so often get the blame? Part of the answer seems to lie in arachnophobia. People who notice a sore and, separately, a spider in the house may jump to the wrong conclusion. Serious arachnophobes often report the feeling, which they themselves may recognize as irrational, that spiders are malicious, conspiring to frighten and harm human victims. Even people without a full-blown phobia sometimes fall into this way of thinking. In fact, most spiders, if they're capable of biting people at all, bite only in defense of self, eggs, or territory, but many people aren't aware of, or even interested in, that fact.

Another source of confusion is folklore. Stories of venomous arthropods circulate so frequently that scientists tend to dismiss them out of hand. Around 2001, I received emails warning of "blush spiders," tiny but deadly red spiders that hide under the seats of toilets on airplanes ready to bite the unwary traveler on his or her most sensitive parts. There's actually no such thing as a blush spider. Its faux scientific name, *Arachnius gluteus,* which would seem to translate into something like "buttocks spider," is an easy tip-off.

In 2004, I received anxious queries about "camel spiders," accompanied by a shocking photo of a massively fanged monster as long as a man's leg. The camel spider, it was said, habitually runs along under

NOT A SPIDER. NOT A CAMEL. NOT DANGEROUS.

camels, leaping up to feast on the flesh of their bellies. Its venom was said to dissolve flesh rapidly. It was claimed that these creatures represented a deadly menace to soldiers at war in Iraq. In fact, camel spiders are harmless, though scary-looking. They are known variously as sunspiders and windscorpions, but are really a little-known arachnid family unto themselves, the solpugids. The largest solpugids in the world are about the size of a woman's hand, which is certainly awe-inspiring, but a mere fraction as large as the trick of perspective in the well-circulated Internet photo suggests. Solpugids don't bite people—their mouthparts aren't hinged the right way, so it's next to physically impossible—and they don't pack toxin. Since their fangs are so massive for their size (proportionally the largest in the animal kingdom), they rely on mechanical injury, not venom, to kill their prey.

These are only two examples of the folkloric nonsense constantly in circulation about arachnids. Specialists are routinely annoyed by pseudofacts claiming that the average person inhales four spiders per year in his sleep or that recluse bite symptoms can be cured with Tasers.

Among the vast diversity of spiders—forty thousand species catalogued so far—only a handful possess the equipment necessary to hurt people: weaponry stout enough to pierce human hide and venom that interacts meaningfully with human biochemistry. But it's hard to be certain which spiders fit this description. Probably no group of animals generates so much disagreement about dangers, even among scientists. Everyone agrees that a few groups have killed people through the systemic effects of their venoms. Many other spiders have been suspected of causing necrotic lesions.

There are certainly a few species that give painful, though essentially harmless, bites: large members of the orb-weaver family, including, for example, the black and yellow garden spider of the United States; the woodlouse spider, a small species with proportionally enormous fangs that bites readily; the redbacked jumping spider of Australia. A few others have been claimed to cause flulike systemic symptoms, including the Australian window spiders and the false widows, which are common in unswept corners of homes around the world. Another candidate for systemic symptoms is the parson spider, a wanderer in gardens and homes. Its small black body is patterned with what looks like white war paint. It's altogether evil-looking, and I'm not surprised people want it to be guilty of something. I once spent fifteen minutes handling a parson spider in an effort to get bitten. The parson would have none of this. I eventually let it loose in my office. If it wouldn't serve for my experiment, maybe it would at least kill a few pests.

The wolf spiders have been slandered for hundreds of years. These hairy, often large hunters can bite, but their looks get them blamed for the deeds of others. In the Renaissance, the bite of one species was supposed to cause "tarantism," a seizurelike mania that could only be cured by dancing. The real culprit was probably a widow spider. More recently, wolf spiders have been blamed for necrotic lesions actually caused by recluses. The Australian white-tailed spider is also falsely accused in necrotic lesions.

Doubts exist because few people can tell one kind of spider from another, and because people so often blame spiders with insufficient evidence. Typically, it is the large, noticeable spider that gets blamed. But a typical American household contains two dozen species of spider in the warm seasons, most of which the human resident never knows about—to say nothing of other arthropods that might bite.

Among the definitely dangerous, we can rank the wandering spiders, bland, earth-toned spiders that in some species achieve five-inch legspans. They move about on the hunt rather than waiting in ambush or making a snare. Several kinds are merely suspected of being dangerous to people. The definite danger comes from members of the genus *Phoneutria,* found in Central and South America. They often come into homes in search of their insect prey, and they may shelter in shoes or in other nooks likely to bring them into disagreement with people. The wanderers bite readily. There's some evidence that the great majority of their bites are dry. When they do inject venom, it causes remarkable pain. Occasionally it causes systemic problems as well. The lungs may fill with fluid; some have died.

People who lack the wherewithal for tightly constructed homes are more vulnerable to many kinds of animals, and that's certainly the case with the wanderers, which often end up in rural huts and the like. But some spiders are small enough to enter even the most modern homes. A recluse spider (*Loxosceles spp.*) has very thin brown legs and drab colors. Its cephalothorax may have a dark symmetrical marking in the shape of a violin. The brown recluse, or fiddleback, is well known in the southern United States; more than a hundred other species occur in Central and South America and the southwestern United States.

Once, while lying on my bed on top of the covers reading, I was startled by a sudden intense pain in my upper arm. I turned my head in time to see a spindly recluse walking at a casual pace away from me. I had a sudden sense of time distorted, for the spider, which must have been the cause of my pain, was about two feet away, despite my having looked instantly when I felt the pain.

My experience illustrates several points about the recluse. Its actual bite, as opposed to the aftereffect of the venom that soon follows, is usually painless. The recluse most frequently bites human beings when arachnid and primate indulge their mutual taste for resting between sheets. In such circumstances, the recluse is often crushed under the mass of its bedmate, and it bites defensively. But its bite is singularly ill equipped to attract the notice of a human being. Its fangs usually gather up a fold of human skin and inject venom between the dermal layers, accomplishing almost no mechanical injury. Most bites are never even discovered. I noticed mine only because the venom caused me some pain after the spider had just about made its escape.

I suffered no lasting effects from the venom; that, too, is typical. In fact, I have been bitten more than twenty times, always without further problems. But perhaps 20 percent of people develop a sore at the site of a recluse bite. It takes the form of a blister surrounded by a red patch, the blister collapsing to leave a divot like the center of a shooter's target. In most cases, this wound heals without incident, though the healing process is slower than for most injuries. Sometimes, instead of healing, the wound gradually deepens and widens, killing some of the skin and underlying tissue—a necrotic lesion. Such lesions resist treatment. Some are so severe as to require amputations. A few deaths from recluse bites are on record, including one case in which the victim died within minutes.

ANOTHER SPIDER BLAMED for necrotic lesions is the hobo spider. It, too, is a brown spider of unimpressive appearance. It is clad in brown herringbone, and its body is typically just short enough to fit on a Lincoln penny. It builds a flat web with a sort of billiard pocket at one corner in which the spider lies at its ease to await prey. People sometimes get bitten by males wandering in search of mates.

In one of the first cases reported in the medical literature, a fifty-six-year-old woman from Spokane, Washington, felt a hobo spider bite her on the thigh. She came down with a migraine-style headache and nausea, and her thinking became addled. In the coming days, a patch of dead tissue sloughed from the spot where she'd been bitten. It was perhaps two weeks before she sought help, but by then it was too late. She was bleeding from the orifices, even from the ears. Doctors found her blood deficient in several basic components. Her marrow had stopped making red blood cells. Having lingered in the hospital for several weeks, the woman died of internal bleeding.

In a case from Bingham County, Idaho, a forty-two-year-old woman felt a burning bite on her ankle. She, too, came down with a headache and nausea, as well as dizziness. The wound blistered and burst, leaving a growing crater. After ten weeks the crater was ringed with black flesh and big enough to accommodate two thumbs. Eventually, more than two years after the bite, the wound had healed into a sizable scar, beneath which the veins were clotted. The woman had trouble standing or walking.

In November 1995, in a suburb of Portland, Oregon, a ten-year-old boy woke with a pair of bites on his leg. The wounds swelled, grew hot, blistered. Dead tissue dropped away. A week after the bites, his leg was swollen and red. He suffered fever, nausea, and debilitating headaches. After a month, the pain of the wounds was mostly gone, but a bruise-like patch of blue remained on his leg. The headaches lasted for four months.

The identification of the culprit in these and other cases is controversial. Skeptics point out that people encountered the hobo spider in Europe for centuries without finding it dangerous. It was only after the hobo showed up in the Pacific Northwest in the twentieth century that it was linked to health problems. It's probable that, like the recluse, the hobo is dangerous only in a minority of cases.

I WALKED INTO the deserted shack and found a web right away. It was a profusion of erratic angles. About two feet above the cement floor its strands became so numerous as to form a loose cloud the color of dirty cotton. Below that, the strands were so sparse I could lose sight of them. Each strand was invisible from some points of view, sheathed in glare from other angles, so that the entire web seemed to shift like a hologram as I walked around it.

Although it was as big as a modest coffee table, it was a simple cobweb of the sort that frequently annoys fastidious housekeepers. The same person who admires the beauty of an orb web in his garden may assiduously destroy every cobweb he finds in his kitchen. This prejudice is a microcosm of human failing. We like the orb web because its kind of order is readily apparent. The cobweb has its own brand of order. It is, as Emily Dickinson put it, a continent of light, a patch of constructed ground from which the spider may never stray. It is also, among other things, an efficient snare.

This particular cobweb advertised its efficacy to anyone who cared to look at the graveyard beneath it. Twenty-six wing sheaths of June beetles lay on the cement. Each sheath—they are really the beetles' front wings, modified into protective armor—was the color of fresh brown

A WIDOW'S BRIGHT MARKINGS WARN AWAY PREDATORS.

shoe polish. They reminded me of the fenders of old Chevys; the place looked like a miniature junkyard.

I looked into the corner of the shack, where the web reached behind an exposed wall stud. There I saw the spider's retreat, a thickened bubble of filthy silk. In the shadow near the retreat hung the spider—a profusion of crooked legs, the spherical black belly marked with a distorted hourglass the color of dried blood. It was a black widow.

In a heap of junk outside the shack I found a rusted chisel. A few yards away was a barbed wire fence, and one of its posts seemed deformed with bulbous tumors. The tumors were really cicadas newly emerged from their hibernation in the ground, most of them still in the gray-brown shells they had climbed the fence post to shed. One of them had already shucked its husk. Its body was tinged with green like the living subcutaneous layer of a sapling—a color that would give way to gold and white if the creature lived another hour. It was trying to spread its wet translucent wings to dry. I rejected this one in favor of a cicada whose shell was just beginning to split down the back. Either one would have suited my need. I suppose I chose the one in the shell because of a vague intuition about justice—no one should die while learning to spread his wings, or some such sentiment.

After gathering up the cicada and the chisel, I returned to the shack to make the capture. These tools were not ideal for the purpose, but they were handy. I tossed the cicada into the web. The slice of green hide showed through the burst seam on its back. The creature resembled some ponderous dinosaur in miniature. The cicada is one of the strongest insects, but the slow churning of its digging claws could not free it from the widow web. The widow emerged immediately from her hiding place, rushing out toward the cicada. When she was too far out to make a quick escape, I slashed at the web with the chisel. The tearing silk sounded like grease popping in a skillet.

My strategy was to maroon the widow on the floor, where she would be easy to capture in a jelly jar I had brought along. Many strands clung to the chisel. When I tried to twist the tool out of their sticky grasp, they wound around it; it was like the paper cone at the center of a swirl of cotton candy. The widow scrambled for her retreat even as all her aerial avenues wrenched about and altered their directions in her claws. She ran along the strands to the chisel where they all converged. She ran up the chisel to the hand that held it. She ran up the hand to the forearm behind it.

I screamed, cursed, danced like an idiot, and ended by dislodging the spider from my arm without getting bitten. She managed to attach a new silk line to my wrist as she fell—the point of attachment tickled as if butterfly-kissed. The line paid out from the spinnerets at the rear of her abdomen, slowing her fall. She flung her legs wide, ready to catch anything that might break her fall. Touching down lightly on the cement, she ran, her globose abdomen making a preposterously large burden. She looked like Santa Claus rushing away with his bag of gifts. Panting with fear, I nonetheless managed to set the jar in her path and prod her into it. Inside the jar, the widow fumbled at the glass like a persistent mime, but she couldn't climb it. She was a robust specimen with a white chevron on her back. The cicada lumbered away on the cement like a windup toy, trailing ten inches of silk.

In pursuing my unorthodox hobby, I've found black widow webs inside broken-down tractors, beneath panels of sheet metal, stretched across the blade of a garden plow, and under railroad ties used for landscaping—the thumb-thick bolt holes in these are ready-made widow retreats. All manner of human implements are fit for a widow's use. Webs have been found in a police call box, in shoes, in well houses and lawn furniture and bureau drawers and wardrobes.

Widows thrive in outhouses—that used to be the most common site of human-widow encounters, before indoor plumbing spread across the country. Cinder blocks and other construction materials are now the most likely points of contact between human skin and widow fang, at least in the industrial West, and the most likely victims are construction workers who go under houses to work on pipes or wires.

The widow is commensal with us. It lives on our labors for free, providing us with nothing substantial in return (most of the insects it eats are not pests) and generally doing us no harm. For every widow we see, many more are ensconced in our castoffs and accoutrements, living their silken lives ignorant of the human forces that shape their landscapes. Because of their comfort in and around human habitations, and the cosmopolitan distribution of the genus, widows have killed more people than any other kind of spider.

The thirty-one species of widow spiders show a variety of coloration.

The black types may be dotted, dashed, triangled, and hourglassed with orange, yellow, and white, in addition to red. There is also a "red" species (in which the cephalothorax and legs are an orange-red, though the abdomen is mostly black), a "brown" species (whose colors put me in mind of milk and chocolate being stirred together), and a white. The familiar Australian redback is mostly black, but with a beaded string of crimson along the dorsal surface of its abdomen. The males are even more various than the females. One specimen I collected resembled the spillings of a lava lamp on a black rug. Others are blond and unobtrusive. The males are considered harmless because their mandibles usually lack the power to pierce human skin, though they do pack venom.

Among the females, the toxicity of the venom varies with the species. The mortality rate for humans bitten by black widows in the United States was about 4 percent in the days before an antivenin existed. With antivenin, it is substantially lower than that. The symptoms of widow bite include severe pain throughout the body, rigid abdomen, sweats, chills, vomiting, diarrhea, swelling of the face, involuntary grimacing, involuntary erection, lowered blood pressure (which may rebound to dangerous heights), and labored breathing. Some survivors say it is the worst pain they have ever endured.

It has always struck me as odd that the widow is simultaneously one of the most beautiful animals in a given landscape and one of the hardest to see. Its dark camouflage is, of course, what makes it so easy to have accidents with. When I capture one, I sometimes have the sense I've bottled a bit of shadow.

SCORPIONS
ORDER SCORPIONES

As I WRITE THIS, a five-inch scorpion is resting in my wife's old shoe. His tail is relaxed, lying almost flat behind him. The stinger at its tip looks like a fat black teardrop culminating in a blond spike. His claws are absurdly muscular. Last night he came prowling the perimeter of the terrarium where the shoe rests. He seized the quick green tiger beetle we'd supplied. One claw pinched a leg; the other severed the beetle's head with a crackle. The claw from which the beetle head lolled was still.

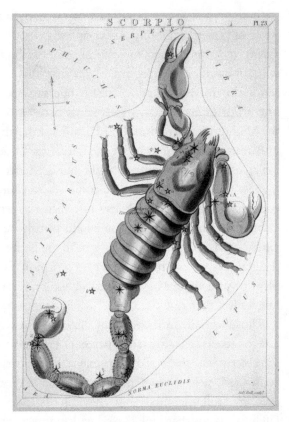

FEWER THAN FIFTY SPECIES OF SCORPIONS ARE SERIOUSLY DANGEROUS.

The other claw tore off pieces and shoved them into the rapidly chewing mouth. Several pieces of the beetle kicked in protest. In the end the scorpion moved on, carrying his pincers spread wide, the way a bodybuilder carries his arms. He left behind an assortment of beetle parts, none easy to identify except the two green forewings with their white spots.

The brute power of this scorpion is what assures me he's a suitable pet. Scorpions with big claws generally find those weapons adequate for subduing prey, but even the biggest scorpion claw can't hurt me much. The ones to watch for are the slender ones, the weak ones, because they tend to rely on potent venoms. Scorpions attack when they feel threatened by a human, who is usually unaware of the arachnid's presence. For example, they may shelter in shoes or between sheets, where people accidentally crush them and force them into defensive stings.

Of the nearly fifteen hundred species, many are harmless, either incapable of puncturing human skin or else possessing a venom ineffective against us. Many others cause local pain, swelling, redness, and itching, without systemic symptoms. Fewer than fifty can inflict anything like serious harm. But many of the dangerous species encounter people often. For example, dangerous kinds occur in well-populated areas of the Mediterranean region, Central and South America, Africa, and Asia.

Authorities disagree about the frequency of deaths from stings. The lower estimates are around eight hundred per year worldwide. The highest reputable estimate I've come across claims that scorpions outpace venomous snakes as killers by a factor of ten. Depending on your estimate of snake deaths, that would put the scorpion deaths at anywhere from 400,000 to 1.5 million. In the United States, where the one dangerous species (the Arizona bark scorpion) isn't especially potent or plentiful and victims have access to good medical care, deaths occur at a rate far less than one per year.

Those who die from stings are almost exclusively children. The death rate for adults is less than one percent of those stung; of those few, most are elderly. Death by scorpion may take less than an hour. When it is protracted, it is among the most painful ways to die. Victims weep; their eyes roll uncontrollably; they can't hold still. Eventually they may fall into spasms that look like convulsions, except that they remain conscious. Their spines curl backward, bringing them head to heels. All the body fluids drain. Death comes from respiratory failure or heart failure. Those who survive may feel an electric current tingling at the site of the bite for weeks.

MITES AND TICKS
ORDER ACARI

HAVE YOU EVER noticed that when you pick up your pillow to put a fresh case on it, it seems heavier than it did when you bought it? Scientists have found that some pillows, even in clean houses, are 40 percent dustmite feces by weight.

Mites are tiny arachnids, many of them microscopic. The tens of thousands of species already catalogued are probably a mere fraction of the total. Their lifestyles are diverse. Some live in water, some in soil. One species lives symbiotically with the Madagascar giant hissing cockroach, cleaning fungi from the insect in return for the privilege of drinking its saliva. Another kind eats human dander; a third resides in the throat of the honeybee. These parasitic arrangements are the ones that interest us, for a few of them harm people.

The house dust mites live on the scalp and in the eyebrows of human beings and in bedding and carpet. More than half of all humans may be infested. The mites survive by digesting skin cells. Both the digestive enzymes found in dust mite feces and the bits of their exoskeletons can provoke allergic reactions in people. It's among the most common of all human allergies.

The sarcoptic mange mites live in the skin, burrowing, laying their eggs, and depositing their chemically irritating feces. These activities cause sores and terrific itching in human victims, mostly between the fingers and toes, in the armpits and the crotch. This condition is the only one properly called scabies, though doctors are sometimes loose enough in their diagnoses and call other, similar infestations by this name.

It has been said that if England had been as rife with chiggers as the southern United States is, English Romantic poetry might have been prevented. I like to think of Wordsworth too busy scratching to recollect his emotions in tranquillity. Chiggers are the larvae of certain mites (*Trombicula spp.*). They bite rodents as well as humans, and, in parts of Asia and Australia, they may transmit the rodent disease scrub typhus to people. This disease causes fever and rash; occasionally it progresses to more serious symptoms affecting the lungs and heart. Modern medicine has made scrub typhus a minor disease, but in times past some outbreaks reached a mortality rate of 60 percent. Similarly, the mite *Allodermanyssus sanguineus* transmits rickettsialpox from house mice. The straw itch mites, or hay mites, are common in grasses and grains. They typically parasitize livestock but sometimes bite people, especially farmworkers during harvest, causing skin irritations. One report suggests that these mites may serve as vectors of "mad cow disease," or bovine spongiform encephalopathy.

Close contact with nonhuman animals may bring a person into contact with other kinds of mites. There are mites specializing in pets—cats,

THE BLACK-LEGGED
DEER TICK SPREADS
LYME DISEASE.

dogs, even snakes; in animals used for their fur, such as rabbits; in food animals, such as chickens. Some fowl mites come to humans when birds abandon the nests they have made under the eaves of buildings and the mites, requiring new hosts, crawl indoors. Others, like the rat mite, thrive in the nests of mice and rats and may spread from there to bite the people who unintentionally share their dwellings with the rodents. These and other such mites bite people and cause skin irritations, itching, and the like. They usually don't thrive on human hosts. It is their vain efforts before dying that cause the trouble.

"DID YOU HURT YOURSELF?" I asked my six-year-old son, Griffin. He was cavorting at the foot of our bed, joking with Tracy and me before saying good night. I'd glimpsed what looked like a scab beneath the strap of his tank top. When I looked closer, I saw that the scab lay in the middle of a red bruise the size of my thumbprint. The bruise, in turn, lay at the center of a baseball-sized rash. The scab was really a hard, dark tick, its jointed legs curved like a crab's, its head burrowed into Griffin's flesh, its body angled out like a shingle on a roof. Tracy brought me tweezers and I seized its body. It held firm. It felt as solid as a staple in my grip. I had to pull hard. Griffin winced and jerked away from the pressure—and the tick was out. It kicked feebly in the grip of my tweezers. Tracy handed me a strip of transparent tape. I pressed the tick flat against it, then folded it over the kicking body. Now it was displayed flat and motionless, like a laminated flower. I knew from experience that it was still alive and would try to crawl away if I peeled the tape apart.

I felt a queasy remorse for my son's pain, but I wasn't done. I ran my fingers through his wild red hair, and quickly another tick appeared, perched amid a red irritation atop his left ear where it joined his head. Griffin seemed to tense and wilt at the same time. His courage was draining away.

"Would you rather have Mom do this one?" He would. My relief was enormous. I stood ready with the tape and packaged up the tick as she pried it loose from his head. She took him off to the bath for further checking.

An hour later, long past his bedtime, he was heard being rowdy with a big brother, apparently in good spirits, but Tracy and I were still worried, our conversation tainted with revulsion.

All ticks are bloodsucking parasites, though fairly few take an interest in people. Typically they latch on to people as they brush by grass or other plants. They crawl to some sheltered site, such as the scalp or a tight spot inside clothing, and bite, usually drawing no notice from the victim. They engorge themselves with blood before dropping off. Depending on species and circumstance, they may take several days to drink their fill, stretching their bodies to many times their unladen size. In most cases, this proportionally enormous meal is an insignificant loss to the victim, who may never be aware of it.

The strangest result of such an attack is called tick paralysis. It occurs when, after feeding for several days, the still attached tick begins to secrete a neurotoxin. The victim begins to feel weak or clumsy. The weakness moves slowly up the legs. Eventually the entire body may be paralyzed, including, in a fraction of cases, the breathing organs. If the tick is found and removed, the paralysis usually clears up spontaneously. Dozens of tick species worldwide have been reported to cause paralysis, most of them in the genera *Dermacentor* and *Ixodes*. Dogs suffer from tick paralysis more often than people do; both dogs and cats can bring the ticks into contact with their human companions.

Like most blood-drinking parasites, the tick is most dangerous as a vector of diseases: Rocky Mountain spotted fever and other rickettsial diseases; Colorado tick fever; certain hemorrhagic fevers; certain viral encephalitis diseases; tularemia; louping ill; pasteurellosis; plague; relapsing fever. What had Tracy and me worried was Lyme disease, a common problem in rural Wisconsin where we live. A bacterium called *Borrelia burgdorferi* or one of its close relatives enters the body when the tiny black-legged deer tick takes its slow blood meal from a human being. The disease begins with fever and other flulike symptoms, and often an inflamed patch around the bite that grows as large as a couple of feet across. Untreated, the disease may advance to the skin, joints, central nervous system, heart, and eyes. Drugs can cure the disease in the early stages. If it has already advanced to the central nervous system, it may leave the patient with long-term health problems. The writer Amy Tan described her own symptoms:

> thinning hair, rapid heart rate, hypersensitive hearing, palpitations, the sense of internal vibration . . . stiff muscles, migrating joint pain, ringing in the ears, sensations of burning and stabbing, a crackling neck, . . . insomnia.

Despite its debilitating effects, Lyme disease is rarely fatal. Victims may die of babesiosis, a malaria-like disease that can be transmitted by the same tick during the same bite. Griffin was lucky: his rash cleared up quickly, and that was the end of it.

THE MYRIAPODS
SUBPHYLUM MYRIAPODA

PARENTING, AS GRIFFIN'S ENCOUNTER REMINDS ME, often comes down to dealing with arthropods. Once when he was a baby, my mid-

SOME MILLIPEDES EXCRETE A FOUL-TASTING FLUID TO DISCOURAGE PREDATORS.

dle son, Beckett, picked something up from the carpet and popped it into his mouth. He put on a sour face, fished the object out, and then grunted angrily at his mother and me, as if we had arranged an unsatisfactory buffet. I found the object to be a brown millipede half an inch long, tightly curled but still alive. The millipede was put into a jar for further study, the baby was pacified with a less traumatic snack, and no further harm ensued, unless I count the noise pollution that accompanied Tracy's insistence on immediately vacuuming the entire house.

A millipede looks like a worm on many stilts. It has two pairs of legs on most of its segments. The number of segments varies among species, with the maximum being about one hundred. The legs protrude from the underside, near the midline. Most millipedes eat vegetable matter. There are eight thousand species. Of these, about sixty have repugnatorial glands. (The great regret of my life so far is that I have never had occasion to use that phrase in conversation.) These glands produce a foul-tasting venom that discourages predators. One dramatically pink Thai species called *Desmoxytes purpurosea* exudes a venom containing cyanide. Though a human being could theoretically injure himself by eating a millipede, no one seems to have died from such a misadventure. Some have reported that the fluid exuded from a crushed millipede stains carpet and hands and provokes nausea. It can irritate the skin and, more seriously, the eyes. It has been blamed for allergic reactions.

The centipedes look similar, but they are mostly predators. They eat small arthropods, and the larger kinds occasionally take rodents, reptiles, birds, bats, and even the formidable goliath bird-eating tarantula, largest of all spiders. The centipedes subdue their prey with a venom injected through scratches, which they make with the specialized first pair of legs. Some centipedes exude repugnatorial fluid, and they can irritate human skin simply by walking across it, their legs scratching in a bit of the fluid. The legs are sometimes equipped with sharp spines that can scratch people on contact. A centipede generally has a single pair of legs sticking out to the sides of each body segment—up to 173 pairs in some species.

In the United States, the so-called house centipede is abundant, though it actually prefers to stay under cover outdoors and encounters people fairly seldom. Entomologists get horrified emails about the never-before-seen creature that slithered across the kitchen tile late one night, all legs and menace. Females of the species have extravagantly long hind legs that, at a glance, obscure their centipede shape and make them appear much larger than they really are—the body length is typically an inch. The scratch of these creatures can hurt like a minor sting from an ant or bee.

Another slightly dangerous species inhabiting the United States and Mexico is the giant red-headed centipede (sometimes known, under different color schemes, as the giant desert centipede). You are not likely to find this creature, even in its native range in the southwestern United States and Arkansas, unless you form the habit of turning over rocks and rotted logs. If you do find one, you will probably be moved by an excitement not altogether attributable to scientific interest. The thing is as long as a man's hand—up to eight inches. Its head is dull red, its body a green so dark it can pass for black, and most of its forty-two legs bright yellow. Sometimes it will slither away under the leaves. Sometimes it will wave its front end about as if to challenge you. If you bother it enough, it will scratch you.

Giant red-heads are the stuff of legend. It's said that people they've walked on, leaving a double row of poisoned footprints, die in delirious pain. (One such case, recorded during the Civil War, sounds suspiciously like an instance of a far more common malady, black widow spider bite.) Dr. William Baerg of the University of Arkansas was intrepid

CENTIPEDES PREY ON
OTHER ARTHROPODS.

in these matters. He tested the giant red-headed centipede on himself, applying one to his little finger and allowing it to scratch him for four seconds. He reported fifteen minutes of sharp pain, then a lessening pain and minor swelling. His symptoms had vanished altogether within three hours.

Mildly dangerous centipedes, many of them belonging to the same genus as the giant red-head, have been reported from Australia, Brazil, China, India, Burma, Malaysia, Sri Lanka, and elsewhere. The symptoms they cause include redness, swelling, bleeding, and intense pain at the site of the wound. Systemic symptoms rarely extend beyond headache. In Turkey, however, a five-inch centipede scratched a man on his big toe, sending him to the emergency room with pain, sweats, dizziness, and low blood pressure. Doctors found that the blood flow to his heart had been reduced by spastic contractions of the arteries that supply it. He recovered from this potentially fatal condition within a few hours.

SWARMS OF LOCUSTS CAN EAT EVERY BIT OF VEGETABLE MATTER IN SIGHT.

15. THE INSECTS

CLASS INSECTA

WHEN ALIENS COME TO EARTH in movies, it's always humans they seek out. Clearly they perceive us as the most important life form on the planet. It's a silly conceit. Any objective observer taking stock of Earth's fauna would note that arthropods—creatures with external skeletons and jointed limbs—outnumber everything else put together. They outnumber us by a factor of 200 million. The million and a half catalogued species are, everyone agrees, a mere fraction of the total. Of these, the six-legged kind are by far the most numerous. Our visitor might reasonably view all the noninsect animals on earth as aberrations.

Of course it might be argued that we are superior to insects because we can squash them. It's true that a one-on-one fight favors the human. But fair fights are rare on our planet, and, as it turns out, some insects are better at killing us than any other animal.

GRASSHOPPERS
FAMILY ACRIDIDAE

. . . the east wind brought the locusts . . . they covered the face of
the whole earth, so that the land was darkened; and they did eat
every herb of the land, and all the fruit of the trees which the hail
had left: and there remained not any green thing in the trees, or in
the herbs of the field, through all the land of Egypt.

Exodus 10:13–15 (KJV)

ONE SUMMER WHEN I was a teenager the grasshoppers were everywhere. Every patch of weeds along the alley would erupt like a pan of
popping corn if I set foot in it. When we drove the highway, we inadvertently slaughtered dozens. The collisions speckled our windshield
with the clear hemolymph that served them as blood. Their wings,
coffee-colored fans striped with yellow at the outer edges, lodged in our
wipers and fluttered in the onrushing air. Sometimes an entire
grasshopper, or most of one, would lodge there as well, struggling to
get free as the wind tore it to tatters.

They could be found in unaccustomed places that summer. I saw two
or three swimming in the dog's water dish. The rosebushes took on the
riddled look of lace, as though the grasshoppers had tasted the leaves
and found them unappealing but serviceable. In the country, the cedar
posts of barbed wire fences seemed to shimmer with heat, but a second
glance showed the effect was no mirage. The posts were simply crawling with grasshoppers moving up or down for no obvious reason. They
moved with great caution, edging past each other. When a stationary
grasshopper got bumped, it would draw its legs in tight and shift its
footing, like a rider crowded on a bus.

Then there was the jackrabbit. We found it beside a dirt road on the
way to the mailbox. It was dead, probably road-killed. Grasshoppers
were thick in the weeds along that road, and dozens clustered on the
carcass. When someone poked at it experimentally, a few of the hoppers
jumped off and opened their wings and were carried away by the wind.
Others crawled off sluggishly. Some stayed put. With the carcass now
more exposed, we could see that its hide was wounded in shallow div-

ots, as if it had been hit all over with buckshot that failed to penetrate. It seemed the grasshoppers had been eating it.

As the season wore on, the grasshoppers grew absurdly thick. Among the metallic green ones there were others, some yellow and spotted, others a brighter green. All these I was familiar with, though I had never made any particular study of them. But I began to see things utterly new to me. One grasshopper was black and flecked with gray, like burned charcoal. Another was black but flecked with a Tabasco red. In outbreaks, the insects are so plentiful that birds and other predators can't keep up with them. That meant grasshopper species rare enough to escape my notice most of the time got relief from predators.

Other things seemed different, too—there were a great many large grasshoppers, thick as lipsticks. One morning on my driveway I found the largest specimen I had ever seen, a yellowish creature longer than a soda can. It was dead—a fact that gave me some comfort. Streams of black ants led up to its carcass. Their presence was the first thing that convinced me I was seeing a once living creature rather than a toy. I turned it belly-up with a stick. Its head and thorax were intact, but its abdomen was riddled with holes. I had not seen this damage at first because its long wings concealed it from above. Through the holes I glimpsed ants working at the grasshopper's half-hollow hull. I returned with a ruler and measured the monster at just less than six inches.

What I've been describing was an "outbreak," a localized population suddenly grown orders of magnitude beyond its usual numbers. A few years ago, scientists documented outbreaks of clear-wing grasshoppers in Colorado at densities of 200 per square yard. These outbreaks occur in irregular cycles influenced by heat and dry weather. In the usual order of things, parasitic fungi on their bodies kill grasshoppers by the billions. But the fungi don't thrive in dry weather, and the grasshopper populations swell. In a normal year in the United States, grasshoppers eat about 20 percent of the fodder on a given stretch of rangeland. In outbreaks, the percentage can increase to 100. Across the planet, one person in ten can find his food supply directly threatened by grasshoppers.

Much of the grasshopper's insides are taken up by reproductive equipment. The yellow ovaries of the female are bunched like grapes glistening with moisture. However, the naked eye is impressed mainly with the fat black strand of digestive tract, narrower in spots, girdled with knotty fibrous lobes near the middle. The dark color comes from chewed vegetation—at a given time, a substantial proportion of the grasshopper's body weight is its unconverted food. Its great capacity for both digestion and reproduction is what makes the grasshopper a danger to us.

When grasshoppers of certain species gather in great numbers, the crowding changes them. Normally they are solitary, avoiding the company of their own kind. Forced together, they try to spread out. But hunger often concentrates them, when a bumper crop of grasshoppers encounters a meager supply of food and they must compete for it. Their changes vary with the species, but in general, their bodies grow to massive size. Their wings grow clear and strong. Their colors shift dramatically—for example, from green and yellow to solid black. Their shape shifts to accommodate flight. Even their smell alters. So profound are their changes that scientists have sometimes mislabeled the two phases, solitary and gregarious, as distinct species.

The creatures behave differently, too. They eat with shocking voracity. They whirl into the air in groups like dust devils, and these join to form swarm clouds. The swarms fly long distances, disrupting ecosystems for hundreds of miles. In the 1870s, one swarm was tracked from Montana to Texas, a distance of 1,500 miles. Polluted layers of glaciers high in the Rockies show that their flight sometimes takes them to altitudes beyond the normal range of grasshoppers. In 1874 a Nebraska doctor used telegraph messages to establish the size of a passing swarm. He found that its area exceeded that of Colorado. Factoring in their rate and the depth of the swarm cloud, he arrived at an estimate of 12.5 trillion grasshoppers. *The Guinness Book of World Records* lists this swarm as the "Greatest Concentration of Animals" yet observed. More rigorous methods were used on a swarm in Kenya in 1954, yielding the figure of 10 billion grasshoppers in a swarm, which happened to be only one of fifty swarms in the country at the time.

This special phase of the grasshopper is called a locust. Swarms of locusts migrate over great stretches of territory, settling down periodically to eat every bit of vegetable matter in sight. Swarms have been recorded since biblical times, when they were classed among the seven plagues of Egypt. Where they occur, locusts represent humanity's most effective competitors for food, the cause of thousands of human deaths annually.

The most vivid firsthand account of such a happening I've come

WHEN NO PLANTS ARE LEFT, LOCUSTS DEVOUR THE
CARCASSES OF ANIMALS—HERE, A CAMEL.

across is that of Laura Ingalls Wilder, the writer who chronicled the life of her family on the American frontier. By 1873, Wilder's restless father had moved the family to a homestead near Walnut Grove, Minnesota. Wilder vividly paints the heat of that summer—the edge of the prairie "seemed to crawl like a snake" with heat shimmer, and the pine boards of buildings dripped their viscous sweat. The family wheat crop, which promised to yield egregiously, was head-high. Then a cloud dimmed the day, moving in without wind. Its particles glittered. The falling insects sounded like a hailstorm, and this sound was succeeded by the multitudes chewing (like the sound of a thousand scissors, some said). Prairie grasses and wheat and oat crops were leveled; beets, beans, potatoes, carrots, and corn were razed; willow and plum trees were shorn. "Not a green thing was in sight anywhere" after a few days, Wilder concludes, echoing the book of Exodus.

Only the family's chickens benefited, snapping up the windfall of easy prey. (Some writers of the period noted that chickens took on a revolting flavor that ruined their meat and eggs. Others noted that the grasshoppers themselves were edible, though the Ingalls family does not seem to have taken an interest in this option.) The family fell on hard times, and at night they could hardly sleep for the sensation of crawling on their skin. On Sunday they arrived at church, their best clothes crawling with grasshoppers and stained with brown spittle. The meager creek thickened with scum; the land twitched with dust devils. The cow's milk went bitter and nearly dried up.

The species that wrought this havoc in the nineteenth century, the Rocky Mountain locust, seems to have become extinct, though there's some debate on that point. It may be the only pest species ever eradicated by human efforts, since the tilling of land along rivers ruined its prime egg laying habitat.

In Africa and Asia, however, swarming species still thrive. For example, the desert locust, which inhabits a wide swath of Northern Africa in its solitary phase, can swarm as far as Portugal on the west and Afghanistan on the east. Individual swarms may cover 460 square miles at a time, with tens of millions of grasshoppers found in each of those square miles. Each locust in a swarm can eat its own weight in a day. Multiplied by billions, this hunger must be the most demanding our planet has known. One estimate has the largest swarms eating 423 million pounds of vegetation per day.

The locust phase of grasshoppers, with its greater mobility, provides a way to survive when food supplies dwindle. In Africa, the desert locust's eggs lie dormant in arid soil for several years until rain triggers their hatching. The hatchling nymphs thrive on the brief lushness desert rains bring. When they've devoured everything in an oasis, they swarm to reach green regions beyond the desert.

It's hard to count the human lives lost to competition with the locust, because the locust is never the only factor in play. For example, thousands died in western India in 1803 and 1804 under the combined effects of drought, war, and locust-induced famine. In 2005, a UN organization announced that six million people in West Africa faced famine because of locusts and drought. In Niger, one-third of the populace was undernourished. Within the past century, desert locusts have produced major periods of swarming seven times, with the longest period lasting thirteen years. Locusts are not an occasional catastrophe, but a continual factor in human survival.

Besides competition, swarms present another danger. Colliding with obstacles and each other, the locusts knock loose bits of their wings, exoskeletons, and feces. These particles linger in the air. The resulting haze can, for brief periods, prove more dangerous than a heavy smog. In the Sudanese city of Wad Medani in late 2003, 1,685 people were hospitalized with asthma attacks induced by a swarm. Eleven died.

COCKROACHES
ORDER BLATTARIA

As I SIT HERE typing this with my left hand, I hold in my right a cockroach just over three inches long and almost an inch wide. It is a member of a docile species, the Madagascar giant hissing roach. It moves more or less constantly, its clawed feet clinging to my skin as it climbs over the fleshy fold between my thumb and forefinger to reach my knuckles. It is searching, I think, for ground that doesn't wiggle and

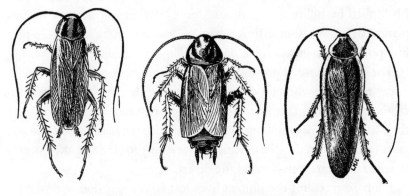

COCKROACHES ARE COMMON IN U.S. HOMES.

shake so much. When I pause in my typing it stops and stands waving its antennae, each thin and segmented, the right one abbreviated by some accident.

I'm sure many readers will find my comfort with the cockroach surprising. In areas where they pose a serious hygiene problem, roaches outrank even spiders as a focus of phobia. But my little friend does me no harm, unless I count his cheddary smell. He is a pet, part of a colony given to my eldest son by a biologist friend of mine. If not for human interference, he would have passed his life in the jungle, having nothing to do with me or any other human. In that way, he and his kind are like most of the 3,500 species of cockroach. But a handful of species live more or less commensally with us; they share our homes and our food. These few species damage us in several ways. There's great diversity even in these few harmful species, so not every remark I'm about to make is true of the cockroach you may have observed in your kitchen yesterday.

First, there's biting. Some roaches eat almost any digestible material, including the eyebrows, nails, and skin of human beings. Frequently they nibble at calluses on the feet of sleepers. One man woke to find roaches had eaten through the soles of his feet to the raw flesh. Cockroaches are attracted to milk around the mouths of sleeping babies. In inner city buildings infested with roaches, it is not unusual to find a child with a rash of shallow wounds caused by their feeding.

Roaches instinctively seek tight spaces for their harborages, a preference that occasionally leads them to invade the orifices of the human body. The ears seem to be the most frequently invaded, and the result is a range of unpleasant sensations, from tickling to severe pain to seemingly psychotic episodes. The legs of roaches are equipped with bristles that can produce great pain on the sensitive inner surfaces of the human body. In *The Cockroach Papers,* Richard Schweid reports a 1997 case from Atlanta in which a baby died by choking on a cockroach.

Next, there's allergy. Scent is social for these insects, and they leave it everywhere—in their feces and saliva, in their eggs and their discarded skins. This dust is the leading cause of asthma in inner city children in the United States. The fact that we sicken and occasionally die by inhaling their dust is simply another twist on animal cohabitation—and not even an unusual one. In fact, people seem to develop allergies to almost any creature they spend much time with—not all people, but a sizable percentage. Most of us can choose not to live with cats or dogs. Living without roaches can be harder to arrange.

Yet another danger of roaches is disease. They walk on, and even eat, such infectious substances as human feces and garbage. They carry dozens of organisms dangerous to people, ranging from the bacterium responsible for leprosy to the polio virus to fungi that complicate surgery to hookworms that can infest the human digestive tract. Roaches in a German hospital were found to carry a strain of *Salmonella* that had sickened some of the patients. Similar evidence links roaches to strep infections, shigellosis, hepatitis, and amebic dysentery. My pet hissing cockroach poses no such risk, because his kind have not adapted to living with humans. It's the ones exposed to our diseases that give them back to us.

BUGS
ORDER HEMIPTERA

ON A COLD OCTOBER EVENING in Wisconsin I remembered that interesting wildlife turns up everywhere. My reminder lay struggling on the walk in a shopping plaza. At first glance I thought it was a lizard, and I signaled my son to watch his step.

"Cool," he said, crouching to observe. Of course it wasn't a lizard—too cold for that. It was in fact an insect so large that the gray glimmer of its scales was visible at a glance. It lay on its wide, flat back, struggling to right itself, its massive front legs churning as if to elbow someone out of the way.

"How big do you think it is?" my son asked.

I laid my car key beside it and noted that the insect stretched from tip to key ring, not counting its appendages. (At home later, we measured the key at three inches.) I looked for water, because I recognized the insect now as a giant water bug. The only water I could see surrounded a fountain a quarter of a mile away. It was a windy night, though, and I imagined the bug had taken to the air and been blown far off course. I was glad I hadn't encountered it while it was airborne.

To the layman, a "bug" may mean any sort of arthropod, but when a biologist speaks of "bugs," she means a group of insects possessing certain specialized sucking mouthparts. Among the bugs are found many familiar insects—water striders and water boatmen, squash bugs and stink bugs. Most are harmless. A few can bite venomously, including some of the assassin bugs, backswimmers, and, yes, giant water bugs. (Some of the giants are much bigger than the one we found. Specimens better than four inches are on record. They can take fish, frogs, and other sizable prey.) Bugs normally use their venom to paralyze prey and liquefy its innards, which they then drink. They use venom on people only when they are handled. The result, usually, is a painful but not serious bite, the effects of which resolve shortly. A North American assassin called the wheel bug bites more painfully than most wasps sting. Some bugs, such as a rarely encountered Middle Eastern species called the afrur, are said to possess a lethal bite.

A few bugs are blood-drinking parasites of people. The most dangerous are certain assassins called kissing bugs, from their habit of biting people on the lips and eyelids as they sleep. These parts of the body are attractive because of their thin, easily punctured skin. Charles Darwin described a kissing bug thus:

> At night I experienced an attack (for it deserves no less a name) of the Benchuca, . . . the great black bug of the Pampas. It is most disgusting to feel soft wingless insects, about an inch long, crawling over one's body. Before sucking they are quite thin, but afterwards they become round and bloated with blood, and in this state are easily crushed. One which I caught at Iquique, (for they are found in Chile and Peru,) was very empty. When placed on a table, and though surrounded by people, if a finger was presented, the bold insect would immediately protrude its sucker, make a charge, and if allowed, draw blood. No pain was caused by the wound. It was curious to watch its body during the act of sucking, as in less than ten minutes it changed from being as flat as a wafer to a globular form. This one feast, for which the benchuca was indebted to one of the officers, kept it fat during four whole months; but, after the first fortnight, it was quite ready to have another suck.

Kissing bugs are vectors of Chagas's disease, which is also called American trypanosomiasis. While crawling around to feed, the kissing bug defecates on the skin of sleeping people. When the feces get rubbed into eyes, cuts, or mucous membranes, the protozoan they carry, *Trypanosoma cruzi,* takes hold. It invades the cells of the liver, spleen, lymph system, and muscles, and sometimes the autonomic nerves. It typically causes a mild illness at first, lives harmlessly within the human body for twenty years or so, and then, sometimes, makes itself felt by slowly destroying the heart or the digestive system. It is the most common cause of heart disease among South American patients. This slow disease only occasionally kills people outright, but it often contributes to poor health and shortens life. Some people develop serious allergies to the bite of kissing bugs.

Bedbugs also parasitize people, giving painful bites. They are small insects, less than a quarter of an inch long. Like kissing bugs, they spend their days in crevices and crawl forth at night to take a blood meal. Each bug needs only a few blood meals in its lifetime. The blood is essentially a dose of added protein to help it reach the next stage in its development. But since a home may have many thousands of bugs, a person can be bitten so many times her skin is mottled with itchy welts. Bedbugs have not been proved to spread disease among humans, though they have been suspected of passing relapsing fever, and the plague bacterium has been found on them. They became rare in the United States for several decades because of devastating pesticides since discovered to be dangerous to people as well. In recent years they have made a comeback in New York and other large cities. Experts predict they will soon be major pests again.

BEETLES
ORDER COLEOPTERA

BEETLES COMPRISE THE ORDER with more members than any other in the animal kingdom. Scientists have catalogued more than 350,000 species. Like most insects, a beetle has four wings. What makes the beetle different is that the front pair are no longer useful for flight. Instead, they have evolved into tough sheaths that conceal the functional hind pair when the beetle is at rest.

The dangers beetles present are minor but diverse. Some occasionally spread bacteria or parasitic worms to people. Others, such as the bombardier beetles and a few of the darkling beetles, behave like miniature skunks. When annoyed, they stand on their heads, elevate their rumps, and spray noxious fluid at their attackers. Only someone trying to handle the beetle is likely to be hurt by this chemical. It causes, at worst, a burning sensation and blisters.

An even less impressive chemical defense is found among the ladybugs (or ladybird beetles). This mostly harmless family of predacious beetles wear orangish wingcases marked with black spots. As a child I handled many without being harmed, reciting the misogynist injunction that the ladybug must hurry home to save her children from a fire. But ladybugs are capable of giving a painful bite. A species imported to control aphids in the United States (the multicolored Asian lady beetle) has become a pest in the upper Midwest, clustering in houses in the winter. (The native kinds cluster in trees.) This species is fairly aggressive and will occasionally bite if handled. Even a brief touch will leave a stink on the human hand; the ladybug deters attackers by secreting its vile-smelling fluid from its leg joints. (All the ladybugs are, I am told, vile-tasting and mildly poisonous, as is common among brightly colored insects, though this deterrent doesn't work on every predator. I have fed them to pet frogs and toads without ill effect many times.) Friends of mine, a mother and her five-year-old son, once suffered an itchy rash that their doctor attributed to an allergic reaction to the bites of these imported ladybugs.

Many other beetles can bite, to minor effect. Especially painful bites come from some predacious diving beetles. My son Parker kept one of these in an aquarium, where he fed it goldfish. It would zip about in the water like a frantic pecan, seize a fish with its forelegs, and devour it so messily that its translucent internal organs fell fluttering to the bottom. The venomous saliva that so easily dispatches fish can make a human dizzy and ill. The larvae, which can also bite, are called water tigers.

But the most dangerous encounters with beetles are caused directly by human beings. For example, certain innocuous-looking beetles in the family Chrysomelidae contain a severe poison. The San people of the northern Kalahari Desert in Africa find the larvae and pupae by digging at the roots of the sand corkwood tree and similar plants. These they may prepare in several different ways, expressing the juice directly or powdering the bodies for mixture with various toxic or adhesive plant saps. They use the product to anoint their arrows. Thus armed, the San bring down large animals such as giraffes. For safety, they cut out the chunk of meat adjacent to the poisoned wound. A human being struck with the poisoned arrow often dies when the toxin paralyzes his heart or lungs.

A poison called cantharic acid is found in certain blister beetles. People have been poisoned by eating frogs that ate these beetles. The poison irritates the urinary tract. Several blister beetles, such as the Eurasian species *Lytta vesicatoria,* are called by the common name Spanish fly. J. L. Cloudsley-Thompson described *L. vesicatoria* as a "handsome green beetle of gregarious habits . . . found in large numbers on ash privet, elder and other trees." A derivative of powdered Spanish fly is used as an aphrodisiac, a homeopathic treatment for irritated skin, even a hair restorative. Cloudsley-Thompson explains how the active ingredients for these preparations are gathered: "The beetles are collected before sunrise, while they are still torpid and unable to fly; but, even then, the collectors must veil their faces and hands while shaking the insects down on to cloths placed on the ground under the trees."

Because of its inflammatory effect on the urethra, cantharic acid really does cause a tingling sensation in one's private parts. Some scientists claim the amount necessary to produce this effect is near the lethal dose.

Incidentally, people have used many insects besides Spanish fly in patent medicines and home remedies. Hundreds of examples could be adduced, from grasshoppers in a treatment for hemorrhoids to powdered cockroaches as a remedy for heart trouble. Doubtless some of these medicines have hurt far more people than they helped.

FLIES

ORDER DIPTERA

ONE OF THE MOST IMPORTANT distinctions between poor nations and rich ones is the ability to fight flies. Good housing, drainage projects, pesticides, medicines and vaccines and people trained to use them—these are among the factors that, on average, make North Americans live half a century longer than Africans. People in less developed countries face many animal hazards rare in the United States, from parasitic worms to predators. But flies come first because, improbable as it may seem, they are the deadliest of our enemies.

The most dangerous flies are mosquitoes. Many, though not all, kinds of mosquitoes take meals of blood from humans and other animals. Only the female mosquito takes animal blood. Both genders normally feed on plant juices, but the female requires the extra protein found in animals when she is ready to produce eggs. She may do this only two or three times in the few weeks of her adult life. But the vast numbers of the insect mean that in tropical and many temperate regions, almost every person exposed to fresh air will get bitten repeatedly. When the mosquito bites, she cuts through the layers of skin with sawlike parts of her proboscis, then inserts its central tube for siphoning. In the process, she injects saliva into the wound. The saliva contains anesthetic substances to prevent the victim from noticing the bite until

MORE THAN ONE HUNDRED AGENTS OF DISEASE CAN RIDE WITH THE ORDINARY HOUSE FLY.

it's too late. It also contains anticoagulants, substances that keep the blood flowing freely. The chemicals in the mosquito's saliva can cause itching, swelling, and irritation.

The regular exchange of blood and saliva makes the feeding cycle of the mosquito an ideal medium for the dissemination of tiny parasites—viruses, protozoa, worms. Malaria is the most important of these mosquito-borne infections. It kills 1.5 to 2.7 million people each year. Millions more survive in chronic ill health. It is endemic in most of tropical Asia and Africa. In the historic past, it reigned over the entire tropical part of the globe and made frequent incursions into temperate regions. The disease is caused by protozoa of the genus *Plasmodium*. The vectors are certain mosquitoes of the genus *Anopheles*. A mosquito acquires the *Plasmodium* by sucking blood from an infected human or other animal. From here the *Plasmodium* takes different forms as its complicated life cycle of sexual and asexual reproduction continues. There is a sort of orgy in the stomach of the mosquito; there is a burrowing into the mosquito's gut wall to incubate; there is a migration to the mosquito's salivary glands. When the mosquito takes another blood meal, *Plasmodia* ride the saliva into the bloodstream of the victim. Once inside the human body, they ride the current to the liver, where they parasitize cells and reproduce enormously. The cells burst, spewing thousands of parasites. The liver bulges. The parasites, now in a new form, return to the blood, this time attacking the red blood cells for another round of multiplication. The body responds with intermittent waves of fever, chills, and sweats. The different species of *Plasmodium* produce different patterns of illness and remission. Some forms cure themselves; others become chronic. Some are fatal, others merely debilitating at intervals.

The most deadly forms of malaria evolved just as agriculture reached Africa. The newly stationary lifestyle farming requires brought people into a different relationship with their parasites. Human settlements developed where water was easy to get, and this meant that villages were always near the breeding places of mosquitoes. Instead of roaming in small and elusive bands, people were suddenly available to the insects in abundance: a ready supply of blood. By six thousand years ago, the bones of humans living in high-malaria areas already showed the modifications brought on by sickle-cell anemia. This condition causes episodes of pain in the belly, muscles, and bones, as well as ulcers on the legs. But it also gives an advantage: the sickle cell in human blood protects people from malaria. All human diseases exert selective pressure on our evolution; malaria has left more obvious traces than most.

History is pocked with the traces of malaria. Some have said it helped topple the Roman Empire. It was present during the U.S. Civil War, infecting more than half the soldiers. In 1923, in Russia, it sickened 18 million people. In 1947, in India, it sickened some 75 million; one million of them died. In sub-Saharan Africa, it killed 1,136,000 people in 2002.

But malaria isn't the only serious disease the mosquito has to offer. Yellow fever is endemic to West Africa. It came to the Americas with slavery, making its first notable appearance in Barbados in 1647. It was a danger to people of European extraction in the Americas and in Europe itself for three hundred years. One outbreak, for example, devastated the French army in Haiti at the beginning of the nineteenth century, killing twenty thousand soldiers and effectively freeing slaves from French rule. People of African heritage were, because of long ancestral exposure, less susceptible to yellow fever. During the Spanish-American War, a team of U.S. Army doctors led by Walter Reed established that mosquitoes spread the disease. That discovery has allowed public health officials ever since to fight yellow fever with quarantines, pesticides, and drainage of mosquito breeding places. A vaccine now exists, though it is not always available in less developed countries. More than thirty thousand people still die of the disease each year in tropical regions of Africa and the Americas.

Mosquitoes transmit at least a dozen notable diseases besides these, including viral encephalitis diseases such as the notorious West Nile fever and several kinds of hemorrhagic fever. Dengue fever alone afflicts 100 million people a year.

But mosquitoes are only one family of flies. Many other fly families are equally rife with bloodsuckers. For example, the humpbacked, thick-bodied black flies populate much of the world. They arrive in my back-yard every summer, and the first sign of them, even before we see them staggering in the air, is the appearance of a ring of itchy red bumps on Griffin's neck. I don't know why he's always the first; perhaps he smells good. The rest of us soon suffer as well. Along with the bumps come swollen lymph nodes, a mild fever, and a malaise that vanishes as the swelling goes down. As the season wears on in black fly country, the bites continue, but they become far less troubling. This partial immu-nity wears off by the following year.

When the black flies trouble us too much, we simply go indoors. But those who must be outdoors can find little relief. Thoreau noted that black flies in Maine "make traveling in the woods almost impossible." An especially annoying species of black fly occurring in Europe attacks en masse, clogging the orifices of domestic animals. It's been claimed that this behavior can choke a person to death. Swarms of black flies are even considered a hazard to aircraft. But black flies are most dangerous in Africa, where they spread parasitic worms. The worst of these is a nema-tode called *Onchocera volvulus*. It moves from fly to human during a bite. It parasitizes the human victim, sometimes causing a disease called river blindness. River blindness currently affects hundreds of thousands of people.

In fact, more than forty diseases are spread by flies. The sand flies, which look like shabby moths, give us such obscure but serious diseases as leishmaniasis and bartonellosis; the biting midges give us worms; horse and deer flies transmit tularemia. About a million people are af-flicted with a parasitic worm called Loa loa, also carried by deer flies. The tsetses, tough flies that often withstand a good swatting, spread the African forms of trypanosomiasis. This protozoan disease, also called African sleeping sickness, once killed two hundred thousand people in a single outbreak.

Flies don't have to bite to serve us diseases. A family called the nonbiting midges is a major reservoir of cholera, a disease that has killed millions. So far, there is no proof that the flies transmit the bacterium *Vibrio cholerae* directly to people, though investigators have established that the adult flies' bodies are richly infested. The bacteria reside in, and feed from, the gelid substance that holds together the flies' floating egg masses. It is the drinking of this infested water that most often passes the disease to people.

The common house fly can transport at least a hundred different disease-causing agents, including microbes and tapeworms. Among the life-threatening maladies associated with house flies are typhoid, cholera, dysentery, and anthrax. The fly walks and feeds on such substances as sewage; the manure of virtually any animal, but especially the accumulated droppings of poultry; rotten food; and carcasses, including human corpses where they happen to be lying about. This circumstance is common enough in war and other disasters.

The house fly is a triple threat, able to infect people and their food three different ways. First, the bristles on its legs and abdomen carry bits of whatever it's recently landed on, so that by merely walking on the human body, it can transmit disease. Second, it defecates indiscriminately, and doesn't mind doing so even on whatever it happens to be eating at the time, or on human skin. Third, its digestion is partly exterior, meaning that it vomits digestive fluids onto a substance, then sucks the half-digested mess up. This procedure allows contaminants from past meals to find their way onto new meals.

BITES ON THE surface of the body are a form of parasitism. But some flies parasitize the human body from within, a practice called myiasis. In his book *Mortal Lessons,* the surgeon and writer Richard Selzer describes one victim—and his parasite:

> His left upper arm wears a gauze dressing which, when removed, reveals a clean punched-out hole the size of a dime. The tissues around the opening are swollen and tense. A thin brownish fluid lips the edge, and now and then a lazy drop of the overflow spills down the arm. . . . [T]here now emerges a narrow gray head whose sole distinguishing feature is a pair of black pincers. The head sits atop a

longish flexible neck arching now this way, now that, testing the
air . . . a dirty gray body, the size and shape of an English
walnut . . . is hung everywhere with tiny black hooklets.

The creature Dr. Selzer so vividly depicts is the maggot of the human
botfly. It infects people, cattle, and other mammals indirectly. First it
captures a bloodsucking parasite in midair—a mosquito, let's say. It
holds the struggling mosquito and squeezes its own eggs onto it, then
releases it unharmed. The mosquito feeds on some warm-blooded
animal—a person, let's say. The maggots, still curled within their eggs,
sense the mammalian warmth. They hatch. They have only a few seconds to act before the mosquito finishes her meal. They crawl off her
body and look for an opening. The wound opened by the mosquito's
proboscis will do, or they can slither down a hair into the follicle. Most
of them won't make it. Once inside the human body, the maggot makes
itself at home. It forms a cyst within which it can grow. It dines on the
flesh and fluids provided by its host. The host is not, at first, aware of
this unwanted guest. He notices a carbuncle slowly growing on his skin.
At some point, he's startled by pain. Some victims, without even knowing what their affliction was, have described a sensation of being
chewed. Eventually, the maggot falls into the sleep of pupation, and the
victim's pain subsides. Then there's an eruption of pus and blood. An
adult fly emerges, dries its wings for a few seconds, and flies away.

That, at least, is what happens when the botfly happens to burrow
into an uncomplicated patch of human skin. Sometimes it invades a delicate area, such as a nose or an ear. The victim may actually hear it chewing into his brain before he dies.

Myiasis can also afflict the eyes, the urinary tract, the gastrointestinal
system, or even the bones, depending on the type of fly and the variety
of bad luck. The maggots may blind a victim by excavating his eyes. Or,
by tunneling the bones, they may leave him deformed. Some parasites,
among the blowflies for example, prefer to enter the human body
through wounds. These are thick-bodied flies with feathery antennae
and often a metallic green or blue tint. A blowfly called the New World
screwworm lays her eggs near open wounds or moist orifices. The maggots hatch and dig into the surrounding tissues, ripping at it with hooks
and lapping up the fluid that oozes forth. They can burrow into carti-

lage and even bone. Each maggot may grow to 17 millimeters, and each female fly may deposit up to three hundred eggs. Once an infestation is under way, the oozing of the wound attracts more of the gravid females, so that a single wound may house thousands of maggots. The infestation is usually fatal if left untreated. The New World screwworm is best known as the killer of hundreds of prisoners at the French penal colony on Devil's Island between 1852 and 1946.

FLEAS
ORDER SIPHONAPTERA

THERE ARE ABOUT two thousand species of fleas, all bloodsucking parasites. Most of them are small enough to pass for lint or dust unless you notice them moving. They are hard to catch, as they hop prodigiously, like popcorn flying from an uncovered pan. When you finally do catch one, pinching it between thumb and forefinger, it looks like a flake of pepper, and you may think you've seized something inanimate by mistake. Only when you loosen your grip enough to see it in profile do you feel sure it's an insect, though it seems to be perpetually tipping forward on to its mustache. Once it has a millimeter of space, it hops away again. To kill a flea, you will have to apply your fingernails; it can withstand the pinch of human fingers.

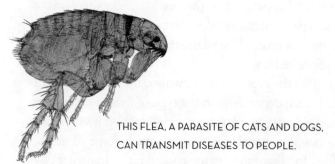

THIS FLEA, A PARASITE OF CATS AND DOGS,
CAN TRANSMIT DISEASES TO PEOPLE.

Many of the fleas specialize in particular hosts, with the great majority preferring rodents. Various species of birds and mammals serve the rest, though an occasional flea wanders onto a reptile and manages to make a go of it. Only about one percent of the species take an interest in humans. Their bites can be itchy and painful. These species include the so-called human flea, which actually seems to prefer pigs; the cat flea, the one most likely to afflict well-housed people in the modern world; and the Oriental rat flea. This last species has served as a prime vector for plague, one of the most important diseases in human history. Fleas can also transmit typhus, trench fever, and other rickettsial diseases; pasteurellosis; relapsing fever; and parasitic worms, including dog flea tapeworms, rat tapeworms, and heartworms.

LICE

ORDER PHTHIRAPTERA

AN ENGLISHMAN NAMED ISAAC ROSENBERG was killed at age twenty-seven, a victim of the First World War. He's remembered now only for his poems. Some of them are about the obvious brutalities of war. The one that strikes me, though, is a funny little poem about soldiers thrashing about "like a demons' pantomime" when they find their clothes "verminously busy" with lice.

THE HUMAN BODY LOUSE,
A HAZARD OF TRENCH WARFARE.

The human body louse is intrinsic to trench warfare. It thrives where humans must crowd together without access to hot water and soap. It is rare in wealthy countries with high standards of hygiene, for it lives in clothing and bedding and is easily dispatched by regular washing of clothes, linen, and body. It's also rare in the tropics, where people don't need to wear much. But wherever people are fully dressed and insufficiently washed, the louse lurks. Homeless people in the United States and Europe sometimes suffer a discoloration of the skin called vagabond's disease—a reaction to the repeated bites of the louse over long periods.

The kinds of lice that trouble people are bloodsucking parasites. Head lice and pubic lice ("crabs") can cause skin irritation. Head lice are transmitted by contact with infected people and by artifacts such as clothing and furniture. Pubic lice pass between people during sexual contact and occasionally spread to infest the eyelids, lashes, and brows. Neither of these species poses any serious health problem, despite the stigma attached to them.

Only the body louse is dangerous. It is less than four millimeters long and looks like the residue of a sneeze—a bloody sneeze, if it has recently taken a meal. Under a microscope, it looks oddly crippled, for its legs curl beneath it and terminate in claws. It's built for clinging and climbing, not walking. When it takes its meal of blood from a human host, it leaves an itchy wound. The scratching victim grinds the dust of the louse's dried feces, or even parts of its crushed body, into his wound. The airborne dust may also infect the victim through his nose, mouth, or eyes; in this way, it can even spread disease to people who haven't been bitten.

Three important diseases pass to us from lice. One of the worst disease outbreaks in history was the epidemic typhus that erupted in the trenches during World War I. It began to torment its victims with a high fever and a headache, proceeded to respiratory symptoms and a rash on the chest, and often went as far as delirium and death. It killed three million people in Eastern Europe from 1914 to 1915. In fact, this disease has erupted in the wake of wars and natural disasters since the fifteenth century. By decimating armies, it has determined the outcomes of battles and entire wars, prompting some writers to call the body louse the most important animal in history.

Trench fever, a close relative of epidemic typhus, first came to the attention of doctors in World War I. In fact, it was the most common disease among entrenched Allied soldiers. The symptoms were fever, dizziness, and diverse pains, including characteristic pains in the lower back and shins. This disease made another appearance in World War II on the eastern front, afflicting some eight hundred thousand men. More recently, it has become common among homeless people in U.S. cities. It rarely kills its victims, but can sometimes affect the heart.

The third major louse-borne disease is relapsing fever, a close relative of Lyme disease. The distinctive spiral bacterium that causes it holds a place in history: it was the first microbe definitively linked to a deadly disease. The symptoms include high fever, chills, head and body aches, and nausea. These symptoms proceed to a crisis, with high blood pressure, followed by a drop into low blood pressure and even shock. If the victim survives, he is treated to a remission of about three days. Then, as the bacteria mutate, temporarily outmaneuvering the body's immune system, another, less severe attack descends. The victim may have as few as one or as many as ten relapses. In some outbreaks, louse-borne relapsing fever has killed an astounding 30 percent of its victims.

BUTTERFLIES AND MOTHS
ORDER LEPIDOPTERA

As YOU MAY HAVE NOTICED by now, I'm something of a specialist in disgust. I enjoy spiders, snakes, and many other animals that give the average American the creeps. An animal that ought to fit into that category, but doesn't, is the butterfly. This thought recurs to me every time I see some painted beauty flexing its wings like a slow dream of sunset while it sips at a pile of dog feces.

Even stranger is the adoration otherwise squeamish people show for the life cycle of the butterfly. Beginning as an egg that resembles moist lint, the creature progresses to a motile bag of muscle hardly distinguishable from a maggot and bent on eating as fast as it can. Having done its duty by gluttony, the creature resorts to sloth, passing a few weeks in the hardened crust of its own skin. Only then does it emerge as an attractive pair of wings attached to a wormy body on jointed legs. This is what entomologists call a "complete metamorphosis," because it takes the insect through a radical revision of its appearance. While I agree that it's spectacular, I find us fickle. Why don't we extend the same admiration to other insects with complete metamorphoses—like the mosquito, which changes from a swimming algae-eater that breathes through its hind end to an airborne sap sucker and blood drinker? Or certain wasps that change from helpless waxy larvae to midnight-blue adults incomparably more graceful than any butterfly?

It may be that people simply don't know how badly the butterflies (and their close but less celebrated kinsmen, the moths) behave. Many are surprised to learn, for example, that caterpillars can bite. That fact surprised me, too, when I learned it at age ten.

I remember the brown T-shirt I wore, because I spent some time afterward trying to imagine how the caterpillar got where it got. We had been shucking corn on the back porch—the green husks squeaking like vinyl as I pulled them off, the crisp crack as I pulled harder to tear the husk from the stalk, then the smaller squeaking as I yanked at the tassel of silk, its filaments unruly and always escaping my fingers. Next came the interminable operation of picking at the renegade filaments threaded between the kernels. The laden ears felt vibrant with life.

We saw the caterpillars as we worked, one in every six or seven ears. They were a nasty surprise, fat green and black strands that felt like dried phlegm. When we ripped half a husk off an ear, the caterpillar would be at the tip among the silk, and its gnawings had made room for it there, deforming the kernels and cob. Such a fouled ear sent a sprinkle of gnawed crumbs tumbling out as the husk parted, but by then it was too late and you might already have touched the caterpillar, which cringed from the light, its body flexing with a kind of slow peristalsis (that is part of their repulsion—somehow they suggest human digestion exposed). If I were outside with my grandfather or my friends, I would have acted boyish and picked them off with my fingers, but indoors, with my mother and sister and aunt, I found the caterpillars daunting. We knocked them carefully into the trash can, and when we were done I carried the trash out to the alley.

Hours later, as I sat on my bedroom floor playing, an acidic pain shot from the right side of my neck down my arm. I groped at my neck. I pictured some poison in my vein, and then, in the succeeding seconds, as less visceral quarters of my consciousness weighed in, I thought of a damaged nerve. But by then my fingers had groped to the source of the pain, a soft warm strand just under the collar of my shirt. My eagerness to remove it did not in the least assuage my revulsion at touching it. As I pulled the invader out of my shirt I felt the tug of tiny mouthparts wrenching loose from my skin. I carried the caterpillar outside, its mint-julep blood staining my hand, its muscular body thrashing. Once outdoors I dropped it to the porch and inflicted violences upon it.

In the bathroom mirror, I saw nothing but a very small red welt, which might well have been the result of my pinching myself in the fracas. A stabbing pain still affected my neck, but in the arm the pain seemed to have dulled to a tingle and sunk to the bone. I told my aunt I'd been bitten by a caterpillar.

"Oh, honey, those things won't bite you," she said. The welt had by that time so completely vanished that it provided no evidentiary value, and probably my story was never believed in that house. The pain in my neck and arm faded gradually throughout the afternoon and evening, and had vanished by the following morning.

Many caterpillars are capable of such surprises. Parker discovered this fact for himself, also at age ten, by handling a woolly bear caterpillar he found in our garden. (The woolly bear is the larva of the Isabella tiger moth.) His pain lingered for an hour or so. Among the caterpillars with biting mouthparts, some have a mild but very noticeable venom. Toxic substances are in fact common among the lepidoptera, and many, such as the famously foul-tasting monarch butterfly, would in theory prove irritating or even dangerous to eat. (People do eat caterpillars in, for example, some parts of Africa, but they know from long experience which are edible.)

Hundreds of caterpillars, including more than fifty species in the United States, are equipped with venomous hairs or spines. The caterpillar of the io moth is bright green, striped with red and white, about three inches long at maximum. It is covered with little caltrops of white bristles like the needles of a prickly pear cactus, and these have caused rashes and irritations to people after a mere accidental brushing. The puss moth caterpillar has, through the touch of its bristles, sent people into shock. A few people have died from contact with caterpillar bristles.

Some moths remain dangerous in adulthood, substituting prickly scales for bristles. In South and Central America, hot, rainy weather brings out swarms of the Hylesia moth, which batters itself against electric lights, bumping into nearby people with irritating results. In Central Africa, the Anaphae moth sheds its venomous hairs in flight. Where the moths are abundant, the air may be thick with clouds of hair. People are sometimes hurt when they put on clothes over which the moths have flown.

Most moths and butterflies live on nectar. A few groups prefer other nutritious fluids—the tears of hoofed animals, for example, or fruit

THE CATERPILLAR OF THE
IO MOTH IS COVERED
WITH VENOMOUS
BRISTLES.

juice. The kinds that specialize in fruit have evolved a piercing proboscis. A group called the vampire moths are not particular about what
they pierce. Sometimes they take a blood meal from an animal. One
thumbnail-sized vampire moth, *Calyptra thalictri,* occasionally drills
into a human victim, causing a few hours of itchy irritation.

ANTS, WASPS, AND BEES
ORDER HYMENOPTERA

As I STOOD ON A LADDER to prune the elm tree in my backyard, I noticed something crawling in the convolutions of the bark. It was a cockroach, a thin brunet one, and he was acting strangely. He was close
enough to feel my breath, but he didn't run away. I stared at him until I

noticed a deficiency: his antennae, which should have been long and whip-thin, were only blunt stubs. I flashed to something I had read, about the habits of a certain wasp, *Ampulex ferruginea*. The wasp bites a cockroach's antennae off; that action renders the roach literally sense-less, unable to comprehend the world around him. It makes the nor-mally skittish creature docile. The wasp can do with her victim what she will.

As I remembered this unusual set of facts, a wasp crawled into view, moving at a businesslike clip. She was leaner than a honeybee, half black and half red. She seized the roach by the stubs of his antennae and led him through the valleys of bark. They traveled only about six inches be-fore the wasp let go of the cockroach and, with a flicker of her transpar-ent wings, vanished. She'd be back. I'd seen the same behavior in the midnight-blue hijacker wasps that dart about on my lawn hunting for spiders. After bringing the prey under their power, they flit between the victim and the grave they mean to seal him in.

The wasp, of whatever species, is a female. She's about to lay an egg, and the final resting place of her victim—it can be a hole in the ground, or, as in this case, a natural crevice in stone or bark—becomes a nursery for her larva. The larva eats the paralyzed prey from within. He becomes shelter and suckle at the same time. The special delight of such arrange-ments is that the prey stays alive through most of it. Otherwise, he would rot and be useless as wasp food. The wasp clan has diversified enormously, so that it can supply parasites tailored for many sorts of liv-ing things—trees and tarantulas, caterpillars and beetles. Some wasps parasitize other parasitic wasps, and these hyperparasites in turn are par-asitized by other wasps, and these by others. Perhaps this hyperparasitic regression goes further, but it's hard to say: at this point, the wasps are too small to be seen without a microscope.

The wasp returned. She was on foot the entire time, never flying. Each time she came back, she would lead the roach a few more inches. I couldn't see the other end of her round trip, the place she had chosen for him. She led the senseless roach around the trunk and out of my sight. I climbed after them a little way, but some idiot had been sawing at the branches, leaving me little to climb on. I strained my eyes gazing at that textured bark, a vast graveyard and nursery.

Most of the parasitic wasps can't control the creatures they mean to use simply by clipping their antennae. They have to paralyze the host with a strategically placed sting. The wasps made a great evolutionary leap when the ovipositor, a tail-like organ for laying eggs, took on this secondary purpose of stinging. This organ, once configured to harm other animals, could be put to broader use as a defensive weapon. It even evolved venoms to enhance its effects. Take, for example, a wasp called the tarantula hawk. When glimpsed from the corner of the eye, it looks like a hummingbird, with its blur of orange wings. The body between those bright wings is black and, in my part of the world, about three inches long. I have collected specimens with quarter-inch stingers. The hawk has a hard, brittle body, but when it moves to sting it curls in with a fleshy delicacy. People who have been stung report that the pain is extraordinary. It is certainly the worst available from any stinging insect in North America. That first blast of pain fades within the hour, but occasionally there are drastic aftereffects. One victim, who accidentally touched a tarantula hawk and was stung on the hand, seemed to recover well. But a few days afterward, her hand turned black. Muscle spasms shook her entire arm. It began to throb. The discoloration and spasms eventually subsided. The aches lingered for weeks. Doctors diagnosed her with nerve damage.

THE HARMLESS END OF A WASP.

• • •

ANOTHER INNOVATION SOME wasps share with their relatives, the ants and bees, is social life. This advance has implications for us humans. I had occasion to mull this matter on a visit to our ancestral home in Oklahoma, where I took Parker for a walk. On a country road we found a patch where the generally fine topsoil was peppered with course bits of stone.

"Look," I told him. "The ground here doesn't have much gravel except in this spot. They've brought it up from below." It is a sign of depth, this gravel, for the burrowers go meters beneath the soil.

He looked closely and noticed the gravel formed a circle. At its center was a hole thick as a pencil. Issuing from the hole were quarter-inch workers, each armed with mandibles like ragged scythes and, harder to see, a stinger like a bundle of fiberglass splinters. I gave him one last warning about the stings, and then with great care he collected a few in a jar for further study. His method was to let one crawl onto a stick placed in its path, then shake it into a jar.

This hole amid a litter of gravel was the portal to a vast society, mostly hidden from view. A colony of red harvester ants may number twelve thousand, most of whom stay inside the tunnels and chambers. The ones we saw on the surface, foraging for seeds and dead insects to feed the whole colony, were the oldest and most dispensable workers. The deepest chambers lay ten feet down. Though the workers die off every year, the queen, and the colony itself, may last for twenty years in the same spot.

But you can't see all this. It's the foraging workers you notice. You have to allow some leeway on their alleged redness. Some are a translucent red-brown, like a blood blister. Some are half red, half black. Looking at one of them up close later on, we saw that her body was three segments with a slender stalk between the last two, giving the effect of beads on a string. She had five legs; I felt a minor surge of guilt as I wondered whether we knocked off the missing one during the capture. Her antennae flopped like dog ears. Two big eyes and a few smaller ones littered the middle of her face like acne. She arched and strained, as if trying to get a better look at something. Her jaws opened wide.

Harvester ants are shockingly durable. Often I have accidentally stepped on one, only to see it continue on its way after a slight stagger, as if shaking off a fit of dizziness.

Once I saw a man try to exterminate a colony of harvesters that had established itself in a driveway. He drenched a square yard of ground with gasoline and poured a few quarts directly into the pebble-ringed burrow. Then the man (who was apparently not conversant with the principles of environmentalism) lit a match and dropped it casually. I gazed into the fire, and inside it the ants were raging, trying to attack the flames with their mandibles. I put a stick into the flames and watched the ants scale it faster and more frantically than the fire could. Their red-and-black bodies turned brown, but they did not wither and curl in on themselves for a long time. I had to throw the stick aside before they could reach me with their stingers. The next day a fresh set of workers, unscathed by flame, cleared away the dead. Others brought in seeds as usual.

As a boy with an unwelcome interest in harvester habits, I was stung many times, the ants anchoring themselves to my flesh with their mandibles and wrenching themselves into preposterous convolutions to bury their stingers in me. They were willing to die to hold their stingers in the flesh. Usually I was stung on my meddling finger. A pain like that of a toothache always lanced through it. After a minute the pain ran through the entire hand, like a hot thread strung from fingertip to wrist bone. The pad of my finger reddened. The pain diminished quickly; within twenty minutes, my finger didn't hurt at all. It only felt as if its bones lay slightly out of alignment.

Once an ant trapped in my jeans waited six hours to take offense, and when it did it managed a great many stings before my mother understood what was wrong with me and, to my embarrassment, depantsed me and threw me into a soda bath. On my thigh a patch of hide the circumference of a baseball protruded like a red relief map. By way of giving comfort, my mother assured me she had ground the offender into the carpet with a shoe.

My adventures affirm the research findings of Dr. Justin O. Schmidt, an entomologist who declared the harvester ant one of the most painful stingers in the insect world. Dr. Schmidt, of the U.S. Department of Agriculture, has been stung by various kinds of ants, bees, wasps, and other creatures. He devised a scale—the Pain Index—to compare the sensations he went through. Four is the highest number on the scale, meaning the most pain. The harvester ant scored a three. I was surprised to read about Schmidt's results. Although I never enjoyed the sting of the red harvester, it rarely counted as the most important event in my day. Practically speaking, the harvester ant is not as dangerous as the fire ant, various kinds of wasps, or even the honeybee, because one harvester ant sting is usually all you get, and it would theoretically take almost nine hundred stings to kill a healthy adult. Still, some people have allergies or other sensitivities that put them in danger. A few have died from harvester ant stings.

One question lingered in my mind after I read about Dr Schmidt's work: Why? Why do tiny animals pack a venom strong enough to hurt big animals? What's the survival value of stinging, a habit that usually leads bigger critters to crush you?

Schmidt has an answer for that one, too. It's a kind of public relations. Social insects pack painful stings just for people and other big animals who may interfere with their dens. The venoms evolve for maximum pain. Among the toxins found in sting venoms are many that tend to provoke allergic reactions. When stings kill people, respiratory failure caused by anaphylactic shock is the usual story. Each worker ant is dispensable, a little kamikaze who will give her life to make sure you never, ever think about bothering a den of harvester ants again. The venom in the sting has no other purpose in the world than deterrence: when you hurt, the ant has made her point.

THE HONEYBEE IS an extreme case of this kamikaze principle. It not only risks its life for the hive, but kills itself outright when it stings. Its stinger has barbs that wrench it from the bee's body by the root when the bee is brushed away. The root is the muscular sac containing venom. It lies on the skin of the victim, a tiny white blister, and continues to spasm, pumping more venom into the puncture.

In June 2008, honeybees came pouring into a home in Lubbock, Texas. All five members of the family within were stung repeatedly, the baby of the house more than thirty times. The hive lived in the walls of the house; no one knows what set them off. This is probably a typical example of miscommunication between species. The bees defend their hive against what they perceive as a threat. That threat can be an actual attack on the hive or on some of its members, but it can also be something we humans see as innocuous—the vibrations of heavy machinery, the scent of perfume, the defensive arm waving of a person.

Sometimes the cause is easier to figure out. In another 2008 incident, five teenaged boys were hiking with a boxer dog when the dog disturbed a nest. The bees retaliated—not just against the dog, but also against his human entourage. One teen tried to carry the dog to safety and was stung some two hundred times, the bees flying into his mouth and crawling on his skin. All the boys lived; the dog died quickly, blood seeping from his mouth. In another case, a California man repairing an irrigation pipe accidentally agitated bees by dumping a load of dirt into a culvert—and onto the hive. The bees flew up from the culvert and attacked him, stinging him more than a hundred times on his head and inside his mouth. The man, who suffered from emphysema, jumped onto a passing pickup truck to escape, but the bees persisted. He died before reaching the hospital. Others have been attacked after mowing over a hive, cutting down a sheltering tree, throwing rocks, or trying to exterminate the bees. In 2008, bee attacks were an unexpected side effect of the real estate crisis in Florida. As buyers abandoned houses they couldn't pay for, bees took up residence, endangering neighbors.

About fifty Americans die from the stings of bees, ants, and wasps every year. Honeybees are responsible for about a dozen of these. As stings go, theirs aren't especially painful (1.0 on Schmidt's scale), and not dangerous except to people with a severe allergy. But en masse, honeybees can be deadly to anyone. The honeybee has been domesticated in Europe for thousands of years, though, like most domestic animals, it attacks people on occasion. In 1957, a wilder strain of honeybee was brought from Tanzania to Brazil. Scientists hoped to cross this African subspecies with domesticated European strains, producing a hybrid better suited to produce honey in the heat of the tropics. They succeeded. But they didn't count on the difficulty of domesticating the African bees. They sting a bit more readily and are more likely to sting en masse, making them somewhat more of a threat to people. The aggressive Africanized bees spread south into Argentina and north throughout Central America and Mexico. They entered Texas in 1990 and have since spread to Oklahoma, Louisiana, Arkansas, Florida, Nevada, New Mexico, Arizona, and California.

But the behavioral differences between races are tendencies, rather than plain truths. In fact, all the honeybees belong to the same species. They can't be distinguished except by a statistical DNA analysis. Even the morphometric measurements sometimes used by labs to distinguish the races are not foolproof. In Brazil, the Africanized bees have even been domesticated to some extent. Nonetheless, U.S. news outlets have been hyping "killer bees" for decades. Much normal bee behavior gets blamed on the "Africanized" race. Americans are suckers for stories about foreign invasions from the south.

A swarm of bees, "killer" or otherwise, can do phenomenal damage. The survivor of an attack in Arizona needed forty staples to close the lacerations in his scalp from a mass attack. "My whole head was like a baseball cap of bees," he said. The insects invaded his eyes, ears, mouth, and nostrils. Rifling through a stack of case reports, I find many instances of people stung more than five hundred times. Amazingly, many of these people survived. In one case from the Big Bend region of Texas, a woman was sitting on her porch swing when a bee stung her on the head. She knew there was a hive in her garden; it had been there for five years, causing no problems. After the first sting, the woman was suddenly swarmed. She ran into her house. The bees followed, attacking her cats. The woman and her husband were so occupied with protecting themselves that forty-five minutes passed before they could call for help. The sheriff who responded to their call didn't dare get out of his vehicle. He saw birds falling from the sky, stung dead. The swarm circled the house for hours.

THOUSANDS OF KINDS of wasps, ants, and bees around the world sting or bite people. Their ways are many. A species called the crazy ant simply sprays its acidic venom at human attackers. Some try to eat human bodies, dead or alive. In 2005, a woman underwent a cornea operation in a Calcutta hospital. As she lay in recovery, ants allegedly ate her eye. It was a fatal trauma.

The image of a human skeleton, sitting inside its clothes, stripped of flesh, is part of our pop culture, the last legacy of nearly forgotten films such as *The Naked Jungle* and their pulp fiction ancestors. The army ants of South America and the driver ants of Africa are portrayed as ineluctable devourers of human flesh. Some species in these groups do form wandering columns that devour other arthropods. They may attack and kill lizards, snakes, birds, and rodents as well, though in many cases they don't actually eat them. These species have painful stings. The driver ants are less notorious for their stings than their bites, which don't inject venom but do puncture the skin. The soldier driver holds its mandibles together so firmly that a person trying to remove it often tears the body off the head without getting the jaws to loosen. The great anthropologist Louis Leakey, who lived in Africa, once heard his baby son cry out in his crib. Leakey and his wife discovered the boy covered with hundreds of driver ants. The ants had climbed the legs of the crib, then crawled onto the boy before beginning their attack simultaneously. The Leakeys were able to save their son. Bedridden people and untended babies aren't always so lucky.

The simultaneous attack, which the ants manage because they communicate by pheromones, is known in other species, including fire ants found in the United States. It's a predatory tactic, designed to kill the prey with mass stinging before it can escape. Fire ants typically prey on small animals like lizards, but they can use the same attack on people who tread on their nests. Children have died of such attacks. A ninety-one-year-old resident of a Texas nursing home received more than six hundred stings. Because of a broken hip, she was unable to flee or summon help. A similar case occurred in Florida, where an eighty-seven-year-old woman died after suffering more than sixteen hundred stings. Cases like these, though rare, qualify the ants as the smallest predators to take human prey.

A TAPEWORM CAN GROW TO 82 FEET INSIDE THE HUMAN BODY.

16. THE WORMS

PHYLA PLATYHELMINTHES, NEMATODA, ANNELIDA, ACANTHOCEPHALA, AND NEMATOMORPHA

SOME NEIGHBORS OF MINE made a startling discovery in their toddler's diaper: a slender segmented worm, transparent except for its grayish strand of gut. After monitoring the situation for a day or two, they realized the worm was not a lone traveler. The boy seemed happy and robust. It was eerie to see him giggle as the disturbing discovery was replicated again and again.

"You'll probably see some vomiting," the doctor said as he handed the mother a prescription slip. He had taken pains to emphasize that a tapeworm infection is easily cured. Now he paused uncomfortably before adding another necessary fact. "You may be startled by the volume of worms coming up." He gestured, involuntarily I imagine: big handfuls. The parents were grateful when the handfuls turned out small.

There was no great mystery about the source of the infection: the family raised pigs. In most cases the exact route of infection is never determined, but my neighbors were soon to be enlightened. As the toddler helped in the pigpen one day not long afterward, his mother saw him look at his dirty hands and then lick them clean.

To THE ORDINARY observer, they're all strands of goo. To the biologist, worms differ in important ways. For example, the nematode has developed a radical innovation not available to the tapeworm: an anus. The worms also vary in their methods for making a meal of human flesh.

Though they seldom intrude on the consciousness of the healthy Western reader, worms are everywhere—in hot springs, in the ocean, in ice, in the dirt of every garden, in the bodies of an enormous range of plants and animals, from fleas to sperm whales. Their eggs have been found in the guts of Egyptian mummies and in the manure of extinct giant ground sloths. Many kinds are microscopic; others can be measured by the meter. The species number in the tens of thousands at least.

Worms can hurt us in two ways. The less common is an injection of venom. The main offenders are bristle worms, aquatic animals that sometimes venture up into the tidal zones to hunt. From each segment of a bristle worm's body protrudes a pair of hairlike filaments. The largest of these worms yet discovered is about a hundred feet long. Some of them have harpoonlike proboscides they jab into prey to deliver a paralyzing venom. They can use this weapon defensively, and several species have had occasion to show its efficacy in discouraging human interference. One, a foot-long blood worm of the genus *Glycera,* causes intense pain. Several others have caused burning sensations, swelling, and numbness, and their stings have led to secondary infections. Still other species, such as the Caribbean fire worm, have injured people with their bristles, which can also inject venom.

The more important danger from worms is parasitism. Let's begin with the leeches, most of which practice ectoparasitism—that is, they feed from outside the victim's body.

One species of leech, *Hirudo medicinalis,* is famous as the bloodsucking agent of backward medieval medicine. It was useful for inducing free bleeding because its saliva contains an anticoagulant. For the leech, this substance helps prevent clotting inside its gut. The theory behind bleeding held that the health of the body depended on its balance of vital fluids, or humors. Some conditions were supposed to be caused by an excess of blood, and leeches were applied to drain this excess. The theory of humors is absurd, but the bleeding was not always harmful. Leech saliva breaks down certain chemical barriers inside the human body, which may have the fortuitous side effect of killing some bacteria. In modern times, leeches have been used to control the pooling of blood in reattached body parts. Nonetheless, medicinal bleeding was implicated in killing people who might otherwise have survived their illnesses. The writer Nikolai Gogol, though already on his deathbed, was probably hastened on his journey by the application of leeches to his face.

THE SALIVA OF THE
MEDICINAL LEECH KEEPS
BLOOD FROM CLOTTING.

People may accidentally encounter leeches by wading in streams, lakes, and swamps. In the tropics it is said some leeches are aggressive enough to burrow through one's socks. Often the leech attaches itself unnoticed; the human victim may at first think his legs are merely covered with a few errant lumps of river mud. But these prove impossible to brush off, and the victim is forced to seize each one and pull. The leech stretches to considerable lengths, its slimy body exhibiting an unsuspected tensile strength. It seems as if it must snap like a watery strand of jerky, but usually its mouthgrip fails first. Blood trickles from the bitten place.

The largest leeches are 18 inches long, big enough to make a difference in your blood volume if you're boarded by more than a few. Most are shorter than a baby's finger. Although some leeches specialize—for example, in fish or in mammals—many dine promiscuously. If they encounter an animal much smaller than themselves, they eat it. If they encounter something more substantial, they latch on to it and suck out all its fluid in the manner of a spider. If they encounter something too big to kill, they simply latch on and suck fluid parasitically. Some are equipped with slicing jaws for this purpose—three jaws in the case of the medicinal leech, which leaves a wound like a peace symbol; others have a proboscis, a sort of syringe with which they draw out fluids. Some leeches can siphon and swallow ten times their own weight at a sitting, and this gorging can last them six months or more.

Most leech attacks on humans are minor events with no lasting consequences. However, some African species, particularly in the genus *Limnatis,* may kill. These leeches swim freely in river water and are, when unfed, small enough for a person to take in unnoticed as he drinks. Once inside, they latch on to the mucous membranes inside the mouth, nose, or throat. As they gorge, each swells to perhaps four inches long and half an inch wide. An infestation with these leeches occasionally kills the victim by suffocation or blood loss. These leeches may also burrow painfully into the eyes of swimmers.

MORE THAN TWO dozen genera of worms are endoparasites of human bodies: they work from within. The parasitic worms probably attack humans more than any other animal; only the mosquitoes rival them, but mosquitoes at least diminish seasonally. At this moment, more than one billion human beings carry within their bodies a nematode worm called *Ascaris lumbricoides*. About one in every thirty humans is under attack from the fluke that causes schistosomiasis; one in six hosts the hookworm. Even in the well-medicated United States, 40 million people are afflicted with pinworms. The results of these diverse infections will vary from no noticeable reaction to excruciating death.

Each kind of endoparasitic worm has its own complicated life cycle. For example, let's consider the genus *Taenia,* which includes beef and pork tapeworms. The bodies of these worms comprise many identical segments called proglottids, and each proglottid makes eggs. When a tapeworm is torn apart, each separated proglottid may still reproduce; in fact, the tapeworm sheds its segments naturally as part of its reproductive cycle. Each proglottid produces perhaps a hundred thousand eggs, most of which are simply wasted. The creature's reproductive strategy is to make so many eggs that some of them are bound to find hosts. Each *Taenia* may have two thousand proglottids, yielding the theoretical potential for 200 million eggs from each parent. (This is not an impressive number for a worm. Some species can manage this many in a day.) The proglottid releases its myriad eggs either before it leaves the human body or afterward, which is why human feces may contain both loose eggs and proglottids strung together like gluey grains of rice.

The life of a new *Taenia* begins when eggs or gravid proglottids from human feces get mixed in with the food of livestock. This is not as unlikely as it sounds; in many places, night soil (human feces) is used to fertilize crops, which then serve as animal fodder. Furthermore, in places where humans are not in the habit of defecating into neatly segregated pipes that lead to sewage treatment facilities—which is to say, most of the world—it is easy for human feces to leach into or otherwise contaminate the water supply. Then, too, the most economical way to raise pork is to let the resourceful pigs run loose, scouring the ground for food on their own. They are not picky eaters, and will dine on such substances as roadkill, table scraps, and the droppings of other animals, including us.

A cow or pig eats the contaminated food. Once it arrives in the animal's intestine, the egg hatches into a tiny larva that burrows through the intestinal wall and makes its way into the blood. It swims this sanguine river until it finds itself in some suitable bed of tissue—it is not terribly picky about the type. Here it goes to ground, walling itself in to form a cyst. If this happens in the muscles or some other relatively innocuous location, the cyst may endure for years, doing no harm, its own life on pause as it waits for our predatory habits to rescue it.

We rescue it when we eat the livestock. Once it arrives in our intestines, the cyst matures into an adult tapeworm. It clamps on to the intestinal wall of a host with its mouth, then absorbs the nutrients floating around it through its skin, which is complicated with tiny knobs that increase its surface area—more surface, more room to take in food. It begins its mass production of offspring. In most cases, it is surprisingly harmless to have a tapeworm producing millions of eggs in your gut. There may be a little discomfort; there's a minor risk of appendicitis or an inflamed bile duct. Most people only discover the infestation when they notice the proglottids in their feces. A human being and his tapeworm may live together comfortably for many years, the worm growing to shocking lengths. An average *Taenia,* left to its business, reaches 16 feet in the human gut. Overachievers, however, have reached 82 feet.

This fairly harmless scenario is not, however, the full story. There is also the condition called cysticercosis. Sometimes the human being is not merely the "definitive host"—the animal within which the tapeworm lives as an adult—but also the "intermediate host." That is, the human fills the role I have described for cattle and pigs, that of host to the larval tapeworms. This happens when the human being somehow consumes the eggs or proglottids—on produce, in water, even by carelessness in cleaning himself when he already has a tapeworm in his gut. The larvae burrow through the intestine and swim the blood, arriving at some comfortable bed of tissue. If it is muscle tissue, the host is unlikely to suffer symptoms, though he may be able to feel the cyst beneath his skin. The cyst will wait patiently for several years for an episode of predation to set him on his journey, and he will probably be disappointed and die of old age. If the cyst forms in the human eye, the host is likely to suffer from blurry and disturbed vision. His retina may detach, leaving him blind. Or the cyst may form in the spinal cord or brain. Here it may cause headaches and seizures. The host may get confused or drift away in a sort of wormy senility. A cyst several years old gets dangerous or even deadly as its own death approaches: its disintegration inflames the brain.

A nematode called the guinea worm causes troubles of a different sort. Let's take a hypothetical, but typical, case: There is a swelling on a woman's foot, like a pecan embedded under the skin. The pain is intense. She bathes it in the river to ease the burning. On the second day the blister bursts. From its ruin something like a soggy strand of spaghetti protrudes. The next time the woman dips her foot into the water, the strand writhes and whitens the water with a milky fluid—eggs released. Let's say the woman is lucky enough to have access to a doctor. He gives her drugs for the secondary infection brewing in the remains of the blister. He tapes the worm to a pencil. Every day he takes two turns on the pencil, wrapping another inch of the worm around it. He dare not pull too fast for fear of tearing the worm apart (if that happens, surgery is the only way to extract the rest of it). An inch or so a day; the worm may be two, three, or even four feet long. The woman will be at this business of slow extraction for weeks, slowly winching the guinea worm out. She will be unable to work for three months. Victims without medical help may be crippled by the secondary infections.

The eggs the worm releases into the water hatch and are eaten by microscopic crustaceans called copepods. People accidentally consume these in drinking water. A copepod can't withstand the rigors of the human digestive tract, but the larval guinea worm can. It burrows through the stomach or intestine to take up residence in the abdominal cavity. When full grown, the worms mate, the male dies, and the female finds her way to the surface of the body, usually on the feet or lower legs. The human body may announce her travels with a fever just before the blister erupts.

There are dozens of other life cycles, involving almost every conceivable part of the human body. Some worms burrow into our feet when we go barefoot; others come into the body on wild berries or garden greens. Many take up residence in the digestive tract, but others are happier in the lungs or liver or even the anus. A worm in its wanderings may cause a condition called cutaneous larva migrans, a peculiar eruption of the skin that resembles the handwriting of an inebriate.

Each parasitic worm has its own preference for hosts. Sometimes a worm is the irritant that provokes the oyster to form a pearl. People have been infected with worms of one sort or another after eating snails, fish, fowl, wild game, and every kind of livestock.

Worms that specialize in people tend to cause fairly minor problems because they are well adapted to our bodies. It's humbling to discover that we can comfortably share several worms with pigs, including *Trichinella spiralis,* which causes the well-known malady trichinosis. This means that from a worm's perspective, humans and pigs are similar and more or less equally desirable.

Worms that specialize in nonhuman hosts are more likely to harm us seriously when they happen to enter our bodies. One such case involved a seventeen-year-old boy from Chicago who lived in a group home for developmentally disabled teens. He began to suffer strange symptoms—clumsiness, sleepiness, a mild fever. Two days later he lapsed into a coma, his muscles growing rigid, his reflexes abnormally intense. His jaws were clenched and his eyes darted. His blood and spinal fluid were full of white blood cells—a sign of invasion, though blood tests did not tell what sort of organism was to blame. When doctors conducted a biopsy of his brain tissue, they found they had also removed a few slices of raccoon roundworm. The logical questions were investigated; raccoon feces turned up in the yard of the group home. The boy lay in a coma for a year, then died.

The raccoon roundworm is extraordinarily common in some populations of raccoon—one survey found 82 percent of raccoons so infested, the nematodes living in their intestines to pass eggs in their feces. The larvae may grow in more than fifty species of birds and mammals, including rodents and rabbits. They return to their definitive hosts when a raccoon preys on or scavenges one of these intermediate hosts. Babies and toddlers can get infected by eating dirt in which a raccoon has defecated. In the human body, the larvae go wandering, sometimes doing incredible damage to the eyes, internal organs (causing fever, asthma, or pneumonia), and brain. No drug has proved effective against the raccoon roundworm.

Some of the most dramatic damage worms wreak on humans is caused by a group called filarial worms. These nematodes use mosquitoes or other bloodsucking flies as intermediate hosts and mammals such as us as definitive hosts. When an infected fly bites a person, the worms crawl onto the skin and into the wound. The filaria best known to most of us is the heartworm that can infect dogs and cats (as well as humans).

A particularly destructive filaria called *Onchocerca volvulus* occurs in parts of Africa, Central and South America, and the Arabian peninsula. This worm, borne by black flies, causes a disease called onchocerciasis. The symptoms include rashes, itching, hard nodules beneath the skin, and disorders of the lymph system. The worms reside in the nodules, each of which may contain many adult worms releasing tiny offspring into the skin and lymph. The nodules may endure fifteen years; an individual worm may continue to breed in the human body for nine years, producing millions of offspring. It is estimated that 17.7 million people are currently infected. A complication called river blindness can occur in people heavily and chronically infected. About 270,000 people are entirely river-blind, while another half million suffer some loss of vision. All this occurs because the worms invade the eyes. Because black flies breed in running water, the worm works its mischief in much greater numbers near rivers and streams.

Lymphatic filariasis is an even more devastating disease. It's caused by three species, *Wucheria bancrofti, Brugia malayi,* and *Brugia timori,* and spread by many kinds of mosquitoes. The disease afflicts more than 120 million people, mostly in Asia, Africa, South America, and the Pacific islands. Fewer than half show overt signs of illness, but some 40 million are disabled or disfigured. Among the symptoms are lymphedema, the swelling of the limbs, breasts, or genitals because of accumulating fluid. A further complication is elephantiasis, the thickening and excessive growth of the skin and subcutaneous tissues. In men, the scrotum may fill with fluid and stretch to gigantic proportions. The disease may ruin the kidneys and lymphatic system; since the latter is integral to the immune system, opportunistic infections are a danger. Pain and sexual dysfunction are common. One's social opportunities are affected—in fact, victims in India are often relegated to the status of pariahs.

OTHER MAMMALS

THE ANTLERS OF A MOOSE
MAY SPAN SIX FEET.

17. THE HOOFED MAMMALS

ORDERS CETARTIODACTYLA AND PERISSODACTYLA

THE ELK'S SHOULDER was nearly as high as my head. When it walked, the muscles rolled beneath its hide. Its antlers had eight points—nine, if I counted one broken short, its splintered end showed like the tip of a whittled stick. The darker fur on its neck looked like five o'clock shadow. Its eyes focused on two-year-old Parker, who was taking an interest in a ragweed right outside its chain-link fence. The closer he got to the ragweed, the closer he got to the elk. Suddenly there was a loud noise, like the puncturing of a tire, and the buck lowered its head, aiming its antlers at my son.

My wife was quicker than I was. She scooped him up and hurried away from the chain-link fence that separated us from the elk. Before she had covered six feet, the elk seemed to relax. She had taken Parker beyond some territorial boundary invisible to us.

"Why you pick me up?" he said. His brow wrinkled.

Why, indeed? The fence would have stopped the elk. My wife had only saved him from a scare. Really, though, she and I had moved on nothing but instinct. I approached the fence and shook it to satisfy myself that the thunder in my ribcage was uncalled for. The fence was sound. But now the elk looked in my direction. I backed away, and again he relaxed.

MOST MALE DEER possess antlers—bony branched horns used for defense and for fighting among themselves. They are for sexual display more than use, and their impracticality necessitates their seasonal shedding in most species. To maintain them through the hard times of winter would cost too many calories.

Bucks duel each other for territory and mating privileges. These fights can go to extraordinary lengths. White-tailed deer bucks have been found in dead pairs, their antlers tangled and locked so tightly they couldn't extricate themselves. They died of thirst or stress. The truculence of deer can go further than that. I know of one case in which a buck was found with the decapitated head of another locked in its antlers. Biologists posited that the living buck picked a fight with an already dead rival and tore his head off.

This truculence transfers easily to humans. In 2005, for example, a man was tending the tomatoes in his backyard near Rancho Sante Fe, California, when a deer appeared. It gored him in the face and head. Bending over to pick tomatoes probably looked to the deer like a fighting stance. The man lingered for three weeks before succumbing to his injuries. In 2006, a seven-point white-tailed buck attacked an elderly man in Pennsylvania, butting and goring him in the head. When his wife came to his defense, she, too, was attacked. The violence stopped only when police shot the buck to death.

Deer kept on farms and in zoos and wildlife parks have also injured people and even fatally gored their keepers. In 1997, in Bell Fourche, South Dakota, a man who kept reindeer as part of his Santa Claus act was attacked by a 550-pound bull in heat. When the bull tried to gore him, the man latched on to its 31-point rack of antlers. The reindeer carried the man—who weighed 370 pounds—in the air for forty-five minutes. Eventually it pinned him to the ground. Five other men tried to pull the buck off. When they finally succeeded, the buck fell dead from its exertions. The owner was not seriously hurt.

The larger the deer, the greater the danger it poses. American elk (also known as red deer or wapiti), like the one my son encountered in a wildlife preserve, often weigh 700 pounds. They occasionally attack people. The largest deer is the moose (aka European elk), which can reach 1,600 pounds. Some hunters consider moose a greater hazard of the Alaskan outdoors than bears, because startling a moose can lead to a fatal trampling. In Alaska, people occasionally get hurt when they try to shoo moose out of their yards. In 1995, a mother moose harassed by students on the University of Alaska's Anchorage campus killed a seventy-one-year-old man.

People have come into conflict with deer while hunting them or walking in the wilderness, but also while minding their own business in town. There are several cases of deer bursting through windows into houses, possibly confused by reflections. One deer attacked a woman waiting for a bus. Others plowed into an outdoor café and an auto repair shop. But the greatest danger deer present is collision. In the United States, four percent of motor vehicle crashes involve animals. The animals most likely to be involved are livestock, pets, and white-tailed deer. More than a hundred people die from collisions with white-tailed deer each year. Other species, including elk, moose, and mule deer, have also been involved in serious collisions. Injuries from deer

THE MOST DANGEROUS
HOOFED ANIMALS ARE
THE DOMESTIC ONES.

collisions have been estimated at nine to sixteen thousand per year. Airplanes have collided with deer on runways, causing damage but not, so far, any fatalities.

The most dangerous hoofed animals are the domestic ones, simply because of their frequent contact with us. The domestic cow is far more dangerous than its image would suggest. In the Old West, it was said that a big semiwild bull was a match for a grizzly bear.

Modern livestock looks less impressive. Beef animals are bred for less aggression and more bulk. They are also castrated to reduce aggression. But even these animals can be ill-tempered. I knew one ranch hand who, charged by a steer, ran for the fence, but turned to ward off the animal with his hands when it became clear he couldn't escape. The impact of the charge knocked him over the fence to safety. Both his wrists were broken. One study found cattle the animals most likely to kill American workers. People have died not only through the obvious mechanisms of butting, trampling, and goring, but also by being pinned against fences or struck by gates as cattle rushed through. Even dairy cattle can dismantle a person effectively when motivated. In 2002, a dairy cow left a Norwegian man with a broken leg, broken ribs, bruises, and cuts.

Sporting events also produce cattle-on-human violence. The most dangerous event in rodeo is bull riding, in which a cowboy attempts to stay mounted for eight seconds. The bull is trained to buck, and the cowboy spurs it to increase its violence, for a good score depends on a wild ride. About half of the six thousand rodeo injuries treated by the Justin Sportsmedicine Team in a year result from this event. Both the competitors and the bullfighters (or, as they were called in my youth, clowns) assigned to protect them get hurt. An article in the *Houston Chronicle* quotes one rodeo expert: "They get anything from a skull fracture to a broken foot." Twenty percent of bull riding injuries involve the spine. In one prominent case, a champion cowboy named Lane Frost was "dry-gored": a bull jabbed him with its blunt horn and shoved him along the ground without actually penetrating his skin. He died of internal injuries within half an hour.

One study reported fourteen fatalities among cowboys in all events over a span of twenty years. Bull riding accounts for the most deaths. At a distant second was bronc riding, in which a bucking horse is substituted for the bull. But safer events like calf roping and steer roping carry their own risks. Many competitors lose fingers when a lassoed animal yanks the rope from their hands. Even ordinary roping of livestock on the ranch can cause this sort of injury. I knew one cowboy who refused to wear his wedding ring while working; he'd seen a colleague lose his third finger when a lariat snagged a gold band.

The sport of bullfighting is, of course, dangerous by design. Few competitors escape without some serious injury. According to Ernest Hemingway, bulls that survived the arena were not used in future fights, partly because they learned the tactics of the human fighters and thus became both less interesting to watch and more dangerous. But in the amateur bullfights known as capeas, financial constraints made the organizers less choosy. One bull killed sixteen men and inflicted severe wounds on more than sixty in capeas. When, in its old age, the bull was sent for slaughter, the brother of one victim volunteered for the work. He gouged out its eyes, spat into the sockets, fatally severed its spine, castrated it, and then, with his sister's help, cooked and ate the testicles.

An annual running of the bulls has been held as a prelude to bull-fights in Pamplona, Spain, since the fourteenth century. Six bulls and a cadre of steers are loosed to gallop 825 yards to a bullring. People run before the bulls, taunting them with red sashes and scarves. Fifteen people died in this pursuit between 1910 and 2008, and many more were injured. Similar events are held in other Spanish towns.

SEVERAL LARGE RELATIVES of the domestic cow, both wild and tame, have injured people, including the gaur, the yak, and the Asian water buffalo. Perhaps the most dangerous wild bovine is the Cape buffalo. The hunter Peter Capstick told of finding a corpse 15 feet up an acacia tree, a massive puncture wound through its solar plexus. Tracks showed the dead man had shot a Cape buffalo bull, then ran for his life as the bull charged him. The bull won the race, goring the man and tossing him into the air. That's when the thorns of the tree caught him. He was out of the bull's range, but it continued to attack the tree itself, knocking the bark off it. Then it trampled the gun the man had dropped.

Large Cape buffalo bulls approach a ton. They have broad outswept horns, with which they sometimes attack people who accidentally startle them. Hunters say the Cape buffalo's durability makes it one of the most dangerous African animals. It often survives a fatal bullet wound long enough to kill the person who inflicted it.

The American buffalo, or bison, is now mostly a captive animal, kept at ranches, zoos, and wildlife sanctuaries. People who keep them tell me they behave much like cattle, but with a streak of wildness and ill temper that never entirely vanishes after generations in captivity. Buffalo keepers are susceptible to the same sorts of accidents that befall cattle ranchers. Tourists sometimes get injured while trying to feed or even pet buffalo in wildlife refuges. In 2008, a Pennsylvania family posed for a photo within two feet of a bull buffalo at the Grand Canyon of the Yellowstone. The buffalo tossed one of them, a twelve-year-old boy, ten feet in the air. His injuries were minor.

In the days when large herds roamed wild, people occasionally came into territorial disputes with buffalo. The buffalo seemed to remember certain places, to which they returned on an annual cycle. Some places were for the mingling of herds; others, sheltered valleys mostly, for wintering. European Americans tried to settle in these places, establishing crops, livestock, and buildings—all of which the buffalo might destroy. One report mentions buffalo razing a log cabin, "taking delight in turning the logs off with their horns." The buffalo were ultimately the sufferers in such conflicts, as is well known, but people died too.

The classic tale of buffalo violence took place in central Pennsylvania at the turn of the nineteenth century. A herd of more than three hundred buffalo returned to Middle Creek Valley to find these winter quarters inhabited by people. They passed a farm held by a family named McClellan. Mr. McClellan shot four cows. The herd passed on to the neighboring farm of a family named Bergstresser, where they broke down a fence to raid the haystacks, in the process crushing and trampling ten cattle and thirty-five sheep. The Bergstressers, aided by Mr. McClellan and some farm dogs, drove the herd away.

McClellan returned to his own farm. The herd was there again, surrounding his cabin so closely as to block it from his view. He waded into the herd in fear for his wife and three children. He shot the lead bull, which fled, breaking through the door of the cabin. The rest of the buffalo tried to follow their leader indoors. Henry W. Shoemaker writes that the buffalo were soon "jammed in the cabin as tightly as wooden animals in a toy Noah's ark." McClellan continued to attack with musket and knife, but couldn't get into the cabin. Bergstresser and other neighbors arrived, drawn by the noise, and helped McClellan tear the cabin apart. The buffalo, Shoemaker writes, "swarmed from the ruins like giant black bees from a hive." Inside, everything had been trodden to pieces. The men found Mrs. McClellan and the three children, all under six years old, "dead and crushed deep into the mud of the earthen floor."

Word spread across the countryside, and soon, as a blizzard descended, fifty men, accompanied by their dogs and wolf-dogs, sallied into the mountains on a mission of revenge. Snow hid the tracks of the buffalo. The men needed two days to find them. The buffalo had gone to ground in a steep hollow, where they were now mired in neck-deep snow. The men waded in to dispatch them with guns and bear knives. Snow and cold made it impossible to skin and butcher them. The men took the only meat accessible in that white and red landscape: they hewed out the tongues and filled their pockets with them.

WE STEREOTYPE ANIMALS, using them as shorthand for human traits—the weasel for duplicitous cunning, the snake for evil, the gorilla for brute aggression. Most of these stereotypes are irrelevant to the behavioral truths of animals.

The domestic sheep, for example, does not neatly fit its image of passive, stupid compliance. There are many varieties of sheep, some more aggressive than others, and the largest grow to hundreds of pounds and can readily display their displeasure with people. It's not unusual for farmers to get knocked down when they step into a pen to offer feed. In 2001, for example, a ram fattening for sacrificial slaughter on a third-floor rooftop in Cairo (where such domestic arrangements are common) butted its sixty-year-old owner, knocking him off the roof and leaving him bone-broken and hospitalized.

In China Grove, North Carolina, in 2000, a mating season frenzy to guard his ewes seemed to motivate a ram who attacked his owners. The couple didn't show up for a family occasion, so relatives went looking for them. They discovered them in the sheep pen, where they had evidently been feeding and watering. The woman, aged eighty, had suffered a broken leg and head trauma. She was already dead. The man, aged eighty-four, was taken to a hospital, where he soon died as well. Police found blood on the head of the ram.

I'M NOT AFRAID of many animals, but the prospect of riding a horse used to terrify me. It all started when I was three and my uncle set me on the back of a brown and white Shetland pony named Snoopy. "Kick him," my father said. I tapped Snoopy in the flanks with my stirruped boots. Nothing much happened. Snoopy gave a shuddering twitch of his thickly maned head, as if bored; the metal parts of his bridle clinked. The sun shone. My mother and sister and cousins and aunt and uncle sat on the porch looking at me as if I'd done something wrong.

"Kick him harder," my father said.

I'd kicked him as hard as I could the first time, so I reasoned that the only way to kick harder was to use the spurs strapped to my heels. I roweled him. Suddenly Snoopy was nothing but motion. A white picket fence separated the yard where we rode from the surrounding countryside. Snoopy made three or four circuits of the yard before he calmed down enough for the men to catch him. I was aboard only for the first circuit. After that, I was lying in the middle of the yard in a patch of sandburs.

I wasn't badly hurt, but I resisted riding after that. I'd been born into

WORKPLACE HAZARDS OF THE 1880S.

an extended family of ranchers and farmers, so my fear marked me as something like a congenital idiot. Further accidents followed. When I was six, the same uncle set me on his stallion Excuse. "Pull on the reins," my father hollered as Excuse and I vanished in the distance, me pulling ineffectually on the reins, he ignoring them. When I was ten, a friend told me he'd cure my fear by riding double with me. When I saw how much fun it was, I'd have to take up riding. He mounted his white pony Shorty first, then guided him to the fence so I could step on. I did. Shorty didn't like it. He reared, and I was mashed into an angle of the fence with my friend on top of me.

I finally overcame my fear when I was twelve and had a chance to ride into Palo Duro Canyon in Texas. I'd ridden into it before, on a tourist train. The ground on top was frosted with caliche and decorated with yucca and prickly pear. The deeper we went, the redder the stratified sandstone walls got. The Red River had bitten deep here. Georgia O'Keeffe called the Canyon "a burning, seething cauldron, filled with dramatic light and color." To me, it was as if we were tunneling into a red velvet cake. The tour guide on the train had given a lecture about the canyon's history—over one thousand horses taken from the Comanche and slaughtered to force them to the reservation—but I was too interested in the rocks to listen closely. The best rock formation was the Sad Monkey, a wind-carved boulder that looked down on the railroad with eyeless sockets, one of them squinted as if against the sun.

I'd read enough about animals by this time to suspect that my fear was itself the reason for all my accidents after the first. I must have communicated my fear to the horses in some mysterious way—through body language perhaps, or through the tone of my voice. So I resolved to act bold. The wranglers were bringing out the horses. One of them brought out a chestnut mare who tossed her head irritably.

"You ridden a lot?" the wrangler asked the man ahead of me in line.

"Yeah, plenty," the man said, and took the rowdy horse by the reins and stepped confidently into the stirrup.

"How 'bout you?" the next wrangler said to me, leading a tall sorrel across the corral. She looked very polite, this horse with the chocolate eyes. I must have hesitated, because the wrangler added, "This one's only medium gentle. You ridden much?"

"Hell yes," I said, and took the reins, and stepped into the stirrup, and tapped her with my heels and headed out into the canyon to see the towers of stone. Hours later I paused in a shallow creek to let the horse drink. Her mobile lips moved among the smooth stones. I loved the horse; I even loved the sunset slathered like violence on the cliff, telling me it was time to turn home.

THOUGH I LOVED my uncle, I was pleased to hear from time to time that Snoopy had bitten him. I guess I harbored a grudge against the man who had so often set me on runaway horses. A horse bite is no laughing matter, really. The animal's incisors are large, and despite being herbivorous, horses can bite through human flesh as if it were butter. In 2004, a stallion pulling a wagon in the streets of Warsaw became aroused by the scent of a mare in heat. When the stallion's owner tried to control him, he was bitten in the neck so badly that he died on the spot, either of a severed jugular vein or of spinal damage.

Most of the cowboys I know have suffered a few horse bites, a few deep bruises or fractures from trodden feet. Many have bad backs or hips that crimp with arthritis in old age, a legacy of being thrown. A few have suffered concussions from head-butts. In the United States, horses kill more than a dozen people on the job every year, mostly by throwing them, crushing them, or kicking them. The figures are proportionally higher in countries where the agricultural life is more prevalent. Such deaths are extremely rare, considering how many interactions people have with horses daily. Most horse people will never sustain a serious injury at the hooves of a horse. In fact, death by horse is a famous "rare event": a probability theorem was written around the example of Prussian soldiers kicked to death by their mounts.

A browse through genealogical materials reveals that in the nineteenth and early twentieth centuries, evidently periods more pragmatic and less sentimental than our own, death by horse was occasionally noted on gravestones. "Killed by horse kicking him in stomach," notes one genealogical document. Newspaper accounts from that period reveal that people were occasionally killed when horses ran away with the vehicles they pulled. One even mentions a death from driving a wagon under a low branch. As methods of transportation, horses and oxen came with the risk of accidents, just as automobiles do now.

. . .

IN TV DOCUMENTARIES, the wildebeest (or gnu) always seems to be the victim, crowding across a stream only to be snatched by a crocodile or getting run down and disemboweled by lions. There's another side to the wildebeest, which hunters occasionally get to see. J. H. Patterson tells the story of a hunter who shot a wildebeest and then tried to photograph its carcass. As he was adjusting his camera, the beast revived and charged. The photographer dodged, but his assistant was gored through the thigh and tossed aside before the wildebeest fell dead of its wound.

Other kinds of antelope have proved even more dangerous to hunt. The bushbuck of sub-Saharan Africa is notoriously eager to defend itself. Its maximum weight is about 120 pounds, its maximum shoulder height less than two and a half feet. But both males and females use their sharp horns to counterattack hunters. Bushbucks have gored people to death. So have sable antelopes. These large, maned, often glossy black antelope with white markings live in the wooded savannas of southeastern Africa. They weigh up to 600 pounds and stand up to five feet at the shoulder; their chests are deep, giving them an almost equine strength. Their scimitar horns can reach five and a half feet. Only lions regularly take the sable antelope as prey. Sometimes the antelope wins.

ONE DAY IN 2009, in rural Curry County, New Mexico, a man was watering his hogs. He reached into the pen to move the hose. That's when his 900-pound boar attacked. It nearly amputated one arm before he could escape. Tests showed the boar was not rabid. The family ordered it butchered.

The pig family includes such formidable creatures as the babirusas and the warthogs. Many of these are dangerous when provoked. Stories of counteraggression against human hunters are on record for the red forest hog. This pig of diverse habitats in central and western Africa is shaggy, with white and black markings on its rusty coat. It grows to about five feet long and has three-inch tusks. Similar stories are told of the giant forest hog, a maned, dark-haired pig of central Africa. This formidable creature reaches seven feet in length and 600 pounds. Its height at the shoulder may exceed three feet. Its rooter (the disk of cartilage at the end of a pig's nose) can be as large as a man's two fists held together. The upper tusks may measure 14 inches. Sometimes the giant forest hog coerces even hyenas to give up their kills.

But the most dangerous pig is the familiar kind found on farms. Most hoofed animals are pure herbivores, but the domestic swine is an omnivore. Using its sensitive rooter, it turns up a wide variety of food: windfall fruit and nuts, insects, fungi, carcasses, live vertebrates such as snakes. Larger individuals can take bigger prey. Because we breed them for size, domestic pigs can attain sizes improbable in the wild; many exceed half a ton. Large pigs, or several pigs working together, can kill a person if they catch him in a tight space. Usually, they aren't hungry enough to bother doing so. They occasionally eat farmers, though it is rarely possible to know whether this represents an instance of predation or merely scavenging after a death by more familiar causes. But they may hurt people in defense of their piglets. Boars, even in captivity, develop a territorial defensiveness that may lead them to attack people.

DOMESTIC PIGS OCCASIONALLY EAT THEIR KEEPERS.

The domestic swine belongs to the same species as the Eurasian wild pig (or wild boar, a confusing use of an otherwise gender-specific term), a furry, long-snouted creature. The domestic form is typically fatter and less hirsute, its snout shorter. These differences are not genetic, but a sort of expanded infancy created by the artificial conditions of captivity over a few generations. The domestic form unravels quickly when pigs escape, yielding the feral form. Feral populations are identical to ones that have been wild all along. They have established themselves in Australia, the United States, and other places remote from their origins. Feral pigs are sometimes called razorbacks—the peaked back is yet another trait muted by domestication.

Wild and feral pigs occasionally attack people, especially in places where easier food is scarce. In the Tai Po district of China, for example, boars have menaced many people. In 2009, one of them attacked a seventy-seven-year-old man, knocking him to the ground and biting him in the groin. In South Korea, wild boars attacked thirty people between 2005 and 2009, killing at least one man. They also slaughtered domestic goats and raided crops. Officials blamed these attacks on a surge in pig population caused by the extermination of its own predators—wolves, tigers, leopards.

The incisors of a pig grow throughout its life. If left untrimmed, they curve upward to form fighting tusks. The teeth readily shear human bones and flesh. A report on pig-related mishaps in Papua New Guinea listed diverse injuries, mostly incurred in hunting feral pigs: penetrating abdominal wounds, compound fractures, collapsed lungs, ripped tendons and severed arteries, joints and genitals ruined by tusks.

AN OLD STORY from Africa's colonial days tells of a group of twenty-one slaves forced to march single file, chained to each other at their necks. A rhinoceros emerged from the bush and gored a man in the middle of the group. The impact snapped the necks of all the others.

I don't know whether this story is true, but it does correctly suggest the power of the rhino. They are much faster than their looks suggest, managing bursts of 45 miles per hour. Even the smallest of the five species, the Sumatran, exceeds a thousand pounds and can generate tremendous force. The white rhino of Africa can weigh eight times that. Peter Hathaway Capstick claimed rhinos had succeeded in derailing locomotives. They have certainly succeeded in pulverizing people.

All of the rhinos are, by human standards, irritable. They attack on what seems to us insufficient provocation. The explanation for this behavior lies in their senses. They have poor distance vision, but good senses of hearing and smell. The elongated head, in fact, accommodates a huge network of nasal cavities. The result is that a rhino may become aware of another animal without knowing exactly what it is. Its solution is to charge. Often, the charges are bluffs, and the rhino will break off well before making contact. But bluffs work only if they are unpredictable—that is, if the bluffer sometimes delivers on his threats.

Depending on the species, a rhino may be armed with tusks or a secondary horn in the middle of the snout. Humans have been butted and trampled to death. But the really dangerous weapon is the big horn on the tip of the snout. The horns are made of compressed hair. They vary considerably in size and shape, the most impressive being the four-foot scimitar of the white rhino. Goring by a rhino is a serious matter. Punctured lungs, evisceration, and other fatal injuries have been reported. A rhino trying to remove an impaled victim from its horn can toss him a dozen feet in the air. Some people have been treated to several tosses.

Though it is the smaller of the two African species, the black rhino is far more aggressive and dangerous. In 2005, a black bull rhino fatally gored a keeper at a wildlife sanctuary near Nairobi, Kenya. It then chased the man's colleagues up a tree. A ranger rescued them by shooting the rhino. In 2004, researcher Kirsten Bond met with another aggressive black rhino at a game reserve in South Africa. It gored her, puncturing a lung, and broke both her legs, probably by trampling. Workers at the reserve rescued her by luring the rhino into a different pen.

A TAPIR LOOKS, to the Western eye, like an amalgam of other animals. In its gross shape and size, it resembles a large pig. It possesses a prehensile snout like an abbreviated elephant trunk. The Malayan species is dressed in black and white like a giant panda. But the beady little eyes and long head of the tapirs give some clue to their true affinity with the rhinoceroses.

Malayan tapirs roam the rain forests of Indochina on trails they themselves carve out with repeated passings, grazing from low brush, sniffing the ground for information, marking their territories with urine, and making characteristic birdlike whistles to communicate with their colleagues. In the wild, these animals avoid confrontations, running away at the first hint of a threat, though local people say they are vicious when cornered. Adults may reach eight feet in length and stand three and a half feet at the shoulder, and their weight crowds 800 pounds.

It was a tapir of this species that attacked a zookeeper at the Oklahoma City Zoo in 1998. The tapir, called Melody (because of its whistling, I suppose), had a two-month-old son. Perhaps she perceived a threat to her offspring in the keeper's motions that November morning. The keeper was, per routine, pushing food into the cage when

Melody latched on to her arm and dragged her in and began to bite her. Colleagues rushed to her aid, but in the few minutes she was in the cage, the tapir inflicted facial injuries, a punctured lung, lacerations, and a few broken bones. It also bit the woman's arm off above the elbow. The arm was too damaged and contaminated to be reattached.

IN ZULULAND IN 2002, a thirty-five-year-old man was on his way home from work after dark when he stumbled into a hippopotamus. It crushed his ribs, collapsed his lungs, and bit off his nose and right eye along with the surrounding tissue. He hiked to a nearby road and flagged down help. At the hospital, he complained of pain in his arm, apparently unaware of his more serious injuries.

A much repeated bit of lore claims the hippo kills more people than any other African species. I haven't encountered solid statistics to prove this claim. I suspect it grew out of the far more supportable contention that the hippo is the most dangerous herbivore in Africa. A hippo ventures onto land at night to feed. That's usually where the trouble starts. It feels vulnerable on land, and it's ready to bolt for the water at the first sign of a threat. If a human happens to walk between the hippo and the water, the hippo panics because its retreat has been cut off. It often gives no warning, but rushes for the water, biting or trampling anyone in its way. Since the hippo may weigh ten thousand pounds, and even an average male may weigh six thousand pounds, no human can withstand its hurtling mass. The tusks of a hippo, up to 20 inches long, can amputate limbs or, as has sometimes happened, cut a person in half.

Hippos have also dismembered swimmers and divers, apparently because they tripped the hippos' territorial instincts or made them feel threatened. They have bitten canoes and motorboats to pieces for similar reasons. In 2000, when competition for food led to conflicts between humans and hippos in Niger, the animals wrecked about a dozen boats. In 1959, a male hippo who lived on the Okavango River in southern Africa harassed so many canoes that a man named Andries Steyn was sent to kill it. Steyn sighted the big male from his boat and shot it. He hadn't counted on its friends. A female hippo Steyn hadn't noticed knocked him from his boat and dragged him under the water. His corpse was never recovered.

VISIT _{THE} ZOO

W P A FEDERAL ART PROJECT PENNSYLVANIA

ELEPHANTS KILL PEOPLE
IN MORE WAYS THAN ANY
OTHER ANIMAL.

18. THE ELEPHANTS

ORDER PROBOSCIDEA

IN 2000, A TWENTY-YEAR-OLD BRITISH WOMAN on vacation near Pattaya, Thailand, amused herself by offering a circus elephant a banana and then retracting the offer repeatedly. Or, according to other sources, it might have been the people seated behind her who made the bogus offers. In any event, the elephant climbed into the stands and repeatedly tusked the woman in the gut and hurled her into the air. She died from blood loss. Her sister and their father, both of whom were seated with her, required surgery for massive injuries.

Elephants are the largest animals on land. They are correspondingly powerful and, as adults, have no predators. Armed human beings are the only serious threat to them, though rats occasionally bite and injure their trunks. (Mice, despite the myth, do not scare them; elephants in mice-infested cages sometimes smash them casually.) One report mentions a Nile crocodile biting an elephant's trunk underwater, having possibly mistaken it for a snake. The elephant dragged its attacker onto the bank and trampled it to death easily. Unattached young males—the most aggressive cohort, in elephants as in humans—sometimes demolish rhinoceroses in the wild, tearing them to pieces. An elephant can destroy a human being with even greater ease. Because of their size, intelligence, and natural armaments, elephants can kill people in more ways than any other animal except the human being itself.

Their most obvious weapon is, of course, the tusk. Less obvious, but more versatile, is the foot. Elephants have killed people by trampling, kicking, stomping, and even accidentally stepping on them. An especially excited elephant may use a more extreme treatment. Here, from his classic essay "Shooting an Elephant," is George Orwell's account of this method:

> The elephant had come suddenly upon him round the corner of the hut, caught him with its trunk, put its foot on his back and ground him into the earth. This was the rainy season and the ground was soft, and his face had scored a trench a foot deep and a couple of yards long. He was lying on his belly with arms crucified and head sharply twisted to one side. . . . The friction of the great beast's foot had stripped the skin from his back as neatly as one skins a rabbit.

Another illustrative incident occurred in October 2001, when a captive Indian elephant named Mya, who had heretofore earned a reputation for docility, was performing tricks for an audience in a London zoo. Suddenly she wrapped her trunk around her keeper's legs and forced him to the ground. She held him down while she crushed his skull with her foot. C.J.P. Ionides reported similar incidents involving wild African elephants: "In one case I investigated witnesses told me they saw the elephant put a foot on a man's head which exploded with a loud pop."

It's hard to convey just how much damage a motivated 12,000-pound animal can inflict. One Vietnamese farmer who disputed with an elephant for ownership of a rice crop was found scattered over an entire hillside, an area of 100 square meters. A neighbor who looked at the evidence said the elephant seemed to have repeatedly tossed and trampled him.

The trunk is an even more versatile weapon. In 2001, a circus han-
dler helping to manage elephants on a movie shoot was killed by a cow
elephant who dispatched him with a single swat. Elephants have also
killed people by squeezing or throwing them. In 2001, a fifty-nine-year-
old Indian man was seized by an elephant and slammed with sufficient
force to kill him. The elephant also pursued and killed his wife and injured their thirty-six-year-old daughter by swatting her aside. In the lore
of big game hunting, there are many reports of hunters who, failing
with their first shot, found themselves dashed against ground, trees, or
termite hills. Elephants have also caused shoulder separation and similar injuries simply by lifting a person with the trunk.

As flies to wanton boys are we to elephants. They sometimes deliberately pluck off the head and limbs of a person—typically a hunter,
though sometimes a lesser offender will do. For example, a South
African elephant tore a fifty-year-old woman to pieces in 2001. She and
her husband had been walking when the elephant emerged from cover
and charged them. Perhaps his motives were territorial. The couple
wisely split up; the elephant pursued the woman. She was found later in
pieces.

CIRCUS ELEPHANTS HAVE KILLED HANDLERS AND SPECTATORS.

Elephants can even use their trunks to manipulate weapons. For example, they can hurl rocks, allowing them to attack people who seem safely out of reach. In one case, a circus elephant pelted a ten-year-old girl in the face, breaking her jaw and knocking out ten teeth. Another circus elephant picked up the security fence meant to separate it from the audience and used it to pin down the first row of spectators, including a family of ten. Two people were injured.

The big pachyderms also know many ways to crush people without the direct use of their trunks or feet. A keeper at Port Lympne Wild Animal Park in Kent, England, was found dead in an elephant enclosure in 2000. No one witnessed his death, but it seemed that a cow elephant had either fallen or deliberately lain down on the man. Another keeper for the same outfit had died in 1984 when an elephant crushed him against a railing. African elephants have killed hunters by kneeling on them. The head, too, is a formidable weapon. Working elephants sometimes knock down trees by pushing them with their heads; flattening the human body presents much less difficulty. Both handlers and hunters have died when elephants pinned them to walls or the ground with their heads and exerted pressure. Or, for a quicker kill, the elephant may simply use a head-butt. Elephants have also wreaked traumatic injuries simply by shaking off riders.

The scope of an elephant's wrath is impressive. One escapee injured its trainer and killed eight people. A different elephant injured twelve people in a single day. Another killed one person and destroyed almost a hundred huts. Numerous reports have elephants toppling walls, dismantling buildings, crushing cars and tossing them aside.

In India, where it serves as beast of burden and bulldozer, the domestic elephant kills more than 150 people each year—far more than such obviously dangerous animals as the tiger. In North America and Europe combined, three or four trainers die from elephant attacks in an average year. The reasons for elephant attacks are sometimes mysterious, but several are well documented. Like people, elephants organize their societies partly according to dominance hierarchies. In managing elephants for service or entertainment, handlers become part of these hierarchies. They can cause the elephants to do their will only by rising to a position of dominance. Practically speaking, this involves beating and whipping the elephants, tactics that sometimes result in retaliatory attacks. But even when the training works and the trainer attains power in the elephant hierarchy, that position is open to challenge, as is the rank of any elephant. So an elephant may attack to improve his standing in the herd. Because humans are so frail in comparison, these challenges can be fatal.

Wild elephants sometimes kill people defensively. Hunters consider the elephant especially dangerous because it frequently charges even after it has been fatally shot. Because of their massive, spongy skulls, many elephants have survived head shots, at least long enough to kill their attackers. It takes a powerful gun to stop an elephant reliably, and even this doesn't necessarily work unless the shot strikes the brain through the thinnest part of the skull. Once an elephant begins its charge, a person's fate depends on the elephant's whim.

It is not necessary, however, for the human being to actually attack an elephant; a counterattack requires only that the elephant suspect the human of harmful intent. Elephants can hear far better than people, which is why a person minding his own business may suddenly find an elephant has taken offense at his presence. The elephant has heard him coming and found him threatening. Elephants surprised by jeeps on African trails have crushed the vehicles, sometimes without first spilling their contents. In 2003, a ranger patrolling for fish poachers in South Africa's Kruger National Park was trampled when he inadvertently annoyed a cow elephant and her calf.

Another circumstance for attack is a condition called musth, or "running amok." The hormones of a male elephant sometimes surge to high levels, causing irritability and aggression. Its urine begins to stink worse than usual, and a secretion oozes from its temples. In this state, it will attack people and other elephants with far less provocation than usual. Startling sounds are especially apt to set it off. The killer elephant Orwell describes was in musth. This condition, which may last only a few days or up to seven months, seems a normal part of the male's life cycle, though biologists don't know exactly what purpose it serves. It is not the same as being in rut, and in fact may run counter to the bull's reproductive interests, since he sometimes kills the females he encounters. But other bulls allow those in musth to ignore the usual territorial boundaries and dominance hierarchies during this time, so the bull in musth may get to mate, even if his usual status would not allow him access to cows.

Elephants, like cattle and deer, are often involved in traffic accidents, with fatal results for all parties. A particularly spectacular example occurred in Bangkok in 2000, when a fuel tanker truck struck an elephant, tumbled off the road, and exploded, killing two people. The elephant left a trail of blood and feces as it ran for cover in the woods. Police found it there, still alive.

In parts of rural India a curious housing trend has developed. Even the poorest villagers are building second homes. The first is a traditional bamboo hut. The second is another bamboo hut, this one high in a tree.

Elephants are the reason. Records of elephants destroying huts and crops go back decades, but starting in the 1990s, the problem took on new dimensions. In Vietnam, China, Bangladesh, Malaysia, and Indonesia, elephants flattened homes, ravaged crops of rice, beans, and other foods, and killed people. In a 2006 incident in Malaysia, a herd of

AN ELEPHANT DRINKING FROM A SWIMMING POOL AT THE IMPODIMO GAME LODGE IN SOUTH AFRICA.

elephants destroyed more than a thousand rubber and banana trees. The same year, a dozen elephants raided a Bangladeshi village, trampling five members of a family asleep in a hut. In various corners of Asia, herds have killed dozens of people in a season. Nor is the problem confined to Asia; in Nigeria and Uganda, where the African rather than the Asian species of elephant is to be found, the same behavior occurs.

Various explanations have been put forward—drunkenness, for example. The inebriates involved were not the humans, but the elephants, who often raid the vats where rice and other grains are fermented for beer. A drunken elephant behaves like a belligerently drunken human with the power of a tank. But of course this hypothesis doesn't explain why the elephants began to go for the vats in the first place. An elephant can learn to enjoy the feeling of intoxication just as many humans do, but the primary motive is hunger. Beer, despite its intoxicating effect, holds a concentrated dose of nourishing calories.

Another theory blamed the vibrations from mining operations. An elephant listens to the vibrations of the ground with its sensitive feet. It makes sense that explosions and the sounds of earthmoving equipment would disturb them. But scientists believe noise is only an adjunct to a more obvious problem: human overpopulation.

Wild elephants thrive only where people don't. As recently as the 1980s, the earth had room enough for both species. It doesn't anymore. Though elephant populations have shrunk under the pressure of poaching, human numbers worldwide have swelled by the billions. Elephants need vast acreage for foraging. People need great stretches of land for farming. Where both species live, the elephants are forced to forage on farms and villages. To the humans who depend directly on crops (and subsidiary products like beer) for a living, the raids of elephants seem like unfounded hostility. But it may be that elephants feel about us as we do about rats in our homes. Some experts report that elephants react with something that looks like rage when they return to traditional feeding grounds and find an infestation of primates.

MUCH HUMAN FOOD IS
CONTAMINATED BY
RODENTS.

19. THE RODENTS

ORDER RODENTIA

MY FIRST VIVID MEMORY OF MICE: I must have been six or seven. We were in a cellar with nests in every corner; in every nest the pink pups lay on their sides, arranged in a circle around a center where the mother could nestle down. I had, against my mother's policy, touched those babies and found them soft as mashed potatoes. It is said that you can eat even an adult mouse whole, its bones no more troublesome than those of a catfish; in medieval England, a mouse on toast was thought to cure colds. I delighted in the delicacy of them, how easy they were to kill with a twig. I was engaged in this activity when my tender-hearted sister, Meg, protested. "Make him stop," she demanded of my mother, and my mother did.

"They're only mice," I protested. Mom had been saying "ew" about them only moments before, as she discovered our stored clothes shredded into mice nests, our photo albums eaten through, plastic covers and all. Her voice held a profound revulsion, and this was what I was trying to say back to her: that she had sanctioned my killing with her revulsion. But I couldn't have gone on with the killing now, even if she'd taken my side. My sister had changed my view. "He's killing the babies," she said, and now I saw them as babies. Their squealing, their helpless softness. The heart had gone out of me. I have killed mice in traps since then, but I never quite lost the vision my sister evoked that day: they are like us.

I found myself, decades later, explaining something like this to Parker, who was then a toddler. A mouse had intruded in our house. I was in my home office, writing at a table. At eye level, peeking from behind the Venetian blinds, was a brown mouse with seeded black eyes. I attacked him with a broom handle, but he was too fast for me. Afterward, everything in the room seemed dirty, not just from his touch, but from my sloppy housekeeping. I noticed how long it had been since I vacuumed; I noticed that the trash can needed to be emptied. I felt, all of a sudden, implicated in filth. I bought two glue traps and placed them along the floorboards. Next day he lay on one rectangle of plastic puddled with glue. His struggles had shifted the trap away from the wall a few inches. I've seen them extricate themselves from this predicament, so I acted quickly. I picked up the other glue trap and pressed it on top of him. He was sandwiched, and he squeaked as I pressed down.

"Again!" said Parker, delighted with the sound. I told him no, that we didn't want to be cruel. We just wanted to kill him, not hurt him. The irony was not lost on me even as I said this, but I bagged the mouse and left him to die in the dumpster anyway. My revulsion lay alongside my feeling of kinship, the paradox unresolved.

THE REVULSION. I was living at the far end of a city where it verged into the creek-threaded woods. I was discovering, all over again, another of the contradictions in my life: a love of the country mixed with a dread of its vermin. Like most Americans, I am capable of delighting in the big wild beast wandering across my yard and simultaneously resenting the intrusion of a smaller, equally wild beast into my cabinets. The trouble with "nature" is that it comes in so many flavors.

Once again it was a mouse that was bugging me. He had taken the bait from my traps and left unscathed. He had skittered around noisily inside my kitchen range, crackling under the foil lining. I think I went a little mad. Finally I turned on the oven, meaning to cook him out, but the smell was soon intolerable, and my wife made me turn it off. I opened the oven—how much work would it be to scrape him off the heating element? None, as it turned out, for I had only cooked his drop-pings. "A mouse's calling card," my grandmother used to say when she found the tiny dark dunce caps in a cabinet. But I had no time for rem-iniscing, because my enemy leaped from the top oven rack and bounced off the open door. It looked like those elaborate gymnastic dives one sees in the Olympics, I noticed, even as I screamed like a child and slapped at the linoleum with a miniature baseball bat.

This happened the weekend of our anniversary. Tracy made me a strawberry pie to celebrate. She went out of town the next day, so only the mouse and I were there to share the apartment. The fridge was full of food, this being also the weekend after our Thanksgiving feast, so the pie sat on the counter, covered in foil. I noticed, as I dished up a piece of pie the next day, that I must have left a strawberry mess on the counter the night before. I relished the first few bites of the pie—its flaky crust, its tart-sweet insides, the seedy counterpoint to the general smoothness of its textures. Yet something was picking at my memory. I pictured the mess on the counter, a random smear of red syrup. But it wasn't random. It held some meaning. It was a code tantalizingly on the verge of coming clear. Doubtless you have already guessed its signifi-cance, but I didn't. I pushed the mystery out of my mind to concentrate on the book I was reading. The fork moved from the plate to my mouth over and over, steadily diminishing the slice of pie. When I had finished, I ran my index finger around the plate a few times, the sticky red adher-ing to me, then the last few crust crumbs sticking to that. I licked my finger clean.

It was so good that I judged a second piece advisable. At the counter again, I wondered when I could have left the smear there. I remem-bered cleaning up the night before. It was in fact quite impossible for a mess to exist there, because only I had been in the apartment. I saw everything then. Through the smear ran a curving line, a drag mark in the red. A tail track. My eyes followed this tail mark to the point where it left the general mess. Yes, it went on, faintly, a slight strand of red curving all the way to the range. I opened the top of the range, and there the mouse was, zigzagging among the burners. I dropped the top. Then, gathering my courage, I lifted it back up, but in that second he had disappeared, presumably finding a hole down into the oven.

It was not nausea that hit me then so much as moral indignation. I know, intellectually, that I have often eaten food on which a mouse or rat has trodden, wallowed, defecated. So have you. One accepts that, if one knows anything at all about the conditions of food manufacture. The FDA specifies how many insect parts are allowed in a jar of apple butter, how many kernels of popcorn may show the toothmarks of rodents before a batch is rejected as unfit for people. The box of macaroni in my pantry may hold nine rodent hairs. A kilogram of wheat is allowed nine milligrams of rodent excrement. These "defects," as the FDA calls them, are unavoidable. When a batch of food is rejected for having higher levels than these, the problem is one of aesthetics, not health. We simply eat, and have to eat, many things we'd prefer not to think about.

This, however, was quite different. Tracy had made the pie for me, an anniversary gift, a token of love. She'd even drawn a heart in the top crust. The mouse had contaminated it. Of course I knew at the same time that this kind of resentment gains me nothing. Mice are mice, and in this world it is impossible to avoid vermin. We are made of them, really: our bodies host headfuls of dust mites, gutfuls of bacteria, a pocket of *Staphylococcus* here, a toenail's worth of fungus there. But I wanted the mouse out of my apartment, even though the word *my* was problematic.

He died early the following morning, his spine broken in a snap trap I'd set days before, one he'd already robbed successfully at least once. The bait was a chunk of peanut butter that had dried so thoroughly it crumbled like a cookie when I stepped on it accidentally—the trap had thrown it clear as it sprang. *Nothing personal, sir,* I thought as I looked at the mouse bent backward in the trap, already dead. *Just you and me wanting the same food.* But what I actually said was "Take that, you little bastard." I was still angry about the half of the strawberry pie I'd thrown away.

•   •   •

IN INDIA IN 1958 and '59, a surge in the rat population led to the starvation of ten to fifteen thousand people. This particular surge was caused by *Melocanna baccifera,* a kind of bamboo that produces fruit only once every forty-eight years. The fruit provides a rich windfall for rats. Their population explodes. When the fruit is gone, they raid stockpiles of human food, including grains, vegetables, and fruits, burrowing through wood floors and walls to get at it. The most recent fruiting of *Melocanna baccifera* occurred in 2006. It has left parts of India, Burma, and Bangladesh in famine. In the Chin state of Burma, rats devoured 90 percent of the rice crop, putting a hundred thousand people in danger of starvation.

And this is only one scenario in which rats and mice compete with us. Across the globe, they eat or contaminate one-third of the food we'd like to think of as ours. Relief agencies providing food to famine-stricken people must often count 10 percent or more of their contribution lost to rodents. Only the red-billed quelea bird and the grasshopper devour human food on such a scale—but those animals are limited to certain regions, climates, and seasons. Our rodent competitors have succeeded in all places and weathers hospitable to humans.

WHEN I WAS a teenager, I visited the farmhouse where my family used to live. My grandparents had lived in it when it was new, and their son, my father, had brought us to live in it when I was two. I remember quite a bit about those times—the color of the walls, the spiders to be found everywhere, the dog we had and the toads that crawled our yard. (I seem to have been less interested in the humans I knew then; they are mostly faceless in my memory, if I remember them at all.) Now the iron gate with its spray-paint red gave me a twinge of nostalgia. The house was split, the rear half of it cleaving away from the front. This was the work of an uncle who had, for reasons never explained to me, moved the house elsewhere, lived in it briefly, then moved it back here. The brick walk that curved around the house was still there, unaccountably covered in the shards of instant coffee jars and jelly glasses. Everything seemed impossibly small, as if my childhood had turned out to be a cartoon after all.

We were about to lose our last claim on the farm, so we had come to take a final look. No one had lived there for a few years now. A farmer was using the place to store sacks of feed for livestock. My cousin Robert had come the day before, and he said the house was full of mice, that he could throw his hunting knife without looking and be sure to hit a few. I assumed he was exaggerating. I imagined the usual signs of mouse infestation in a house, only magnified—feces scattered along the floorboards, and that scent, like urine on dust, that accompanies mice in numbers.

Robert opened the back door, and I followed him in. My sister Meg came cautiously behind me. There was the red linoleum floor of my youth, faded to a dusty pink. Scattered across it was an enormous quantity of feed pellets, and against the far wall were three or four hundred-pound sacks of the feed. Mice were still scrambling away from the opening of the door, running across and around the scattered feed, some of them describing psychotic esses in their flight, as if they were constantly being frightened into changing their trajectories. Their claws ticked on the floor. They aimed to hide, but they were so numerous that dozens of them could not find holes to hide in. They rushed in a wild panic, bumping into each other and reversing direction until they met with new collisions. They were like pool balls. Some made overtures in our direction, then panicked again and reversed. But my attention was drawn by a sound like the ticking of a hundred clocks out of sync. I looked up and beheld a parade of mice scrambling along a ledge, just above head level. Something was wrong, and I kept staring at the ledge to place it. Soon enough it came to me: the file was already passing, dwindling to a laggard few, but the sound, the ticking of tiny claws, went on and on. They were inside the wall, hundreds of them, perhaps thousands.

"I'm getting out of here," Meg said sensibly, and exited before she had even taken her hand off the doorknob.

My hackles had risen the second I walked in. The smell of the mice was palpable. They whirled in every corner—gray, brown, cream, black, mottlings and combinations of all, but averaging toward that indistinct color I can only describe as mouse.

Robert and I moved toward the living room, going slowly so that all the mice could get out of our way. There the creatures were sparser, a solid line of them along each wall, and a few of them scattering across the middle of the room. Our steps were loud on the wood floor. The windowsills were covered with mice, and as I moved closer to one window, a cascade of them fell across it. On the facing atop the window, a few milled, chittering in panic. The fallen ones must have been up there too, pushing and rushing in their efforts to escape us.

It was impossible to avoid them all. Robert walked among them boldly now. He didn't seem to care when they skittered across his boots. In every room we entered, they were in a state of disorganized flight, which had presumably begun when they sensed us. They ran in every possible direction, even toward us. I kicked the nearest ones away as I walked.

All day Robert had been saying he didn't hurt living things. The question had first come up when he refused to kill a wasp that was troubling my grandmother and instead insisted I do it, but he had managed to repeat his nonviolent philosophy several times. Now I saw how recent his resolution was. On the inside knob of the front door, three mice lay draped, dead, like the darkening skins of bananas. I found a loose board to poke them with: they yielded, and the uppermost fell to the floor, his body retaining a ghost of the doorknob's curve when he hit the floor, like a leather glove that keeps some shape of the individual hand.

I heard a thunk. Robert had moved on to the hall—impossibly narrow compared to my recollections. I caught up with him as he was retrieving his hunting knife from the floor. Another mouse lay bloodlessly dead, bludgeoned by the haft of Robert's knife.

"You said you didn't kill things," I said.

"Mice don't count," he said.

I looked into the bathroom. The bottom of the big tub was covered with mice, many of them dead, others futilely trying to climb the sides.

Down the hall was the billiard room, where my father and my uncle and other men used to gather and laugh outrageously and advise each other on shots between the clacking of the balls. That doorknob was stacked with mice too, and so was the doorknob of my parents' old room. I arrived at last in the room I had occupied, the one with the pink-painted floor. This was at the dark end of the hall. I went in, but it was too dark to see well. A water stain spread down from the window. Next to the door (I was turning to go, the darkness having boosted my mouse-unease past the point of tolerance), I saw a shape crayoned on the wall. It might have been a human figure. A swell of nostalgia took me. Could this have been my drawing, or my sister's?

Then I noticed the damage caused by my uncle's house-moving experiment. A thread of afternoon light seamed the wall, like frozen lightning. I could still hear the motion of the rodents. They were invisible now, sunlight blinding me to what moved in the dark.

Teeth define the rodent.

Rodents lack canine teeth; the space where these occur in most mammals instead serves as maneuvering room for the animal to bring objects between its front teeth. The front teeth—the incisors—are long and coated with hard enamel only on the front, so they can grow continually, allowing the rodent to chew through dense and tough materials—including concrete and steel, in the case of some rats. In fact, a rat possesses an inexhaustible desire to gnaw, and will chew through wood until a building collapses. It will chew into pipes, causing basements to flood, or into power cables, causing blackouts. Investigators say rats may cause a quarter of all electrical fires by chewing on wires.

Murinae, the subfamily of rodents that includes mice and true rats, is only about five million years old, yet accounts for a disproportionately high number of both species (well over five hundred) and individuals, many with a cosmopolitan range. The murines are about as old as our own genus; we have evolved together, often as commensals, and our relationship with them has continued to unfold even over the course of book history. Rodents are, historically speaking, second only to insects as shapers of human destiny.

Besides competition, disease is their main influence on us. This fact is surely behind the revulsion I felt for the mice in my house and for the disgust most of us feel at the thought of rodent contaminants in our food. In surveys, rats often rank among the scariest animals. The idea of a haunted house, vital to the Western imagination since ancient Rome, has something of the rodent in it: the real reason old houses make noises in the night is that rodents inhabit them—the older the house, the more thoroughly have the rodents colonized its walls and excavated beneath its cellars. (Virtually every important writer of horror stories, from Edgar Allan Poe to Bram Stoker, made use of the rat.) And the reason certain old houses seem to breathe death is that the rodents within their walls are sometimes ripe with contagion. Such, at least, is my materialistic explanation of these feelings.

What draws rodents to us, besides our food, is our leavings. In cities, where garbage provides masses of food, rats grow larger and are more prolific than their country cousins. Among the urban populations of rat, sickness is no more common than it is among urban populations of humans. But the rats spread what microbes there are far more effectively than we could do alone. Each rat may run a nightly beat, carrying the infections of one man's garbage to his neighbor's house. Rats and mice are social, and disease can spread quickly through their ranks.

The array of rodent-borne diseases is staggering: various kinds of viral encephalitis and hemorrhagic fever; tuberculosis; parasitic worms and mites and fungi; *Salmonella* infections and rickettsial diseases; *Hantavirus* and Rocky Mountain spotted fever; and more, including some you probably haven't heard of. But the most important is plague.

Some 200 million people have died of plague. Among infectious diseases, only malaria has killed more. But malaria most often simmers, killing a small part of the population at a time. Plague has exploded several times, killing huge numbers across the globe in short order before subsiding. This explosive pattern has given plague a decisive hand in human history. Scholars have blamed it for the fall of the Roman Empire and credited it with the birth of the Renaissance.

One early outbreak, called the Plague of Justinian after the Roman emperor of the day, ran from about A.D. 541 to 590. It killed perhaps 100 million people, reducing the population of a wide band of Europe and Asia by a third. Crusaders brought the disease back to Europe at the close of the eleventh century; hundreds of thousands died this time. But these were mere preliminaries. An outbreak known to history as the Black Death dominated Europe and Asia from 1347 to the 1380s. "In the face of its onrush," noted the poet Giovanni Boccaccio, "all the wisdom and ingenuity of man were unavailing." The death toll this time was about a third of the population of the planet. The absolute number of deaths may have been 75 million in Europe alone.

Ecosystems shifted to accommodate the mass mortality. The slow-growing disease leprosy virtually disappeared from Europe, the victims it had fed on wiped out by the quicker disease. The Black Death was disastrous for rats, too. Black rats had spread from Asia on ships and other human vehicles to conquer the world. They had taken up residence in human houses across Asia and Europe. They became the main hosts for the Oriental rat flea, which was the main vector of the plague. But plague killed many of the rats. In fact, the first clear sign that plague had come to a city was the sudden litter of rat carcasses in its streets.

RATS BITE MORE THAN 40,000
AMERICANS A YEAR.

Eventually, the ravaged populations of the black rat were supplanted by a larger, more resourceful Asian species called the brown rat. The browns took up residence in human houses; the blacks were forced into less desirable outdoor niches. The brown has remained our most frequent commensal rat ever since. The triumph of the browns disrupted the spread of the disease. It helped bring the pandemic to a close.

But microbes evolve fast, and the plague was back for another world tour by the 1660s. The Oriental rat flea remained the vector of choice, but the brown rat was now its main vehicle. The Great Plague appeared in Turkey in 1661 and spread through Europe and England. At its height, it briefly dispatched some one thousand or fifteen hundred people per day in England. The final death toll in England was about seventy thousand. The "Great Fire" of London curbed the disease by drastically reducing overcrowding and disrupting chains of transmission.

The next major outbreak occurred in the early nineteenth century. Constantinople was among the cities hard hit. Some one hundred thousand people died. A century later, plague struck India and China. But the world had changed. Better sanitation spared the richer nations of the West from the worst, though global travel brought minor subsidiary outbreaks to such far-flung places as San Francisco. The crisis lasted until about 1948. The toll was 12 million. It was during this outbreak that scientists linked the disease to the bacterium *Yersinia pestis*.

Y. PESTIS IS at home in a great many animals, but rats, because of their communal living arrangements, provide an especially hospitable reservoir. From rats, the disease can travel to people along various routes, the most powerful of which is the bite of bloodsucking insects. Like other flea species, the Oriental rat flea regurgitates or leaks some of its previous blood meal onto a new victim, who then scratches the itchy bite and may grind the vomitus into his wound. This system provides microbes with a convenient ride into new bodies. But plague bacteria multiply enormously in the flea's foregut, blocking the flow of new blood meals, so that the flea becomes hungry and seeks more and more meals until its sucking knocks the clog loose, releasing the now numerous bacteria into the new victim. In this way, the bacteria increase their odds of transmission. The Oriental rat flea is especially susceptible to being used in this way because of a creel of spines in its foregut. The spines, which are not found in all flea species, make a handy frame on which the bacteria congregate and clot.

In the human body, the bacteria can cause three forms of plague. In the bubonic form, the lymph nodes swell painfully as the bacteria lodge there and multiply. Fever, chills, exhaustion, headache, and delirium ensue. Without modern medicines, the mortality rate in this mildest form is 40 to 60 percent. Other people, especially caregivers, may get pneumonia after inhaling the bacteria. This pneumonic form, if untreated within the first day, kills virtually all of its victims. (Plague is thus a plausible weapon for bioterrorists, though so far no one seems to have used it successfully.) If the bacteria invade the bloodstream rather than the lymphatic system, the victim may get septicemic plague, the worst form. It kills virtually all of its victims within hours unless treated with massive intravenous doses of antibiotics.

Plague continues to thrive on all continents except Australia and Antarctica, its main reservoir being wild rodents such as prairie dogs and ground squirrels. The World Health Organization reports more than sixteen hundred cases annually. Plague simmers consistently in the

United States (with about a dozen cases a year), Brazil, Peru, Vietnam, Myanmar, Madagascar, and Congo. Larger outbreaks have recently struck India and Vietnam.

A FRIEND OF mine who supervised a warehouse where produce was stored used to tell me of his troubles with rodents. He would set out trap cages for them in the evening. In the morning these were populated with legless mice. The rats were too smart to be trapped, but the mice weren't; and once the mice were caged, the rats would come to feed on them. The cages protected the mice except for their legs, which could be reached through the mesh. In fact rats take meat eagerly, and any helpless animal will serve their appetite.

Another acquaintance of mine claimed to have seen a prone dog swarmed by junkyard rats. He wasn't certain whether the dog died before the swarm attacked. He had neither the heart nor the courage to stay and watch the rats' progress. Human beings have no special immunity from such assaults. Near Chicago, in 1978, for example, a man fell in his basement and found himself unable to climb the stairs. The rats that inhabited the basement soon attacked, and though the man was able to fight them, they persisted at intervals, gnawing his extremities. After two weeks the man was rescued. Doctors amputated part or all of seven fingers. The rats had merely nibbled the tips of some of them, leaving them open to infection, and these the doctors took at the extreme knuckle. Others the rats had gnawed to the bone, and these the doctors had to amputate entirely. More severe were the infected wounds on his legs, requiring amputation at the knee.

Even robust adults are not exempt from the attacks of rats. In Philadelphia, a pack of rats rushed out of an abandoned bar to assail a woman walking down the sidewalk minding her own business. A man witnessed the attack and helped her fight off the rodents, whereupon he himself became the object of their attentions. After he too had escaped, the animal control people he summoned found the rats abundant in the bar, which had been undisturbed by human beings for months.

But children have the most to fear from rats. One of the subsidiary horrors of Hitler's genocides was that the Nazi death camps exposed starving children to their depredations. In Auschwitz particularly, rats were said to have taken children. The same circumstance occasionally occurs wherever poverty is worst. In 2001, a South African couple took their baby to an emergency room in gastric distress. Doctors instructed the parents to leave the child for what might turn out to be a long stay. When the couple returned the next day, they found rats feeding upon the corpse of their child in her hospital bed. The hospital issued a statement to the effect that the baby had died of her illness and that the rats had merely scavenged the corpse. The parents were not mollified and filed suit.

Lepers are especial victims of the rat. Leprosy does not, as is commonly supposed, cause the tips of fingers, nose, and toes to fall off. Instead, the disease leaves these extremities insensate because of nerve damage. In this condition, the leper is vulnerable to mishaps, infections—and nibbling.

Though outright predation on humans is rare, skirmishes between people and rats are common. Rats bite some forty thousand people in the United States each year, for example. Most bites are inconsequential, but some of them result in infections. Two separate diseases, caused by entirely different bacteria, are called "rat bite fever." One, caused by *Streptobacillus moniliformis,* produces systemic symptoms, including fever, pains, rash, chills, and vomiting, progressing if untreated to complications with the lungs, heart, and central nervous system. The other, caused by *Spirillum minus,* causes a recurring swelling and irritation of the original wound site long after it has healed, along with fever, headache, and swollen lymph nodes. The tissue around the wound may eventually slough. Poor people who must live at close quarters with rats, especially children, are frequent victims.

THE OTHER RODENTS can seem comical, but their big incisors make them dangerous on occasion. An adult beaver will attack when rabid. That happened to three people in 2005, in the water at a state park near Bel Air, Maryland. I have known of several people bitten while hand-feeding healthy squirrels. In 2006, a squirrel scurried up the leg and onto the back of a mail carrier in Oil City, Pennsylvania, biting and scratching her before she could throw it off. Gophers come into conflict with people when they damage gardens or lawns. People trying to dig out or otherwise kill the gophers sometimes receive blood-drawing bites.

Prairie dogs build large colonies on the plains of North America. One colony in Texas may have included hundreds of millions of individuals. They don't directly hurt people in the wild, because they take shelter at the first sign of danger, though their burrows are a tripping hazard for horses and riders. Kept as pets, they can become aggressive during rut, biting or scratching their owners. They have spread disease, including plague and monkeypox, to people.

At a Groundhog Day ceremony in 2009, New York mayor Michael Bloomberg discovered the biting power of seemingly comical rodents. Bloomberg offered a corncob to a groundhog at the Staten Island Zoo. It bit through his glove and bloodied his index finger.

PORCUPINES ARE, OF course, well known for their quills—modified hairs that lodge in the flesh of an attacker, splintering and hooking. The porcupine cannot launch these quills, as is often claimed, but it can run backward at an attacker, the quills stabbing on impact. Carnivores often get quills in the mouth, snout, and forelegs. A lodged quill is painful, and it may fester unto the point of death. When I was a boy my father would present me with a cup of quills he'd pried with pliers from the snouts of our dogs. They seemed not to learn from their pain, for they eagerly attacked the next porcupine they met. The quills were about the length and girth of a toothpick.

In Asia and Africa, however, the predators are bigger, and porcupines go better armed. Their quills may be a foot long. Kenneth Anderson, who hunted dangerous wildlife in southern India in the mid-twentieth century, reported finding a dead tigress, emaciated and pierced by twenty-three quills. One quill had destroyed her right eye. She died after winning a fight with a leopard. Anderson thought she'd nearly starved because the quills had crippled her. That's why the fight with the much smaller cat finished her.

Since the days of Jim Corbett, who gained fame dealing with dangerous wildlife in India in the early twentieth century, hunters have claimed that porcupines help make big cats dangerous to people. Several man-eating tigers, lions, and leopards have borne quill wounds. Corbett:

> I have extracted, possibly, a couple of hundred porcupine quills from the man-eating tigers I have shot. Many of these quills have been over nine inches in length and as thick as pencils. The majority were embedded in hard muscles, a few were wedged firmly between bones, and all were broken off short under the skin.

He mentions specifically the Muktesar man-eater, which killed twenty-four people:

> This tigress, a comparatively young animal, in an encounter with a porcupine lost an eye and got some fifty quills, varying in length from one to nine inches, embedded in the arm and under the pad of her right foreleg. Several of these quills after striking a bone had doubled back in the form of a U, the point, and the broken-off end, being quite close together. Suppurating sores formed where she endeavoured to extract the quills with her teeth.

When Corbett killed and skinned the Mohan man-eating tiger, he found more than two dozen quills embedded in it, and "the flesh under the skin, from the tiger's chest to the pad of his foot, was soapy, and of a dark yellow colour."

Similarly, a leopard that killed forty-two people in Gummalapur, India, left distinctive tracks caused by walking on the edge of its right forefoot. After Anderson killed the leopard, he skinned it and found the foot deformed by old but imperfectly healed quill wounds.

Both hunters deduced that these injuries left the cats unable to kill buffalo and other formidable animals. With limited options, the wounded cats had turned to the easiest prey they could find.

MILLIONS OF MEXICAN FREE-TAILED BATS EMERGE FROM
A CAVE NEAR SAN ANTONIO, TEXAS.

20. THE BATS

ORDER CHIROPTERA

DUSK IN THE RUST-RED Gloss Mountains of Oklahoma. Suddenly a
few bits of something were floating in the air between two buttes half
a mile from where I stood. They might have been shrapnel rising from a
slow explosion. The bits of shrapnel became more numerous, forming
a column that broadened at the top to resemble a silent tornado. The
tornado moved toward me. Suddenly the twilight sky over my head was
pocked with uncountable puncture wounds, moving without a noise to
the east. The silence was relative. To some of the insects and birds out
that night, the conglomerate of sound must have been louder than
nearby thunder. It was simply too high-pitched for me to hear.

One bit of shrapnel flew a little lower than the rest, and I could see
the shape of the thing, its rapid wings appearing as short, sharp triangles
cowled in the ghost of their own motion. A few moments before, I had

been only subliminally aware of the insect life around me—moths popping out of the undergrowth, gnats venturing too close to my eyes, an occasional mosquito bite. Now I was acutely aware of the absence of insect life. This one colony, comprising perhaps a million bats, is said to scour tons of insects from the sky every night, each bat devouring half her body weight or better to maintain her flying heart rate of 900 beats per minute. I couldn't see their messy eating in the high darkness, but biologists have told me of gazing up into a snowfall of amputated moth wings.

The wind changed, and the bats turned to the south. They were still streaming out of the cave, and now, seen from a different angle, they looked like particles swept along an invisible river into the darkness.

Even larger colonies of Mexican free-tailed bats are known, including one in Austin, Texas, estimated at 20 million. These bats do no harm to people unless handled; in fact, they incidentally help us by controlling insect pests. The danger they pose is a rare and peculiar one. In caves, the feces of populous colonies builds to great depth—deep enough to engulf a human being, in theory. It is a gleaming black tar. Certain beetles live in and consume the guano. These specialists eat nothing else, and their digestive process transforms the guano into a rich fertilizer. They are like a multitude of tiny methane plants.

The danger of this arrangement is the airborne spore of a fungus called *Histoplasma capsulatum*. This fungus turns up in many places, often spread with the feces of birds as well as bats. But the great accumulations of guano beneath a colony of Mexican free-tailed bats form an especially hospitable ground for such spores, and they build to a heavy concentration in the air of a bat cave. A human being venturing into such an environment without protective gear inhales the spores. The resulting infection, called histoplasmosis, may cause knots of fibrous tissue to grow in the lungs. A pneumonia-like illness may follow, or swollen joints, or spots on the skin; the liver and spleen may swell; the linings of the circulatory system may thicken. The problems may even spread to the eyes, brain, and spine.

Decades ago, doctors sent tuberculosis patients to caves so that they could benefit from the cool, humid air. Some of these patients died of histoplasmosis, which was misidentified as a worsening of their tuberculosis.

• • •

BATS SEEM, TO our human way of thinking, anomalous. They're the only mammals that really fly. Early systematists like Linnaeus didn't know what to do with them; they were classed variously with the primates and the rodents. They must be an aberrant variety of some normal animal—but who knew which one? Centuries of further research have revealed bats to be even stranger than we knew. Among them are, for example, the only male mammals that habitually lactate for their young.

Their apparent strangeness, along with their nocturnal lifestyle and seemingly erratic flight, imbue bats with the power of phobia. I have fallen victim to this sensation several times, as when a little brown bat went swooping around my kitchen and I stood swinging a broom at it as if I were a troglodyte defending myself against some primeval bear. The bat, unscathed by me, exited through the open door of my cave—I mean, house. The only damage was to walls I'd scarred with the broom.

There are more than nine hundred species of bat. Many of them live in colonies of hundreds or thousands, and that's what makes them ideal laboratories for the creation of new diseases. Viruses and bacteria can spread rapidly between hosts, mutating as they spread. Since bats may fly for miles in a night, they can spread microbes abroad. Our own swelling population brings us into contact with bats and their diseases.

For example, the Nipah virus, a relative of the microbes that cause mumps and measles, has its natural reservoir in fruit bats of the genus *Pteropus*. As farms expand into previously unsettled areas of Malaysia, India, and Bangladesh, domestic pigs come into contact with the feces of fruit bats and the fallen fruit from which the bats have eaten. The pigs contract the virus, which causes them to get sick with respiratory symptoms. Humans who contact the pigs have come down with similar symptoms in some outbreaks; in others, encephalitis has been the main manifestation of the disease. A 1999 outbreak in Malaysia killed 105 people. Half a dozen other outbreaks are on record, some of them killing 75 percent of known victims. There's good evidence that some people have caught the disease from fruit contaminated by the bats themselves.

Other exotic diseases, including the notorious Ebola fever, probably originated in bats, though other animals have also been involved in their complicated routes of transmission to people. In the United States, bats are the most likely way for a person to get rabies. Fewer than one percent of bats actually carry the disease, but the sick ones are more likely to meet people; they stay out in the day and become too ill to avoid human contact.

THE FLESHY NOSE OF A VAMPIRE BAT SENSES HEAT.

IN THE MOVIES I favored as a child, the undead transformed them-selves into bats that looked like winged jackals. But real vampires are small—three inches or less in length, their wings spanning about eight inches. Their noses are not lupine, but flattened and fleshy, their convolutions serving as part of a heat-sensing apparatus. With this they find the portions of a host's body where blood runs close to the surface, like men witching for water.

The targets of their nocturnal hunts are most often hoofed animals— horses, deer, cattle. Cattle are especially vulnerable, because we gather and pen them. We make them a food court for the vampires. Once located—by smell, sonar, and ordinary sound—the host is approached on foot, for stealth. The vampire is ungainly on the ground, using the thumbs of its wings to help it crawl. A short hop brings it to the blood-rich body part identified by its heat sensors—the tip of a nose, ear, or toe; the obtruding angle of a steer's leg; the brood patch beneath the breast of a chicken. Once aboard, the vampire makes a nipping incision with its sharp teeth. As the blood begins to flow, the vampire licks it up. It does not actually suck. Its slaver contains anticoagulants and an anesthetic. The vampire requires about two tablespoons a night, which it may achieve in one feeding or several. It may take a mass of blood equal to 60 percent of its beginning weight. Its stomach is built of thin muscles capable of far greater expansion than is typical of mammals.

Blood is their only food. After their nightly rounds, they return to a communal roost, where the females lick the lice from their fellows and regurgitate blood into the mouths of those who have failed in the hunt.

Typically, the victim of this bloodletting feels nothing. A human usually does not wake. Though it's a vast quantity of blood compared to the bat's own mass, it is an insignificant loss for an ungulate or a large primate. But a victim may be parasitized by more than one bat, or on successive nights, leading to anemia. Cattle occasionally die from bat-induced anemia. That's rare in humans, who eventually realize what the trouble is and take steps to stop the feeding. However, because they deal in body fluids, the vampires serve with special efficacy as vectors of disease. In some regions of the Amazon, there's an outbreak of bat-borne rabies every year. In 2005, at least twenty-three people died from rabies in Brazil after nocturnal visits from vampires.

PET RABBITS HAVE BITTEN OFF HUMAN FINGERS.

21. A MISCELLANY OF MINOR MAMMAL DANGERS

As MY FRIENDS AND I peered into the sheltered part of the hutch where a big New Zealand white rabbit had given birth, one of the boys suddenly said he could see the mother eating the kits. Someone opened the wooden door and we jostled each other for a glimpse. Tommy reached in to separate the survivors from their mother, then yanked his hand out with curses that sent his chew of tobacco sputtering out onto the ground. He held the wounded hand in the other, blood welling out to cover both. I only glimpsed the wound: a red valley between the greasy rolling hills of his knuckles.

It is not terribly unusual for captive rabbits to bite, and the strength of the bites belies the rabbit's image as a cuddle toy. In 2004, for example, a captive rabbit bred as food for a pet python nipped a twenty-month-old boy. His index finger was, according to a news report, "bitten off past the finger nail." His father tore open the rabbit's gut, but couldn't find the fingertip. Other such amputations have been reported as well.

In 2002, people in Santa Rosa, California, reported that they had been attacked by a wild jackrabbit. One man was bitten on the hand when he attempted to pet the animal; he chose to undergo rabies shots as a precaution. In another incident, the same jackrabbit chased a woman up a hill. This second attack seems to have been entirely unprovoked. There was also a peculiar news report from Germany, in which it was claimed that a big hare attacked a moped, biting into the rear tire. When a friend of the driver tried to remove the hare, it attacked him, biting through his shoe into his foot. The man was obliged to kill the hare with a stick. It tested negative for rabies.

As CHILDREN, MY sister and cousins and I once chased a cottontail rabbit into a pit beneath iron pipes. We could see it trying to hold invisibly still in the green weeds four feet down, but we couldn't reach it. Its body pulsated like a heart. We poked and shouted until the rabbit came bounding out of the pit, zigzagging up the dirt road. Meg caught it, first clumsily in both hands, then moving her grip instinctively back behind the head, safe from its biting.

We took the rabbit in to show my mother. I meant to keep it as a pet. She said, "Oh, look at its eyes." They were rimmed with a gummy pink irritation. "I think it's sick. Take it back where you found it and let it go. And then come in and wash your hands."

We took it back to the road and set it free, but I chased it down again immediately. Meg chastised me and reminded me of the instructions, but my cousin Faye and I walked on down the road, taking turns at petting the quivering rabbit.

"It won't hurt to hold it a little while longer," I said.

"We need to get it far away from the dogs, at least. Otherwise they might kill it," Faye said. We continued in this vein for some time, mere excuses to keep holding the rabbit. It shivered and shifted in my grip, its eyes staring in what looked clearly enough like fear, and my petting and soothing talk did no good. I wanted, I guess, to make a connection with it, but it wanted nothing to do with me. Eventually Faye lost interest and told me to free the thing. I lingered a while alone on the road, my compeers having gone on to something else. After a moment I set the rabbit down and watched it bound off into the twilight and the weeds.

No harm came to me, but the diseases my mother feared are in fact the worst danger we face from rabbits. Hunting regulations in many areas allow the taking of rabbits and hares only in seasons when disease is least likely. Rocky Mountain spotted fever simmers among rabbits and occasionally passes to people through ticks. It causes confusion, headache, and muscle pain as well as fever. Five to seven percent of its human victims die. Others suffer neurological damage, deafness, or paralysis.

The rabbits and hares, especially cottontail rabbits like the sick one I caught, are also reservoirs of tularemia. People get it by eating the flesh of rabbits, by skinning them, by handling them—even from being parasitized by the same deer fly or tick. A victim of this malady may find his skin mottled with ulcers, his groin and armpits and neck lumped with swollen nodes, his eyes inflamed, his mouth breaking out with sores. He may suffer diarrhea and even pneumonia. In the United States, about a thousand people a year get this disease, and about fifty of them die.

RABBITS ARE NOT the only harmless-looking mammals to make trouble for us. The platypus lives along the banks of eastern Australian lakes and rivers, where it dives for crayfish and grubs. It usually holds its eyes and ears shut underwater and finds its prey with its flexible, leathery bill, which is highly sensitive to touch and can even detect the electrical fields that surround living things. It has formidable claws. A male possesses a spur on each hind leg, and the spurs are supplied by venom glands. This apparatus seems mysteriously connected with reproduction, for its development finishes just as the male reaches sexual maturity, and the venom gland swells in the spring, when the males are ready to battle each other for the right to copulate. Biologists think platypuses use the venom mainly against each other in such fights. It might have some use in bringing the female into submission. Platypuses have been observed to kill each other with venom, though this can hardly be a common occurrence. In lab tests, the venom has proved fatal to rabbits and mice, which, if sufficiently dosed, give every indication of pain before they fall into labored breathing, thence into convulsions and death.

The platypus also uses the spurs for defense. It scissors an attacker with its hind legs, driving in the spurs and squeezing venom through ducts into the wound. Dogs have died from such counterattacks. In at least one case a human antagonist had to kill a platypus to get loose. Human victims are typically spurred on the hand. The result is immediate, intense pain, followed quickly by swelling that may reach the shoulder. The swelling may last a week; the pain and sensitivity can linger for months, and are often severe enough to render the arm useless. People so affected sometimes emerge from their ordeal peculiarly asymmetrical, long disuse having caused the envenomed limb to dwindle.

KANGAROOS AND HUMANS SOMETIMES COME TO VIOLENCE ON
THE SUBURBAN LAWNS OF AUSTRALIA.

KANGAROOS MAY EXCEED six feet in height. In the days before such spectacles were frowned upon, promoters sometimes pitted kangaroo against human in boxing matches. The spectacle worked because the roos naturally box with each other in dominance rituals. They often defeated their human opponents. Without the gloves, however, a kangaroo's jabs can inflict gouges on a human opponent, a fact that has come to public notice in recent years because roo and human frequently meet on the suburban lawns of Australia. Besides jabs with its front paws, a kangaroo can deliver powerful kicks with its massive hind legs. These, too, are armed with claws. They can disembowel dogs and other kangaroos. A kangaroo's teeth, designed for cropping and grinding grass, are not ideal for injuring people, but will do in a pinch.

In 1996, a thirteen-year-old boy searching a golf course in Grafton, New South Wales, for an errant ball was mauled by a kangaroo. He suffered wounds to his face, belly, back, and legs; schoolmates called him names. For his sufferings physical and nomenclatural, he was recompensed after legal action. A larger kangaroo attacked a couple in Monto, Queensland, in 2003. Helen Crouch suffered a kick to the gut and cuts to her face, back, and groin. Her husband, John, endured a sprained hand and assorted scratches and bruises. Mr. Crouch finally killed the kangaroo with an ax. A newspaper quoted him as follows: "It was kill or be killed." Indeed, one human death has been attributed to a kangaroo attack.

Kangaroos are also a traffic hazard, much as deer are in the United States.

The only armadillo found in the United States in modern times is the nine-banded species. Its leathery armor is made of ossified skin. This primitive mammal resembles an inverted bronze gravy boat with a head and tail. An adult runs about the size of a football, but much heavier.

Armadillos delight not only in carrion, but also in the grubs and maggots that accompany it, like prizes in a box of Cracker Jack. They dig for insects and carrion compulsively, and that trait has given them a folkloric reputation as robbers of human graves in the American South. Such sarcophagy may explain how armadillos came to carry leprosy.

They transmit leprosy to people only when we handle or eat them. The symptoms of leprosy, also known as Hansen's disease, start in the nerves. Patches of skin lose feeling. For some people, that's as far as it goes. For others, things get much worse. Grainy, ulcerating lesions appear on the hands, feet, back, and, in men, testicles. Nerves degenerate, causing the glands that oil the skin to stop working. The skin cracks, leaving the extremities vulnerable to secondary infections. People lose fingers and toes—not because of the disease itself, but because they don't notice that they're too close to a fire or that rats are nibbling at them. The dead nerves create an array of odd postures—the claw hand, the staring eye that cannot be closed. The respiratory system is invaded; a slimy discharge issues from the nose. The eyes succumb to infection and eventually to blindness. The disease progresses slowly, the first lesion following the actual infection by three years or more, the worst manifestations developing years after that. But these horrific symptoms occur in only a tiny minority of those infected, and most people are not susceptible to infection at all. "*M. leprae* is almost the perfect parasite," one researcher pointed out, because it so rarely destroys its host, and then only very slowly.

Armadillos maintain a low body temperature as mammals go, about 86 to 95 degrees Fahrenheit. It's this coolness that makes them ideal hosts for leprosy. They get it more thoroughly than human beings do. Organs that remain untouched in the worst human cases are loaded with bacilli in the armadillos. With their twelve-year life spans, armadillos live long enough to develop full-blown cases. But they seem to get the disease only where they range into swampy areas.

Charles Darwin described armadillo as "a most excellent dish when roasted in its shell." The meat resembles pork.

SOME OF THE small burrowing mammals called shrews possess venomous saliva, which they deliver with a bite to people who harass them. The effects are merely painful. Their West Indian cousins the solenodons are larger, more aggressive animals, up to the size of a house cat. Their bites are also painful, though less toxic than those of some shrews and not a threat to human life. Moles annoy some humans addicted to the unnatural perfection of their lawns, but I can't hold the little creatures responsible for an affair that occurred in Berlin in 2007. A man drove electrified spikes into the ground to kill the moles that damaged his garden. After the current was applied, the man lay dead, but the moles remained.

GORILLAS ESCAPING FROM ZOOS HAVE INJURED PEOPLE.

22. MONKEYS, APES, AND THEIR KIN

ORDER PRIMATES

ONE MORNING AT THE TURN OF THE MILLENNIUM I headed north across Lake Pontchartrain in a fog that yielded only reluctantly to the rising sun. Once over the lake, I got lost. On my left hand lay a wilderness of oak and kudzu punctuated by narrow paved roads, on my right a wilderness of convenience stores and fast food joints. Eventually I found my turn among the trees, and then it was down a country road until I came to a flat grassy stretch, several acres wide, ringed with high fences. The acreage was cut up in chain-link grids, and it might at first glance have seemed some sort of sheep ranch. But in place of the sheep were monkeys.

I made my way through a guard station, and once inside the complex of buildings I presented proof of my identity and received a visitor's pass. I was to be accompanied at all times. From this perspective the place seemed less like a ranch than an army base. Soon I was joined by my host, a research biologist who specialized in leprosy and tuberculosis. The closest approximation to the course of these diseases in humans was to be found among our fellow primates.

The monkeys I saw that day had already finished their life's work. They had been infected with leprosy and other diseases; when the experiments ended, they had been cured. Government rules dictated that they never leave this place. The reason was fear of some mistake—fear that a research animal might not really be cured, might turn up in some zoo later on to spread disease to people. So I saw, for example, sooty mangabeys, with their dark faces and startling white brows, looking out of cages they would know for the rest of their lives. Various arrangements had been made for their comfort. There were jungle gyms to play on, and even outdoor runs, though the monkeys seemed uninterested in either this tepid January morning.

There were reasons, beyond an ordinary measure of caution, for the perpetual boarding of these monkeys. Over a stretch of several years, researchers at facilities across the country had discovered something they weren't looking for in captive chimpanzees and mangabeys and rhesus monkeys: AIDS. In nonhuman primates, the microbe is called simian immunodeficiency virus, or SIV, but it is indistinguishable from HIV and can be transmitted across species boundaries. That, in fact, is how AIDS became a human disease—by transmission from other primates. All the captive research animals accidentally discovered to have SIV could be traced back to the Yerkes primate research facility in the American state of Georgia. This is not, in retrospect, too surprising, since Yerkes supplied a majority of the primates used in research in the United States. But there was the sinister possibility that workers at Yerkes, while researching AIDS, had somehow infected their primates before sending them out across the country. No evidence ever turned up to support this scenario, and in fact it is now accepted that AIDS crossed the species barrier when people ate wild chimpanzees and mangabeys in Africa, but the government set up rigorous rules to make sure that nothing of the kind ever happened. No one wanted monkeys infected with AIDS or other lethal diseases scattered across the country.

Half a world away, in a place also coincidentally named Georgia, the scenario that worried the U.S. government was playing out for real. The

Republic of Georgia had boiled over with civil war in 1992. In the city of Soukhoumi, in the seceded region called Abkhazia, had stood a research and breeding facility similar to Yerkes. Among the animals held in residence there, some had been infected with AIDS, and some perhaps with other diseases dangerous to people. When the war reached Soukhoumi, the facility was shelled. Of the 7,000 primates, only 270 could be accounted for when things settled down. Some had died; some had been stolen; some had escaped. The escapees lived on in the woods nearby, raiding henhouses and gardens, attacking people and taking their food. Some impoverished local people made extra money by capturing monkeys and selling them to foreign dealers. These recaptured monkeys went, presumably, to zoos, circuses, and perhaps even other research labs. It's too early to know whether AIDS and other diseases will follow in the wake of this diaspora. In fact, even if such a thing happens, it's unlikely we'll ever know for sure where the infection came from. Diseases are always breaking out anew, and only rarely can their wanderings be traced.

It would be a mistake to think that things like this happen only in war zones. In fact, at the facility I visited in Louisiana, monkeys have escaped several times, though so far without any known serious repercussions. But the danger is more than theoretical. Other diseases besides AIDS have crossed the species barrier between us and our fellow primates, often with hideous consequences. For example, macaques carry a type of herpesvirus closely related to the one that causes cold sores in people. In the macaque, this virus causes only sores in or near the mouth. When it passes to a human body through bites or lab accidents, it becomes serious, with a fatality rate near 100 percent. Dozens have died of this virus.

And hundreds have died of Ebola hemorrhagic fever acquired from other primates. The most recent outbreak of this disease killed ten human victims in the Republic of the Congo. The first to die in this outbreak were hunters who had touched the blood of monkeys or apes.

ALL PRIMATES ARE equipped to bite and scratch, and all of them have prehensile hands that can grasp and throw objects. This latter point is not trivial. There is at least one case of a monkey killing a man by hurling a flowerpot onto his head.

ANY CAPTIVE PRIMATE
CAN BE DANGEROUS.

Any captive primate can be dangerous. Monkeys are common pets across the globe, but poor ones. They often bite their keepers or strangers. Sometimes they fly into a rage and bite everyone in sight. Some have been known to wait on roofs or in trees and ambush people passing below. Though most monkey attacks yield only minor bites, some are serious. In Brakpan, South Africa, a pet chacma baboon escaped from its owner, took a baby from its carriage, and fatally bit through the child's skull before the mother could come to its defense. In Los Angeles, a monkey whose species is not mentioned in the news reports "disfigured and permanently disabled" a volunteer zookeeper. In New Delhi, a monkey mauled and tore the throat of a zookeeper, killing him. In Houston, a pet capuchin monkey inflicted near-fatal wounds on his owner and bit off her thumb and some of her index finger. In Sibu, Malaysia, a pet monkey escaped its chain and mauled a three-year-old girl, sending her to the hospital with wounds to her head, face, eyes, and legs. In Hillsborough, Florida, a capuchin monkey bit her owner fifty times in a single attack. In Mexico, a capuchin monkey bit actor Salma Hayek on the arms and hands, inflicting nerve and ligament damage. Hayek was filming a biography of the painter Frida Kahlo, who kept and painted—and was bitten by—pet monkeys.

Of special note among the captive monkeys is the Barbary macaque. It is about the size of a two-year-old human child, and of similar temperament. It was known to the ancients as a reasonable substitute for a human corpse in anatomical dissection. It can be boldly aggressive toward people, depending on its upbringing. In recent years Parisian youth gangs, deprived of attack dogs by law, have substituted ven-

omous snakes and Barbary macaques. The snakes, though not susceptible to training, become weapons of intimidation in muggings. The
macaques can be trained to attack rivals as well as targets of robbery.
They often hurl themselves at the victim's head, and their teeth and nails
make them a serious threat. The males seem to perceive human males as
threats to their place in the dominance hierarchy, and will bite their
genitals.

Monkeys in the wild are generally far less dangerous, but there are exceptions. In areas of Asia and Africa where they are habituated to
human presence, langurs, macaques, and baboons sometimes become
aggressive toward people. This is particularly a problem in India because the Hindu faith forbids the killing of monkeys. The monkeys invade homes in search of food. They bite and otherwise harass people.
They have destroyed crops, gardens, orchards, and even livestock. They
have thrown rocks at cars, cyclists, and pedestrians; they have invaded
hospitals, yanking the IV tubes out of patients. In times of drought or
famine, baboons have proved especially aggressive, attacking children
and, in one case, stealing water vessels. In 2001, a baboon snatched a
two-year-old Saudi Arabian girl from her father. She was later found
dead. Infants strapped to their mothers' backs have also been snatched.
In fact a number of cases of child snatching have occurred; sometimes
the child is found alive. One much-retailed story, which originated with
the hunter and writer P. J. Pretorius, tells of a big male yellow baboon
in Tanzania that habitually preyed on humans.

The bites of monkeys, like the bites of humans, are septic. Alexander,
the king of the Hellenes at the end of World War I, is probably the most
famous person to have died from a septic monkey bite. The bite occurred when he tried to break up a fight between his dog and someone
else's two pet monkeys. One monkey bit his leg. He survived for four
weeks as the infection progressed. Doctors operated seven times, to no
avail. Since his death caused foreign powers to shift their alliances in the
Greco-Turkish war then in progress, this particular monkey bite altered
the course of history. Winston Churchill said, "It is perhaps no exaggeration to remark that a quarter of a million people died from this monkey bite."

· · ·

ONE DAY IN 2009, Travis the chimpanzee was out of sorts. His human companion, Sandra Herold, had been trying to calm him down all morning, even serving him tea laced with the anti-anxiety drug Xanax. She called her friend, fifty-five-year-old Charla Nash, for help. Travis knew Nash well; they had always gotten along. When she stepped out of her car, he leaped on her and gnawed her face off. She tried to protect herself with her hands: he chewed her fingers off as well. Herold bludgeoned Travis with a shovel, but she couldn't stop him. She tried a butcher knife next. At some point she took refuge in her vehicle and phoned the police, telling them that Travis had ripped her friend apart and was eating her.

When police arrived, Travis attacked them. Officers took refuge in their cars. Travis tore the side mirror from one car, then opened the door and entered the front seat to attack an officer within. The officer shot him in the chest repeatedly. Travis retreated to the house. There were some tense moments as the police followed his blood trail, hoping they weren't walking into an ambush. But they found him dead in his room. Nash lost her fingers, lips, nose, palate, and eyelids in the attack; afterward, doctors removed her ruined eyes. She showed signs of brain injury.

Because they are so visibly like us, the violence of chimps occasions special horror. Travis's attack struck many with particular force because he had been a beloved minor celebrity in his adopted hometown of Stamford, Connecticut, performing in TV projects and riding around town in his owner's vehicles. He played with babies and logged on to the Internet to look at pictures.

TV and newspaper reports quickly latched on to a couple of "explanations" for the attack. One was Lyme disease; the ape was being treated for it. A doctor interviewed for one of these reports claimed the disease can cause psychotic behavior in people. Other theorists pointed to the drugs used to treat the disease, or to the Xanax Herold administered. In fact, no such explanation is required, because, surprising as the attack may have been to Travis's friends, it is normal behavior for a captive primate.

Adult chimps, especially males, are simply prone to solve their problems, and even their passing irritations, with violence. Dozens of violent encounters, both in zoos and in the wild, attest to this. A wild chimp in his early teens, like Travis, would be roughing up the females in his troop, training them to submission. He would then progress to finding his place in the hierarchy of males, using violence and perhaps political alliances to secure as high a rank as he could. These energies, turned on humans, are devastating. The jaw of a chimp is built for shearing meat; its canines are imposing. Because its muscles are anchored differently than a human's, its power is far greater, despite the similar size of the two species. One captive chimp weighing about 160 pounds lifted an 1,800-pound object.

PEOPLE HAVE LONG been fascinated with the notion of raising a chimp baby as a human. There is a substantial pet trade in chimps, and scientists have been similarly inclined to cohabit with them for research purposes. An estimated four hundred chimpanzees live in private homes in the United States. Almost always, adolescence changes a chimp from a lovable family member to a violent and dangerous malcontent.

The violent potential of chimps was not well appreciated in the late 1960s, when St. James and LaDonna Davis of West Covina, California, adopted a chimp they named Moe. Hunting had orphaned him. The couple called him their son and treated him accordingly. He wore clothes, used the toilet, and washed himself in the shower. He first came to public attention in 1998, when he flew into a rage and the police intervened. Moe bit one officer; his hospital bills eventually ran to a quarter of a million dollars. The next year, Moe bit a visitor badly enough to amputate part of her finger. The Davises fought for the right to keep Moe. But the court found him dangerous and mandated his removal. He ended up in a facility for primates with similar stories.

In 2005—more than five years after he'd been incarcerated—Moe was one of seven caged primates in residence at Animal Haven Ranch. On his thirty-ninth birthday, the Davises visited him with a cake. Moe was locked in his cage, but Mrs. Davis handed him cake through the mesh.

Two teenaged male chimps escaped from a nearby cage. Perhaps provoked by the preferential treatment of Moe, they attacked. One of them bit off Mrs. Davis's thumb. Her husband tried to protect her. The two teens then concentrated their attack on him. He lost a foot, all of his fingers, his testicles, part of his buttocks, an eye, and parts of his nose, cheek, and lips. When a worker at the Ranch shot one of the attackers dead, the other dragged Mr. Davis down the road. The worker shot this chimp dead as well.

Mr. Davis's condition was critical. Six months of complications and reconstructive surgery passed before he was allowed to return home. More surgery and rehab awaited him. He was confined to a wheelchair, unable to feed or clean himself.

Moe was unable to intervene in the attack because he remained caged. In the weeks following the mauling, LaDonna Davis described him as despondent. He was transferred to another sanctuary. In 2008, he escaped into the forests of Southern California. He hasn't been seen since.

Though many news reports portrayed the Davis attack as unprecedented in its violence, other attacks by chimps have taken a similar form. For example, in 1998, in Rishon Lezion, Israel, a chimp attacked a zoo worker, amputating his nose and some fingers from both hands and injuring his back, buttocks, and arms. In 2006, construction workers entered a wildlife sanctuary in Sierra Leone and were attacked by the resident chimps. A BBC news report said one man was "killed and mutilated." Four others were hospitalized; one of them had injuries requiring the amputation of his hand. The chimps seemed to perceive these workers as a rival troop invading their territory.

Researchers working with chimps in the wild have also been hurt by chimps that seemed to perceive them as rivals or invaders. In 1998, Gary Larson, the cartoonist best known for *The Far Side,* was roughed up by Frodo, a wild chimp under the study of Jane Goodall. Larson emerged with scratches and bruises. In 1989, Goodall herself had suffered a more serious beating from Frodo, including stiff blows to the head.

Caged chimps have bitten and scratched many lab workers. Goodall lost the tip of a thumb when a chimp bit her during her visit to an experimental facility in New York State. Washoe, a chimp famous as one of the first to learn sign language, bit several people, including a surgeon whose finger had to be partly amputated. Washoe apologized for the incident.

• • •

So far I've been talking about chimp-human conflicts that amount to social misunderstandings, though with horrible consequences. These are not true predatory attacks, though in some cases the chimps apparently swallowed some flesh. But wild chimps occasionally prey on children.

Chimps are omnivores, supplementing their vegetable foods with grubs, ants, and termites; perhaps an occasional lizard; bird eggs and hatchlings; and whatever mammals are available, including small antelope, bushpigs, and monkeys. Goodall even observed a family of cannibal chimps. The relations between chimps and baboons are changeable. The young of both species have been observed playing together. In one incident, notorious because it was among the first human observations of chimp carnivory, an adult chimpanzee intervened in a playgroup by seizing a young baboon and dashing its head against a tree. It then ate the baboon, taking special relish, as is the chimp way, in the brain.

PIONEER FIELD
RESEARCHER JANE
GOODALL.

Since then, chimps have been observed hunting hundreds of times. Their usual method of dispatching a fellow primate is to bite it in the brain or neck, or wring its neck with both hands, or else, as in the case above, seize it by the hind legs and slam its head against the ground or a tree. Chimps have been seen to tear off the head and dig into the base of the skull, where it joins the spine, to get at the brain. Or they may simply prize the forehead open with teeth and fingers. They lick the inner surface of the skull clean. Next, after perhaps a little pruning away of obstructive limbs, come the viscera, and then the trunk. The chimp cracks the ribs into manageable slabs, perhaps flensing some of the hide. He will eventually devour everything—bones, teeth, hair, the humors of the eye.

The primates eaten by chimps are typically under 20 pounds—a category that includes human babies. A study published in 2004 said chimps had, in the seven years preceding, attacked at least sixteen children in Tanzania and Uganda. Eight of the children died; among the survivors, the injuries included amputations and disfigurements. In one case, a woman was working in a potato field with her three-month-old son. A chimp appeared, pursued her when she fled, tripped her, and wrested the baby from her. A man with a spear managed to drive the chimp away, but it had already eaten the baby's upper lip and nose. The child survived another week.

Frodo, the notoriously aggressive chimp studied by Goodall, killed a baby in 2002. The wife of a researcher who worked in the park where Frodo lived came to see her husband. She brought her fourteen-month-old daughter, who was carried by the woman's niece, age sixteen. The party came upon Frodo feeding on oil-palm fronds. He seized the baby and scampered away with her. A researcher spotted him shortly thereafter, perched in a tree and eating the baby. At sight of the human intruder, he dropped the baby and retreated. Park officials decided not to kill him.

EARLY REPORTS OF white missionaries portrayed gorillas as man-eaters who perched in trees and used their pendulous arms to hoist unsuspecting humans to their deaths. Subsequent experience has proved that gorillas, though far more powerful than humans or even chimpanzees and equipped with impressive fangs, eat only plant matter, inverte-brates, and eggs. The largest male gorillas reach six feet when standing. Zoo specimens may weigh 600 pounds, though wild ones are much leaner. They do not hunt humans or any other large animals. In the wild, they have attacked people only in defense of themselves or their troopmates. I find no well-documented cases of humans killed by goril-las, though it's certainly possible that this has happened a few times among the many unrecorded illegal hunting incidents. In a typical hunt-ing scenario, a hunter shoots a female gorilla, then either runs away to avoid the counterattack of the silverbacked male, or meets his charge with the other shotgun barrel. Males have also charged people in de-fense of territory. The attack of a male gorilla is usually meant as a bluff, however; it typically stops short of actually harming a person or other large animal, relying on fear to drive invaders away. In one case, a sil-verback charged a man on foot who was carrying an orphaned baby go-rilla. The male claimed the baby and adopted her into his own clan. It appeared that the male would have fought the man for the infant, but the man dropped it in time and was spared.

Aside from hunting, most dangerous encounters between human and gorilla occur in zoos. It's hard to keep an intelligent animal captive. Day after day they observe the routines of their keepers and the struc-ture of their cages. If they want to escape, they often find ways. Some-times they need only their physical prowess. That was the case in a gorilla escape at the Dallas Zoo in 2004. It began with teasing. The per-petrators were two unidentified teenaged male humans; the victim was a teenaged male gorilla. The teasing, according to news reports, ex-tended to pelting the gorilla with ice or rocks. (Further evidence that human intelligence is not equally distributed in the species.) This must have seemed to the boys a safe enough diversion. The gorilla was inside a 12-foot moat ringed with a 14-foot wall. For extra assurance, the wall was topped with an electric wire. The gorilla cleared moat, wall, and wire with a single running leap. His antagonists fled.

The gorilla first entered the aviary, where women and their children were looking at exotic birds. The people fled, but one mother was trapped on a staircase beneath the gorilla. She began lifting children into the bird enclosure, hoping it would protect them. The gorilla con-fronted her and roared in her face. Her four-year-old son stood near a tree, and she told him to stay there and hope the gorilla didn't see him. Eventually the gorilla headed to the other end of the aviary. The woman saw a chance to escape. She hefted the children out of the enclosure and sent them toward a door in a direction opposite the gorilla's. She had to carry the four-year-old; he wasn't fast enough to run down the intervening stairs.

When the door opened, the gorilla saw it from the far end of the aviary. He had, it seemed, been looking for a way out, and he came running on all fours. Every child was out the door except the smallest. The woman hurled him through and then rushed out herself, trying to shut the door behind her. The gorilla hit the door with awesome force, slamming it open. The woman hit the outside wall along with it. The gorilla seized her and sank his teeth into her upper arm repeatedly.

Next the gorilla approached a party who happened to be standing outside the aviary. It picked up a three-year-old boy and bit him in the chest and head. His mother leaped onto the gorilla's back, hitting it with her fists. The gorilla tossed the boy against a wall and attacked the mother. It bit her on the legs before hurling her, too, against the wall. Then it ran off. Other zoo visitors dragged the victims to safety, all the while begging them to stifle their screams so the gorilla wouldn't return. One man phoned the police. The dispatcher asked him if he was serious.

The gorilla, meanwhile, had inflicted a minor bite on a ten-year-old boy before disappearing into the trees and bamboo that served to make the jungle area more realistic. When police arrived, the zoo staff supplied them with safari rifles meant to drop big game in its tracks. The usual police-issue handguns probably would have sufficed, but nobody wanted to take the risk. The tranquilizer guns and pepper spray the zoo kept on hand weren't deployed because the staff was busy evacuating the place.

Two police officers were poking through the bamboo when the gorilla reappeared, stepping into view with a pair of child-sized white sandals in its hand. It charged. They fired three shots, and the gorilla lay dead.

The ten-year-old bite victim was treated on the spot and sent home. The two women went to the hospital with minor injuries. The three-year-old boy was listed in critical condition, but he made a full recovery and returned home in eight days.

This was not the first time a gorilla had harmed a human being at the Dallas Zoo. In 1998 a gorilla walked out of a cage accidentally left open and mauled a keeper intermittently for half an hour. Bites to the arm and torso put her in the hospital with more than thirty puncture wounds. At the Bronx Zoo in 1992, a gorilla said to weigh 500 pounds broke free while being transferred between cages. He sent two keepers to the hospital with bite wounds. In Miami in 1992, a gorilla unlatched his cage and bit a keeper.

The Franklin Park Zoo in Boston was the site of an escape in 2003. A gorilla there climbed a 20-foot wall but was quickly recaptured. A month and a half later, the same gorilla once again escaped. This time he seized a child from her mother's arms, hurled her to the ground, and stomped on her. He also bit a volunteer on the back and tried to assault workers who locked themselves in a ticket booth. He left the zoo grounds and remained at large for two hours before being brought to ground with tranquilizers. The girl survived.

ORANGUTANS KEPT AS pets or performers have a reputation for a peculiar form of play in which they bite the fingers of humans, sometimes to the point of amputating them. Why this should seem amusing to them is yet another quandary of interspecies relations.

In zoos, orangutans, like many primates, have found disturbing ways to relate to their captors. A zoo volunteer of my acquaintance says a certain male orang used to greet her each day by sexually assaulting a boulder in his cage. Improbable as it seems, wild orangs have also evinced sexual interest in human females, even descending from the canopy to seize them; but apparently such contact has not seriously hurt anyone, nor proceeded to the lurid conclusion pulp fiction would suggest.

Orangutans come from Indonesia and Malaysia. They are generally a bit larger than chimpanzees and certainly have the power to hurt people—but they rarely do. An orang escaped its cage in Rochester, New York, in 2003, seized a volunteer, and carried him around for a while before releasing him without serious violence. In Gulf Breeze, Florida, in 2000, a female orang escaped and battered a keeper, biting her repeatedly, sometimes bone-deep, on the leg. Both of these escapees returned to their cages voluntarily.

GRIFFIN, ME, AND BECKETT WITH OUR FRIENDS TIGER LILY AND FERGIE.

"You're all a bunch of apes," I told my wife and sons as we sat down to dinner the other night.

"Well, you're a squid," said Griffin, who's now seven.

"No, something grosser," said Beckett, ten. "You're a toad, Dad."

"Perhaps a dung beetle," offered Parker, fourteen.

"Actually, I'm an ape too," I said. "We all are."

"You're just now figuring this out?" said Tracy.

"A hagfish," said Griffin.

"It's official," I said, spearing a steak from the common platter. "We're in the family Hominidae."

"Are we still Grices?" Beckett said.

"Yes, but also great apes."

"I'm a great ape, but the rest of you are mediocre," Parker said.

"I'm a greater ape than you," Griffin said.

I looked at them all with a sudden twinge. I had always meant to bring my boys up someplace like my childhood home. They'd grown up while I was working out the details. After supper we would go our separate ways—Beckett to build a swing in the backyard, Griffin to the computer to make a slideshow called "Wildlife of North America," Parker to the garage where his frog farm awaited.

"I'd better feed my crows," I said after a while, gathering the table scraps for the feeder I'd rigged atop the shed.

"Tell them not to chase my bluebirds anymore," Tracy said, and opened the blinds to let the sunset in.

REALLY, IT IS nothing new to call us apes. In the eighteenth century, when Linnaeus invented the system for naming living things we still use today, he classed us among the primates. He was immediately criticized on religious grounds. Nonetheless, biologists have considered us primates ever since. Within that group, our position has shifted. We started out distinct from the other primates—the lemurs and monkeys and gibbons and great apes. We might fit into a group of animals, but at least we stood out within it. But this notion fell away in recent decades as scientists got better at analyzing DNA. We have obvious similarities to the chimpanzees, orangutans, and gorillas. Analysis proved that among this group of four, the orangutans diverged first. Gorillas diverged next. So not only are we mixed in with the rest, but we're first cousins to the chimpanzees. A chart of the evolutionary relationships used to show us as a side branch, jutting far from the family tree. Now we're mixed in with the other leaves. Of course nothing real has changed; what's in a name?

People resist calling themselves apes because it runs counter to our deep intuition that we're fundamentally different from other animals. Western thought has spent a great deal of effort trying to make science support that intuition. So far, science has resisted. Such distinguishing features as language, tool use, and the opposable thumb have turned out not to be so distinctive after all. Creatures as diverse as wasps and otters use simple tools of one sort or another; raccoons and monkeys manipulate objects as well as we do; the crows of the air and the whales in the sea speak to one another in languages we have yet to comprehend.

Even more disturbing, gorillas and chimps sign to us in languages we do understand.

But one distinction remains to us: we're the best killers. In a recent year, homicide took 520,000 lives; war took another 310,000; suicide took 815,000, and law enforcement killings took 14,000. The total damage: 1,659,000 lives. This total doesn't include many other kinds of death, such as traffic accidents, that might reasonably be attributed to human causes. We have no near competitors as killers of human beings. All the venomous snakes combined kill fewer than a hundred thousand people per year. The mosquitoes kill perhaps two million by spreading disease, but we spread our own diseases far more effectively. Besides, it's our violence that occasions our perverse pride.

Even there, we'll have to be disappointed. Our worst behaviors can be observed in many other species. War, for example, has its analogues among chimpanzees, hyenas, wolves, and lions, among others. Something similar happens even among ants. The behavior extends easily to something resembling genocide. In a war among chimpanzees, for example, the victorious side hunted down and killed members of the losing faction even after they presented no threat. We find the murder of mates among brown bears. The killing of young by male mammals is common; it occurs, for example, among domestic cats and lions. It appears that this violence is usually, though not always, directed at the offspring of other males. Male lions that take over a pride by killing or ousting the incumbent male typically kill his offspring. The situation among humans is much the same; men are far more likely to kill their stepchildren than their biological children. Cannibalism, a behavior rare among human cultures and among individuals within cultures that do not generally tolerate it, occurs among at least a hundred species of mammal. It is well represented among many other animal classes as well.

I don't mean to slight the moral implications of these acts among humans, or to place moral significance on the acts of other animals. I only mean to show that we're hardly the aberrations the moralists would have us believe. We might even learn something about our own worst traits by looking at our fellow animals.

The reason for our proficiency at killing isn't, then, a special inclination. It's the quality of our weapons. Weapons are, of course, a class of tools. Many animals use them. Elephants pelt people with rocks; monkeys have killed people by dropping objects on them. But no one can match our technology. Our weapons are unusual both in their inherent destructive power—here I'm thinking especially of fire, which no other animal uses—and in their complexity. Many advances in technology have yielded obvious results in higher mortality—the Gatling gun, mustard gas, atomic bombs.

Our most effective method of killing each other will probably turn out to be environmental destruction. Here again, there is no use pretending to be special. Many animals, from the red-billed quelea to the desert locust, devour all available resources. In the usual course of things, excessive appetite limits itself by causing mass die-off. If locusts strip the land of food, it will not support them the next year, and they will die back to more manageable numbers. Many animals, in fact, live in boom-and-bust population cycles. Humans do too, in the poorest conditions. Technology is to blame here as well. Because we've found ways to produce and store food and energy more effectively, the wealthiest among us manage to survive even when, theoretically, we ought to die back a bit.

It used to be estimated that the planet could accommodate no more than five billion people. We have, through such technological tricks as mass crop production, managed to exceed that number by a third. So far our technology has showed us how to wring maximum yield from the planet, but it has not showed us how to dispose of all the waste the technology itself produces. In the relatively clean and wealthy lands of North America, the waters show traces of prescription drugs and the cities exude an air caustic enough to disable a fraction of the populace several days a year. In the poorer countries of the East, thousands have died from industrial accidents like those at Chernobyl and Bhopal. The planet groans at the seams; the very weather seems to protest. But of course the weather, in one form or another, will be here for billions of years to come. We may not.

ACKNOWLEDGMENTS

I'm grateful to the many who helped make this book.

I could fill another book with the names of biologists and other professionals who answered my questions and, in some cases, took me into their labs or into the field to learn about the animals. Others told me about their encounters with animals. I know it wasn't always easy for them to talk about those events. I hope they'll accept this meager thanks for their many hours of time and trouble.

Some passages in this book first appeared in different form in magazines. I thank the editors of those magazines, particularly Burkhard Bilger, formerly of *Discover;* Louisa McCune of *Oklahoma Today;* Michael Ray Taylor and Marck Beggs of *Arkansas Literary Forum;* and Ian Jack, formerly of *Granta.*

My agent, Elyse Cheney, and her staff undertook more than the usual amount of insanity in helping me finish this project. Vincent Virga managed the daunting business of selecting and securing illustrations. Susan Kamil and Noah Eaker at Dial shepherded the book to completion. Lynn Hamilton and Thomas Massaro sent photos from Africa.

As usual, my family ended up appearing in my work, whether they liked it or not. I appreciate their tolerance. My mother, Gloria Grice, was tireless in helping me with photos and memories of my animal-rich childhood. Tracy, Parker, Beckett, and Griffin spent many hours talking through the stories with me. Jim Turner, James Twiggs, and D'Arcy Allison-Teasley were the sort of friends every writer ought to be lucky enough to have. Parker and D'Arcy helped with the photos.

Finally, I owe my thanks to James Addison Conrad, whose music helped in more ways than he knows.

GENERAL SOURCES

On animals that kill people, the twin standards are Roger A. Caras's *Dangerous to Man* (Chilton Books, 1964; rev. ed, Holt, Rinehart & Winston, 1975) and James Clarke's *Man Is the Prey* (Stein and Day, 1969). Caras leans to the scientific approach, Clarke to the view of the hunter, but both are thorough and admirably skeptical. Of Peter Hathaway Capstick's marvelously entertaining books, the best is probably *Death in the Long Grass* (St. Martin's, 1989), while the one most thorough in its cataloguing of dangerous animals is *Maneaters* (St. Martin's, 1981). Also valuable is Edward R. Ricciuti's *Killer Animals* (Lyons Press, 2003).

C.J.P. Ionides is best known as an authority on snakes, but he had much firsthand experience with elephants and big cats as well. I recommend his memoir, *A Hunter's Story* (W. H. Allen, 1965). Donna Hart and Robert W. Sussman address the question of early man as prey in *Man the Hunted* (Westview Press, 2005). Edward E. Leslie tells of humans in trouble with animals, and many other dangers, in *Desperate Journeys, Abandoned Souls* (Houghton Mifflin, 1988).

For sheer volume and entertainment value, no book matches Alex MacCormick's anthology *The Mammoth Book of Maneaters* (Carroll & Graf, 2003). MacCormick includes everything from historical cases of cannibalism to newspaper accounts of children beaten by baboons. So long as you don't believe every piece of lore in this vast volume, it's great reading.

For several years, the best place to find news stories about human-animal conflict was The Animal Attack Files, < http://attack.igorilla .com >, edited by Igor Eximel. The site is rarely updated these days, but its archives make for fascinating reading. To learn about animals in general, not necessarily engaged in violence, my favorite site is the Animal Diversity Web, maintained by the University of Michigan Museum of Zoology, <http://animaldiversity.ummz.umich.edu/site/accounts/information/Animalia.html>.

Charles Darwin remains an entertaining guide to the natural world. His *Journal of Researches into the Geology and Natural History of the Various Countries Visited by H.M.S.* Beagle, sometimes published as *Voyage of the* Beagle, tells of dangers as diverse as the jaguar and the kissing bug. It's available on my website, www.deadlykingdom.com.

THE CARNIVORIDS

Biologist David Mech explains wolf behavior in several books, including *The Arctic Wolf: Living with the Pack* (Voyageur Press, 1988). Barry Lopez's *Of Wolves and Men* (Scribner Classics, 2004) has much to say about human cultures as well as the biology of wolves. Peter Steinhart takes a journalistic approach to wolf issues in *The Company of Wolves* (Knopf, 1995). Rick McIntyre's anthology *War Against the Wolf* (Voyageur Press, 1995) details the history of wolf-human conflicts in North America. For tales of individual wolves, the reader may enjoy Rick Bass's *The Ninemile Wolves* (Clark City Press, 1992) and Farley Mowat's *Never Cry Wolf* (Little, Brown, 1963). On coyotes, my favorite, after all these decades, remains *The Voice of the Coyote* (Little, Brown, 1949), by the legendary Texas journalist J. Frank Dobie. William Least Heat-Moon's *PrairyErth* (Houghton Mifflin, 1991) contains a fascinating chapter on coyotes, "After the Sixteen-Sixty-Six Beast."

There are lots of good books on bears. In *Man Meets Grizzly* (Houghton Mifflin, 1980), F. M. Young and Coralie Beyers gather bear stories from eyewitnesses old and new. Larry Kanuit's *Alaska Bear Tales* (Alaska Northwest Publishing, 1984) collects accounts from contemporary survivors. Doug Peacock captures the thrill—and horror—of encountering predators in the wild in his memoir *Grizzly Years* (Henry Holt, 1990). Scott McMillion takes a journalistic approach in *Mark of the Grizzly* (Falcon Publishing, 1998). The definitive scientific book accessible to popular audiences is Stephen Herrero's *Bear Attacks: Their*

Causes and Avoidance (rev. ed., Lyons Press, 2002). Bill Bryson's *A Walk in the Woods* (Broadway Books, 1999) is mostly about hiking the Appalachian Trail, but it manages to impart a lot of information about black bears along the way.

The best books about human encounters with carnivorids came out of the colonial experience, and while many of them are vastly entertaining and informative, they can also offend modern sensibilities. With that caveat, let me recommend a few of the best. The ultimate true story of encounters with lions is J. H. Patterson's *The Man-eaters of Tsavo* (which you can find for free, in full or in an abbreviated "just the good parts" version, at my website, www.deadlykingdom.com). The hunter Kenneth Anderson wrote many accounts of deadly tigers and leopards (and an occasional bear or hyena); the handiest way to sample his work is *The Kenneth Anderson Omnibus,* which collects half a dozen of his books. Jim Corbett was a nature lover who found himself called on to kill the tigers and leopards no one else could. *The Man-eating Leopard of Rudraprayag* (Oxford University Press, 1947) is his magnum opus, a gripping tale of one predator and its effect on thousands of people. Corbett describes several leopards and tigers in *Man-eaters of Kumaon* (Oxford University Press, 1944). The Victorian missionary David Livingstone wrote memorably of encounters with lions and other wildlife, particularly in *Missionary Travels and Researches in South Africa* (also available on my website).

For contemporary books, I'll refer the reader to two new takes on carnivory in Tsavo. *The Lions of Tsavo* (McGraw-Hill, 2004), by the zoologist Bruce Patterson, is scientifically rigorous. For a more casual approach, there's Philip Caputo's *Ghosts of Tsavo* (National Geographic, 2002). Robert R. Frump's *The Man-eaters of Eden* (Lyons Press, 2006) tells the story of lion attacks in South Africa's Kruger National Park.

On tigers, my favorite contemporary book is Sy Montgomery's *Spell of the Tiger* (Houghton Mifflin, 1995). On cougars, David Baron has written the definitive account of the Scott Lancaster case in *The Beast in the Garden* (Norton, 2004). Kathy Etling's *Cougar Attacks* (Lyons Press, 2004) is a thorough survey of cougar-human trouble.

Those interested in learning more about hyenas will enjoy Hans Kruuk's study *The Spotted Hyena* (University of Chicago Press, 1972). While Kruuk was researching it, his subjects fell under the scrutiny of

Jane Goodall and Hugo van Lawick, who described their findings in a chapter of *Innocent Killers* (Houghton Mifflin, 1971). Both books are well worth seeking out. I found Joanna Greenfield's extraordinary essay about surviving the attack of a striped hyena in the anthology *Women in the Wild,* edited by Lucy McCauley (Travelers' Tales, 1998).

Among more general works about carnivorids, my favorites include Kruuk's *Hunter and Hunted: Relationships Between Carnivores and People* (Cambridge University Press, 2002). David Quammen deals with human-eaters of various kinds, including tigers and brown bears, in *Monster of God* (W. W. Norton, 2003).

AQUATIC DANGERS

Edward R. Ricciuti's *Killers of the Seas* (Lyons Press, 2003) and Peter Benchley's *Shark Trouble* (Random House, 2002) survey the dangers of the deep.

Richard G. Fernicola's *Twelve Days of Terror* (Lyons Press, 2002) and Michael Capuzzo's *Close to Shore* (Broadway Books, 2001) recount the famous Jersey Shore shark attacks of 1916. The *Indianapolis* disaster is the subject of several fine books, including Thomas Helm's *Ordeal by Sea* (Signet, 2001), Don Kurzman's *Fatal Voyage* (Atheneum, 1990), Raymond B. Lech's *All the Drowned Sailors* (Stein and Day, 1982), Richard F. Newcomb's *Abandon Ship!* (HarperCollins, 2001), and Doug Stanton's *In Harm's Way* (Henry Holt, 2001). Further information about the *Indianapolis* appears on the U.S. Naval Historical Center's website, < http://www.history.navy.mil/faqs/faq30-1.htm >, and at U.S.S. Indianapolis.org, < http://www.ussindianapolis.org/woody .htm >. Robert D. Ballard's *Graveyards of the Pacific* (National Geographic, 2001) adds some information about the presence of sharks at other Pacific theater battles.

John Long's anthology *Mark of the Shark* (Falcon, 2003) contains many fascinating narratives, including Bret Gilliam's account of his brush with oceanic whitetips. The International Shark Attack Files, < http://web.cyberia.net.lb/lebscuba/english/sharks/sharks-attacks .html >, provides interesting statistical information on sharks. Shipwreck narratives supply a wealth of information on encounters with sharks and other sea dangers; of these, I recommend *Albatross,* by

Deborah Scaling Kiley and Meg Noonan (Houghton Mifflin, 1994), and *A Furnace Afloat,* by Joe Jackson (Free Press, 2003).

On shipwrecks caused by whales, I suggest Bill Butler's *66 Days Adrift* (International Marine/McGraw-Hill, 2005); Steven Callahan's *Adrift: Seventy-Six Days Lost at Sea* (Houghton Mifflin, 1986); Nathaniel Philbrick's *In the Heart of the Sea: The Tragedy of the Whaleship* Essex (Viking, 2000); and Dougal Robertson's *Survive the Savage Sea* (Praeger, 1973). Richard Ellis's *Men and Whales* (Lyons Press, 1991) is a great source for further reading on the whaling industry and its dangers.

Wade Davis's inquiry into Haitian ritual, *The Serpent and the Rainbow* (Touchstone, 1997), led him to several aquatic dangers. Richard Ellis's *The Search for the Giant Squid* (Penguin, 1998) was written before the fascinating discoveries of recent years, but still makes for compelling reading.

THE REPTILES AND BIRDS

After half a century, Lawrence M. Klauber's *Rattlesnakes: Their Habits, Life Histories, and Influence on Mankind* (University of California Press/ Zoological Society of San Diego, 1956) is still the definitive work. The same press published a shorter edition geared to lay readers in 1982. For sheer fun, though, J. Frank Dobie's *Rattlesnakes* (University of Texas Press, 1994) is hard to beat. On the other venomous snakes of the world, the classic twentieth-century authors Sherman A. Minton and Raymond L. Ditmars remain the most entertaining. A good starting point for Minton is *Venomous Reptiles* (written with Madge Rutherford Minton; Scribner's, 1969). *Reptiles of the World* (Macmillan, 1937), by Ditmars, is beautifully illustrated. Mark W. Moffett wrote a compelling account of death by krait: "Bit" appears in *Outside Magazine* (April 2002).

David Quammen's *The Song of the Dodo* (Touchstone, 1996) includes information on the Komodo dragon. The greatest work of art in the genre of dangerous-animal books is surely *Eyelids of Morning* (Chronicle Books, 1990), in which Alistair Graham's acerbic text and Peter Beard's awe-inspiring photos pay tribute to the ultimate predator of humans, the Nile crocodile. Hugh Edwards's *Crocodile Attack* (Harper & Row, 1989) deals with the saltwater species.

My favorite books on birds are by Bernd Heinrich. He recounts the defensive powers of the great horned owl, along with much other information, in *One Man's Owl* (Princeton University Press, 1987).

THE ARTHROPODS AND WORMS

Richard Conniff's *Spineless Wonders* (Henry Holt, 1996) provides beautifully gruesome reading on creepy things. Robert Gale Breene III is the author of the entertaining pamphlets *Spider Bob's Animal Odysseys I* (SB Island Science Press, 1994) and *II* (American Tarantula Society, 1997). The photographer Catherine Chalmers has produced two fascinating books of (mostly) arthropod images, *American Cockroach* (Aperture, 2005) and *Food Chain* (Aperture, 2000). I wrote a short essay for the latter, but I'd recommend it even if I hadn't.

P. D. Hillyard's *The Book of the Spider* is a good general source. *Spiders of the World,* by Rod and Ken Preston-Mafham, is a gorgeously photographed volume. Neither of these is specific to the venomous spiders, however. My earlier book, *The Red Hourglass: Lives of the Predators* (Delta, 1999), details the habits of widow and recluse spiders and tarantulas. The Spider Myths Site, maintained by Rod Crawford of the Burke Museum of Natural History and Culture, <http://www .washington.edu/burkemuseum/spidermyth/index.html>, is a dependable debunker of nonsense, which is what most stories about dangerous arachnids are.

J. L. Cloudsley-Thompson's *Insects and History* (St. Martin's, 1976) tells of disease-transmitting insects, as well as the toxic Spanish fly. *Mosquito* (Hyperion, 2001), by Andrew Spielman and Mark D'Antonio, is an accessible account of its subject. Richard Schweid's *The Cockroach Papers* (Four Walls Eight Windows, 1999) is wonderfully informative, but not for the queasy. If you're into queasy, however, check out Stanford University's Myiasis page by Anna M. West, <http://www.stanford.edu/class/humbio103/ParaSites2001/myiasis/ Anna West's Myiasis Page.htm>. You will never look at parasitic maggots the same way again. While I'm recommending grue: Richard Selzer's *Mortal Lessons* (Touchstone Books, 1976) is mostly about the human animal and has only one selection about maggot infection—but what a selection it is.

Laura Ingalls Wilder tells the quintessential story of humans versus locusts in *On the Banks of Plum Creek* (HarperTrophy, 1994). Her eye for detail does justice to both sides. It's not just for kids.

Any reader curious about some hideous arthropod in his or her home may want to check out *What's That Bug?*, <http://www.whatsthatbug.com/>, where critters are identified and, usually, fears allayed.

You might be shocked how many great websites have been built around worms. Many are for specialists only. For the general reader, let me suggest the parasitic disease page at the U.S. Centers for Disease Control and Prevention, <http://www.cdc.gov/ncidod/dpd/index.htm>, where you can choose technical or plain-English accounts of these parasites. Handy charts, too.

OTHER MAMMALS

Ernest Hemingway's *Death in the Afternoon* provides a detailed account of the business of bullfighting. David Dary wrote the definitive account of the American bison in *The Buffalo Book* (Swallow Press/Ohio University Press, 1989). I've mentioned Peter Hathaway Capstick already; he wrote often of encounters with antelope, Cape buffalo, and other hoofed dangers, as well as elephants. He details the Cape buffalo incident mentioned in this section in *Death in a Lonely Land* (St. Martin's, 1990).

Cynthia Moss details the lives of elephants in *Elephant Memories* (University of Chicago Press, 2000). Her *Portraits in the Wild* (University of Chicago Press, 1982) deals with black rhinoceroses and other animals as well as elephants. George Orwell's classic essay "Shooting an Elephant" appears on my website, www.deadlykingdom.com.

Robert Sullivan's *Rats* (Bloomsbury, 2004) deals mostly with urban rat populations. Marilyn Chase describes the role of rodents in spreading disease in *The Barbary Plague* (Random House, 2004). Barbara Hodgson's collection *The Rat: A Perverse Miscellany* (Ten Speed Press, 1997) is an entertaining compendium of lore and images.

Jane Goodall gives firsthand accounts of chimpanzee behavior in several fine books, including *In the Shadow of Man* (Mariner Books, 2000). Dale Peterson's *Jane Goodall* (Houghton Mifflin, 2006) includes much information on both Goodall and her research subjects. Peterson's *Eat-*

ing Apes (University of California Press, 2003) delves into the bushmeat trade. Craig B. Stanford's *The Hunting Apes* (Princeton University Press, 2001) explores the chimpanzee as carnivore. Dian Fossey's *Gorillas in the Mist* (Mariner Books, 2000) and George Schaller's *The Mountain Gorilla* (University of Chicago Press, 2000) elucidate the lives of the gentler primates.

ILLUSTRATION CREDITS

Italicized page numbers indicate illustrations.

ABOUT THE AUTHOR

GORDON GRICE has written for *The New Yorker, Harper's, Discover, Granta,* and other magazines. His first book, *The Red Hourglass,* was named to best-of-the-year lists by the New York Public Library and the *Los Angeles Times.* His work has been anthologized in *The Best American Essays.* He lives with his family in Wisconsin.